WORDS OF COMME[ ]

"Christians often speak of our [ ] is being a resident of the New Jerusale... ... . of what the Bible says is the believer's destiny? What are we to make of statements such as that of the Apostle Paul to the Romans that not only are we heirs of God, and joint heirs with Jesus, but that we will be glorified together with Jesus with a glory not yet revealed? (Romans 8:17-18) In THE REVEALING: UNLOCKING HIDDEN TRUTHS ON THE GLORIFICATION OF GOD'S CHILDREN, authors Gary Huffman and S. Douglas Woodward argue that there is much more to the believer's "hope of glory" and our life AFTER the rapture than is currently being taught. In fact, the glory of God and Jesus the Christ has a clear purpose in its manifestation through and in the children of God! Don't spend another day not knowing what your destiny is as a son and daughter of the Most High God!"

Dr. Mike Spaulding. Pastor, Calvary Chapel of Lima and Host, *Soaring Eagle Radio*

"I am always amazed at the depth of insight and timeliness shown in works connected to Doug Woodward. THE REVEALING: UNLOCKING HIDDEN TRUTHS ON THE GLORIFICATION OF GOD'S CHILDREN, by Gary Huffman and S. Douglas Woodward, shows how God's eternal purpose is the ultimate motivation for the church – to make known to the principalities and powers, the manifold wisdom of God. This book is not a call to retreat, but a much-needed call to engage."

Pastor Larry Spargimino, *Southwest Radio Church* and co-author *FINAL FIRE*

"Beloved, now we are children of God, and it does not yet appear what we shall be." (1 John3:2). That is exactly what Gary Huffman and Doug Woodward have explored for us in this exciting volume, pulling back the curtains of Scripture on the future destiny of God's redeemed children. You will be stirred and challenged by this study on what awaits us the children of God."

Dr. Kevin Clarkson, host *Prophecy in the News*, Pastor First Baptist Church, Moore OK

'THE REVEALING provided deep, detailed insight into many questions about end times Bible prophecy and the destiny for believers in Jesus Christ. This new book by Gary Huffman and Douglas Woodward is well-researched, thought provoking, and absolutely stunning! Well done."

Lyn Leahz, host *Lyn Leahz YouTube Channel*, author *SOUL DECEIVER*, and Director of FreedomNationNews.com.

"Within the pages of this book, Gary Huffman and S. Douglas Woodward provide a clarion call to the Remnant. Now that we have assessed what the enemy has done, it is time to return to the biblical mandates of a pure faith, a holy heart, and a clear vision of the Messiah in the lives of His people" (from the Foreword).

Dr. Michael K. Lake, author THE SHINAR DIRECTIVE and THE SHEERIYTH IMPERATIVE, President and host, Kingdom Intelligence Briefing

"Yet another volume from Woodward (and co-author Huffman) that challenges readers to rethink foundational biblical beliefs. Woodward, McGriff, and I did this in THE FINAL BABYLON when we proclaimed that America comprises Mystery Babylon today. The Church must get beyond 'being born again' (John 3) and 'cheap grace' (Bonhoeffer). It's time for us to grow up. It's about sanctification and getting holy – now! Only mature sons and daughters will shine bright when God's children are revealed.

THE REVEALING is a wake-up call for the Body of Christ. Know this: we will NOT face the Great White Throne Judgment, but we shall surely face the Judgment Seat of Christ, where we will account for those works done in our earthly bodies. Paul ran the race that was set before him – but are we in that race? If not, it's high time we don the track shoes. We must run 'so as to win the prize.'" (1 Cor 9:24)

Douglas W. Krieger, author of many books and President, *TribNet Publications*.

"Attempts to identify the Antichrist, Gog of Magog, the False Prophet, or Babylon the Great dominate our study of the end times. While Christian authors who write such books do great good, generally they overlook subjects that are most relevant to the questions we should be asking, such as: "What should we who follow Jesus Christ be doing now to "prep" ourselves for what comes next? What is the connection between living "in Christ" now and "with Christ" later – after the rapture of the Church? Is the afterlife for Christians just a time of bliss? Or do we believers, who have been glorified at the "revealing" (the resurrection/rapture), still have work to do on earth?"

Authors Gary Huffman and S. Douglas Woodward explore this question which frankly, I don't know if anyone has asked before. And they tackle sanctification (becoming holy) through sharing a basket-full of biblical material seldom touched by our most familiar prophecy authors today. Prepare to have your eyes opened and your priorities reset!"

Derek Gilbert, Host, *SkyWatchTV*, author of *The Great Inception*, and host of the popular podcast, *A View from the Bunker*.

The REVEALING

"For I consider that the sufferings of this present time are not worthy to be compared with the glory which shall be revealed in us." (Rom 8:18)

Unlocking Hidden Truths on the Glorification of God's Children

GARY L. HUFFMAN
S. DOUGLAS WOODWARD

FOREWORD BY DR. MICHAEL LAKE, Th.D.

THE NEW JERUSALEM AND THE RIVER OF LIFE
Beatus de Facundus, 1047
Madrid Biblioteca Nacional
(Public Doman, from Wikipedia Commons)

The Revealing

Unlocking Hidden Truths on the
Glorification of God's Children

GARY L. HUFFMAN
S. DOUGLAS WOODWARD

Foreword by Dr. Michael K. Lake

FAITH HAPPENS BOOKS

Oklahoma City

CONTENTS

ACKNOWLEDGEMENTS vii

FOREWORD ix

PREFACE.. xiii

INTRODUCTION..3

    WHAT IT TAKES TO PUBLISH A BEST SELLER 3

    OUR PRIMARY ASSUMPTIONS... 5

    PUTTING FIRST THINGS FIRST 8

    ITS ABOUT THE AFTERLIFE, AFTER ALL................................... 9

    DIVING INTO THE DEEP WATER 10

    FINAL THOUGHTS 11

1: GOD'S PATTERN FOR RESTORATION 13

    ONE SHINY PENNY... 13

    HEAVEN IS NOT OUR REWARD 15

    GOD'S ETERNAL PURPOSE: THE ULTIMATE MOTIVATION............ 19

    THE HOPE OF GLORY 21

    DEEP DIVE: THE REVEALING OF THE MYSTERY IN PAUL...... 25

    THE GLORY OF GOD 28

    DEEP DIVE: THE GLORY OF GOD 29

    THE PATTERN 33

    DEEP DIVE: TYPOLOGY 33

    JESUS CHRIST: GOD'S PATTERN FOR RESTORATION 34

    THE TRIPARTITE NATURE OF SALVATION FOR HUMANKIND....... 37

DEEP DIVE: THE LEAST UNDERSTOOD PHASE OF
SALVATION – GLORIFICATION 44

2: THE TABERNACLE IN THE WILDERNESS 49

THE RELIGION JESUS BROUGHT TO US 49

THE OUTER COURT 50

THE HOLY PLACE 55

THE HOLY OF HOLIES 61

DEEP DIVE: EXCEEDINGLY BEYOND EXCEPTIONAL 62

THREE TYPES OF LIGHT 65

DEEP DIVE: BEING MADE "PERFECT" JUST LIKE JESUS 67

3: THE FEASTS OF THE LORD 71

THE THREE FEASTS IN SEVEN PARTS 74

THE DAY OF ATONEMENT 90

THE FEAST OF TABERNACLES 93

DEEP DIVE: THE SHEKINAH [KABOD] GLORY OF GOD 103

TABERNACLES IS THE FEAST OF FEASTS 105

4: THE GLORY OF GOD 107

THE KINGDOM OF GOD AND THE KINGDOM OF HEAVEN (GOD'S
GLORY REVEALED) 107

THE KINGDOM AND THE GLORY OF GOD 114

THE RESURRECTION OF THE DEAD 122

WHAT HAPPENS IMMEDIATELY AFTER THE RAPTURE? 126

DEEP DIVE: A NEW BODY IS LIKE MOVING INTO A BRAND-
NEW HOUSE 133

DEEP DIVE: REPLACING THE PRINCE OF THE AIR AND HIS POWERS AND PRINCIPALITIES WITH THE GLORIFIED CHILDREN OF GOD 135

A STARRY-EYED GROOM AND GLORIOUS BRIDE MEET ABBA ... 137

GOD'S PROMISE TO ABRAHAM HAS MULTIPLE MEANINGS 139

DEEP DIVE: BECOMING AS THE STARS OF HEAVEN 139

5: THE INHERITANCE 143

WHAT AWAITS THE MANIFESTED CHILDREN OF GOD 143

THE ADOPTION OF SONS 147

DEEP DIVE: THE CREATION WAS SUBJECTED TO EVIL FOR OUR GLORY 153

WHAT IS AVAILABLE TO US TO WALK IN THE SPIRIT? 157

GOD'S FAMILY BUSINESS 158

PARALLEL TRUTHS 162

DEEP DIVE: PREACHING "TOTAL" SALVATION TO UNBELIEVERS 163

6: THE PAROUSIA 165

THE PAROUSIA AND THE OLIVET DISCOURSE 165

THE ANGEL, THE NAME, THE PRESENCE 175

THE GREAT TRIBULATION (THE DAY OF THE LORD) 177

JACOB'S LADDER IS A PROPHECY FOR THE CHURCH 186

7: ALL ISRAEL SHALL BE SAVED 193

ARE YOU SAVED IF YOU ARE BORN A JEW? 193

WHAT IS GOD'S PLAN TO BRING ISRAEL TO FAITH? 198

THE REJECTION OF ISRAEL AND THE RETURN OF THE KING......202

THE TRIGGER POINT FOR JEWISH REPENTANCE 205

DEEP DIVE: THE FLIGHT OF THE REMNANT FROM
JERUSALEM AT MID-TRIBULATION 206

OH WHERE, OH WHERE CAN ARMAGEDDON BE? 213

8: THE WOMAN ISRAEL AND HER MALE CHILD 219

A GENERATION LOST AND FOUND.................................219

SO HOW CAN A SON WITH NO NATURAL CHILDREN – BE AN
EVERLASTING FATHER?...222

DEEP DIVE: THE BODY OF CHRIST.................................224

THE SEEDS OF TWO BIRTHS...227

CHRIST IN YOU, THE HOPE OF GLORY 229

THE CHURCH WILL RULE WITH A ROD OF IRON?...............230

THE SIGN IN THE HEAVENS – COULD THE CHURCH BE THERE?233

THE SIGN OF THE SON OF MAN.....................................239

THE DAY OF ATONEMENT 244

9: MANY SONS ARE BROUGHT TO GLORY: THE BOOK OF
HEBREWS 251

JESUS CHRIST BUILDS A NEW HOUSE FOR HIS BRIDE...........251

EVEN CHRIST HAD TO "LEARN" OBEDIENCE......................254

A SUPERIOR PREISTHOOD – THE ORDER OF MELCHIZEDEK.......255

A NEW TABERNACLE, A PERFECT WAY INTO THE HOLIEST
PLACE..257

HOLD THE ROPE – DON'T GIVE UP HOPE – THE KING IS
COMING...261

OBTAINING THE PROMISE, IN PART, NOW THROUGH FAITH 262

RESISTING SIN, RUNNING THE RACE, & "KEEPING OUR FEET"...265

THE HEAVENLY TABERNACLE 268

SPIRITUAL WARFARE IN THE COSMOS 271

THE PICTURE OF THE COSMOS THE TABERNACLE SUPPLIES......273

DEEP DIVE: GENESIS 1 AS TEMPLE TEXT IN THE CONTEXT OF ANCIENT COSMOLOGY..275

DEEP DIVE: THE NEW JERUSALEM.................................281

10: CONCLUSION – FINISHING STRONG WITH THE BODY OF CHRIST 285

OUR UNITY – A TESTIMONY TO THE TRUTH OF THE GOSPEL 286

AS THE DEW FROM HEAVEN – THE REFRESHING OF THE SPIRIT 289

PRESSURE, PAIN, PERSECUTION: THE APPOINTED PATH TO PARTAKING OF THE DIVINE NATURE 290

DEEP DIVE: THE CORPORATE GLORIFICATION OF THE BODY OF CHRIST 294

THE FAMILY AND THE CHURCH................................297

APPREHENDING THE HEAVENLY LIFE IN CHRIST 301

DEEP DIVE: THE NEW CLOTHING FOR WHICH WE PERSEVERE 302

THE CALLING IS UNIMAGINABLE AND WEIGHTY 307

DEEP DIVE: THE WEIGHT OF GLORY.................................309

FOR FURTHER READING 315

ABOUT THE AUTHORS... 317

ACKNOWLEDGEMENTS

Author Gary Huffman: I would like to thank the following:

- My wife, Paula, for her long-suffering (this took a long time – looks like we made it to "just before" the Day of the Lord!)

- The late brother Bob Baker, for his early encouragement and ideas in the formation of this book.

- Brother Doug Woodward, for his openness to new ideas and catching the vision for *The Revealing.*

Author Doug Woodward: I would like to express my gratitude to:

- My wife, Donna, who continues to put up with our dining room table covered over with my work, many research papers, and a stockpile of no less than two dozen books (although at any given time, many more reside there).

- All the friends of Faith Happens Books that gave of their valuable time to review and comment on the manuscript. And to Ann Christopher who put up with her aching back to help proof this book.

- All those who provided approbations extoling the virtues of this book. Their kind remarks are appreciated so much.

- And to my new friend and brother in the Lord, Gary Huffman, for waiting so patiently while I completed my previous book, *Revising Reality,* and gave only a small slice of my time until this spring, 2017. Gary had volunteered to proof *Revising Reality* and did a tremendous job. He has been a pleasure to work with. His grace and accommodating spirit made this mutual endeavor great fun and rewarding. I learned a lot from you Gary! Thank you.

Together, we also should acknowledge that our work has been enhanced greatly by the scholarship and writing of Drs. Michael S. Heiser, Michael J. Svigel, and John H. Walton. We very much appreciate Lambert Dolphin (and have included one portion of his fine work). Of course, we have brought to the reader's attention some great works from much loved Evangelical scholars that have gone on to be with our Lord, such as DeVern Fromke, William G. Moorehead, G.H. Pember, Arthur Pink, T. Austin-Sparks, Ray Stedman, and John Walvoord. We believe that those readers not familiar with them will benefit greatly by being introduced to their work. Note, "For Further Reading" lists the works of these gentlemen referenced in this book and also several others that we believe would be excellent books to add to the reader's library.

And a very special thank you to Dr. Michael K. Lake, for his willingness to pen an excellent foreword for our book. His contribution is so very helpful. We commend Dr. Lake's works to the reader as his material is cutting edge while at the same time deeply grounded in the Scripture.

FOREWORD

Dr. Michael K. Lake, Th.D.

[19] "Repent ye therefore, and be converted, that your sins may be blotted out, when the times of refreshing shall come from the presence of the Lord; [20] And he shall send Jesus Christ, which before was preached unto you: [21] Whom the heaven must receive until the times of restitution of all things, which God hath spoken by the mouth of all his holy prophets since the world began. [22] For Moses truly said unto the fathers, A prophet shall the Lord your God raise up unto you of your brethren, like unto me; him shall ye hear in all things whatsoever he shall say unto you. [23] And it shall come to pass, that every soul, which will not hear that prophet, shall be destroyed from among the people." Acts 3:19-23

IT HAS BEEN TWO THOUSAND YEARS since Peter uttered these words recorded in the Book of Acts. When you understand the significance of what he was sharing, this apostle of old took us from his day all the way to the Valley of Armageddon.

There are precious few in the Church that recognize the prophetic significance of the Feasts of the LORD. These powerful appointed times (*moedim*) were divine rehearsals and would find their fulfillment in Messiah. The first time that Jesus came He fulfilled the Spring Feasts: He was the Passover lamb, the unleavened bread come down from Heaven, and the first fruits offering. We are currently in Shavuot (Pentecost), were Messiah is empowering us to be His witnesses in all the Earth. And finally, we are racing toward the Fall Feasts, which we find played out in the Book of Revelation. I believe the apostle Peter was alluding to the Day of Atonement. We find in Leviticus:

> [27] Also on the tenth *day* of this seventh month *there shall be* a day of atonement: it shall be an holy convocation unto you; and ye shall afflict your souls, and offer an offering made by fire unto the LORD. [28] And ye shall do no work in that same day: for it *is* a day of atonement, to make an atonement for you before the LORD your God. [29] For whatsoever soul *it be* that shall not be afflicted in that same day, he shall be cut off from among his people. Leviticus 23:27-29 (KJV)

There is a prophetic correlation between the Day of Atonement and the Valley of Armageddon.

Day of Atonement	Valley of Armageddon
Those that have not humbled themselves and been brought under the blood of the lamb sacrificed for atonement will be cut off.	Those that have not humbled themselves, yielded to the Gospel of the Kingdom, and been brought under the blood of the Lamb of God for salvation will perish at the brightness of His return.

As we have progressed toward the restitution of all things, each generation since the Early Church has been given the holy tasks of maintaining the faith that was first delivered to the saints (Jude 1:3) and to grow by standing on the shoulders of past generations, until we finally reach the *measure of the stature of the fullness of Christ* (Eph. 4:13). To be honest, the history of the Church has revealed many dark times in which Jesus could hardly be seen at all. Yet, in the midst of that darkness, the Almighty would release a spark of truth that would ignite the Remnant in that generation; the results were *repentance, revival, and reformation.*

In our day, the ancient directive that was established in the plains of Shinar is now in full swing. The globalist agents of the Mystery Religions have labored for well over a century to pervert our faith, entrap God's people within a *Laodicean* materialistic prison, silence the preaching of the Gospel of the Kingdom, and prepare the hearts of mankind for the arrival of the Son of Perdition. However, as the world races toward darkness, God's flame of truth is reigniting within the hearts of the Remnant once again.

As the Remnant awakens, we have several tasks before us:

- Assess the plans and progress of the enemy.
- Regain the faith that was once delivered to the saints.
- Return to the process of growing in our walk in the Kingdom.
- Seek to reach the stature of the fullness of Christ.

There is a "showing" coming before the "showdown" in the Valley of Armageddon. As the agents of the kingdom of darkness labor tirelessly to fulfill the promise of the serpent in the Garden, Heaven is preparing to release a fresh anointing to manifest the fullness of Christ through His Body on the Earth. The greatest hour of the Church is nearly upon us. The world is about to truly see Jesus glorified through His people. As the mark of the beast is being prepared, citizens of the world must be given a clear choice: the Kingdom of God or the kingdom of darkness. Within the pages of this book, Gary Huffman and S. Douglas Woodward provide a clarion call to the Remnant. Now that we have assessed what the enemy has done, it is time to return to the biblical mandates of a pure faith, a holy heart, and a clear vision of the Messiah in the lives of His people. Gary and Doug have powerfully presented these truths as salvation, sanctification, and glorification, *but from a unique eschatological point of view.* So, Remnant of the Most High God, it's time to roll up our sleeves and get about the business of the Kingdom. May the Lamb of God that was slain receive the reward of His suffering!

Michael K. Lake, Th.D.
Kingdom Intelligence Briefing   May 2017

PREFACE

Gary L. Huffman

"My little children, of whom I travail in birth again until Christ be formed in you" (Galatians 4:19)

In 1971, this study started for me when traveled from Seattle to Akron, Ohio with a Christian musical group called "The New Men." We had a free night, so we went to a Billy Graham movie at a neighboring town. The couple at the door handing out flyers for the movie was friendly. We talked to them afterwards thinking we would tell them about the Baptism of the Holy Spirit (as we would often do). Well, they said they had the Baptism, but did we know that there was something more after that? We were shocked! We thought we had it all and were out to tell the world, but then we heard that there was a third experience (salvation, baptism, and "the third stage"). They called it the "Feast of Tabernacles."

They invited us to their home and we heard many interesting things that night that I will never forget. Some was off the track of truth, but some was right on. This started me on the Bible study which I will share with you throughout this book. There will be concepts that may challenge some of your old established beliefs (dare I call them pet doctrines?) If the truth be told (and I aim to do that), Church pulpits and hymns have taught these doctrines for hundreds of years. However, you may still find some of what I will share here surprising. Please reserve judgment until you have read the entire study. Something that concerns you or is unclear in one chapter will likely become clearer in the next. While I don't claim to know everything about sanctification and glorification – for we see through a glass dimly – I have learned a great deal in my Christian experience and in persistent study in the Word of God. I pray the insights shared here inspire and influence you toward greater holiness and a closer walk with our Lord. I pray you come to understand the glory that awaits.

Humanity was not originally designed to live apart from the manifested *presence* of God. But something deferred God's ultimate plan for His people (both Israel and the Church) for perhaps 6,000 years so far. However, God has a strategy to bring humankind back into His glorious presence. All Christians know a good portion of that plan; however, what they have learned is rather paltry when compared to the whole body of truth. For sure, they know that plan begins with justification – the work of Christ reconciling the world to Himself – but is that where the story ends? Is the requirement only believing in the cross to take away our sins, with the promise we go to heaven after we die? Hardly. Indeed, it is a poor facsimile of the promises concerning what lies in store for those who believe. So, it is this *full story* we attempt to answer in *The Revealing*.

Note that much of the book connects the dots between scores of passages in the Bible. That's intentional of course. We are focused on what the Word of God teaches about the manifestation of the glory ahead for the children of God. So, to begin, here are the essential points I seek to establish with my co-author Doug Woodward:

- God has revealed a pattern for *His Plan* to restore and complete the Church.

- The fulfillment of God's Plan primarily consists of revealing His Glory in and through the Church to a dying world.

- This Plan includes revealing Jesus as the Messiah to Israel through His Glorious Body – the Church, which is itself, the "revealing."

- Understanding God's plan in depth, in its fullness, will motivate the Church to unity and maturity, to face the difficult days ahead.

However, as another important word of preface, I must make clear that the subject we discuss in this book has often been distorted into harmful admonitions, if not outright heresies. While the subject, rightly presented, stands at the pinnacle of the Bible's message to the Body of Christ, there have been well meaning teachers like George H. Warnock, associated with "the Latter Rain Movement" that taught the truth of Israel's feasts in good faith, but wound up going down the wrong path. Some of his best teaching has influenced me positively and is reflected in our study. As such, I believe we should not throw out the baby with the bathwater. Nevertheless, we must not overlook how the teaching in *The Revealing* has been, and could be again, misinterpreted.

Here is what I think Warnock got wrong: he taught that the typology of the Feast of Tabernacles, aka the "manifestation of the sons of God," applied only to a small group and perhaps *only one individual*. Such "individualist" teaching comprises one of the most aberrant traits of a cult. That is indeed heresy – we can't find that teaching anywhere in the Bible.[1] To expound on this further: here is a concise summary of the matter from *Theopedia*, in its article addressing the false teaching of the "Manifest Sons of God" (which was a defining belief in the Latter Rain movement):

- An elite group of believers will be revealed in the end times to prepare the world for the millennial reign of Christ.

- These believers will become a literal incarnation of Christ on earth and, while still living, will obtain immortal spiritual bodies;

- With these new bodies they will be invincible, able to change their appearance, to speak any language, and to teleport;

---

[1] The teaching that an elite group of believers will be changed and get the world ready for the Second Coming of Christ, is a very dangerous deception. These teachings have "manifested" in the modern movements such as the Third Wave/New Apostolic Reformation, Dominionism, Kingdom Now, and The Seven Mountains Movement.

- They will have the ability to perform signs, healings, and miracles greater than those of the Apostles;

- They will complete the Great Commission by (causing) the greatest revival of history, converting the majority of the world to Christ.

These affirmations stretch every aspect of what the Bible teaches about the manifestation of the sons of God. However, it is our premise that Christians need to have their understanding of the glorification of God's children stretched a bit, but within the bounds of biblical teaching, of course.

I hold that the prayer of Jesus in John 17 (which Warnock misinterpreted), will be answered only when *there is complete unity in the Body of Christ*. Understanding "the Mystery" of the Body of Christ will in fact be the antidote to the fallacious teaching characteristic of those apostasies that we see too often, frequently emerging from Pentecostalism, where excesses have too often surfaced.

To conclude this preface, please know that The Feast of Tabernacles (as the consummate work of God's grace, building on justification and extending through sanctification) will be, instead, a corporate, *inclusive* event as the Body of Christ comes together in the wake of coming tribulations, persecutions, and even martyrdom. I hope our teaching in this book corrects such errors as discussed above while disclosing, among many other key truths, the relevance of the feasts of Israel for the Church *at the end of this age*. This is especially so for the feast we know as Tabernacles, where I began my remarks.

Gary L. Huffman
Great Falls, Montana   May 2017

The Revealing

"In my opinion, whatever we may have to go through now is less than nothing compared with the magnificent future God has planned for us. The whole creation is on tiptoe to see the wonderful sight of the sons of God coming into their own. The world of creation cannot as yet see reality, not because it chooses to be blind, but because in God's purpose it has been so limited—yet it has been given hope."

Romans 8:19-20 (Philips)

1

INTRODUCTION

S. Douglas Woodward

WHAT IT TAKES TO PUBLISH A BEST SELLER

The bestselling books on eschatology sell well primarily because they are ultra-sensational, not because they are, at their core, thoroughly Biblical. Fearsome images of destruction, fantastic predictions about doom, little-known facts about ancient giants, exposing the diabolical and paranormal, along with controversial stories peppered with speculation about extraterrestrials and UFOs, dominate the eschatology genre today. Not that these subjects are off-base. Nor are they necessarily wrong-headed. I would be the first to admit, I have written a number of those books myself and often recommend them. Nevertheless, does eschatology demand we focus only on stupendous if not supernatural subjects? Reviewing the most successful titles today certainly suggests this is so.

However, in this book, *The Revealing*, author Gary L. Huffman (with a little help from me along the way) takes a very different tact in exploring what we affirm is the most important topic in Bible prophecy; that is, *what believers can expect when Christ comes for them in the clouds and how we prepare ourselves for this transition to the next life.*

As you will see, we proclaim that there is, basically, a third work of grace (as "holiness" groups might term it). But there is no real need to affix any label. For the essential issue is connecting the various meanings of the *Feast of Tabernacles* (aka *Booths* or *Succoth*) to the process of *sanctification* – culminating in our *glorification*. Consequently, we will study many Old Testament passages and unite them with New Testament truths that explain their meaning. However, the process works both ways. We will show how we can derive great value in grasping the meaning of Old Testament symbols and "types", allowing them to disclose to us what the deeper biblical teaching in the New Testament actually is.

More specifically, the authors will answer questions like, "What will we be like after the Rapture happens? What will "the raptured" be doing next? Will we just rest, retire, refresh relationships with friends and family, and merely repeat song after song singing of God's lovingkindness and grace?" I certainly want to engage in those things. However, will we be left out of the battle taking place on planet Earth? Or will the newly glorified saints discover instead that we are stepping up our efforts to reach unbelievers and especially the ancient people of God? Joining with the two witnesses, will we also display signs and wonders to convict and convince a dying world that God earnestly desires those that don't know Him to become His children? This book argues that is exactly what we will be doing. And the case will be made that this is what the Bible teaches.

Those of us who believe that the Rapture of the Church happens some time before His visible return at the Second Coming will find the most unique assertion of this book fascinating. In other words, those who believe the Rapture precedes the visible Second Coming by some allotted period, will be particularly blessed by spotlighting this truth. Therefore, Pre-Tribulation, Mid-Tribulation, and Pre-Wrath Rapture adherents can more easily adopt the "Huffman Hypothesis" without altering their perspective on the timing of the Rapture. The "time gap" between the Rapture (when the Church is snatched up to be with Jesus – the Second Coming, Phase I) and the visible return of Jesus (the Second Coming, Phase II), could be as much as ten years or as little as 30 days (as my friend and former co-author Douglas Krieger espouses). No matter. The unusual interpretation, discussed later in this book, can be adopted by any of these positions.

On the other hand, Post-Tribulation Rapture believers will reject the premise of our particular proposal for how the Church is involved during the Great Tribulation. Despite disagreeing with our supposition about what happens after the Rapture, the good news is that these brothers and sisters can nevertheless benefit from all other subjects taken up in this work, which is about 95% of the material readers will find here. This is so since the majority of our subject matter deals with sanctification and glorification, perhaps the most under-studied, misunderstood, and nearly abandoned doctrines of our day – especially for those committed to the study of prophetic themes.

OUR PRIMARY ASSUMPTIONS

Right up front, I wish to present other key presuppositions of the book, besides the distinction between the Rapture and the Visible Second Coming I've already disclosed.

First, the typology of the Old Testament is crucial to the conclusions drawn in this book. Explicit passages (on what was originally only Huffman's view of the role of the Church during the tribulation period) are few, but the typology is plentiful. As the reader will discover, the many scholars we reference also support many aspects of his (and now my) conclusions, although at your first encounter you may be stunned.

Secondly, both Gary and I affirm that salvation involves spirit, soul, and body. Our deliverance by the power of God is through regeneration of the spirit, sanctification of the soul, and glorification of our body. But what we usually miss is how *sanctification connects to glorification*. As I asserted at the outset, there is great interest in fossils of giant humanoids, in the burgeoning appearance of flying saucers, in the frightful cases involving the paranormal, and in the many proofs of the Christian worldview. Think of the Shroud of Turin, or archeological finds that verify challenged geographical facts and historical dating of the Bible. While these intriguing matters attract our attention, *think how little we concern ourselves with developing holiness in this life and exploring the nature of our life after this one.* In other words, little interest exists in how we become holy – and whether we should even bother with it, since God is loving and forgiving anyway! Consequently, we have little grasp of how deepened holiness sought after now, translates into glorification at the resurrection (or for those alive when the Lord comes, the aforementioned event we all call *the Rapture).* Does this seem smart?

In dramatic contrast, about 100 years ago, sanctification was serious business and on the heart of most American Christians. A breakoff denomination from Methodism, the Nazarene Church, taught its members the "Second Blessing." While Pentecostals connected a "second work of grace" known as *the Baptism of the Spirit* evidenced by speaking in tongues. (the first work of grace was justification), the Nazarenes taught "entire sanctification." In essence, their teaching was this: if you worked hard enough at being holy, one day God would eradicate your sin nature and you would BE *completely holy from that point forward.* My loving grandmother (my father's mom) was indeed a saint, but she could also be ridden by guilt if she did something she considered a sin. That usually amounted to little more than watching the famous CBS TV Western, *Gunsmoke,* which ran from 1955 to 1975, the longest running action series ever in the United States. This was one of her guilty pleasures, featuring Miss Kittie's infamous saloon, The Long Branch. Should she be watching a TV show where many of the scenes took place in a saloon (and brothel!)? My grandmother Minnie's concern for living a sinless life, in my view, went just a bit too far and became an unhealthy obsession as she fretted over vices and entertainment, like playing cards and dancing. (At least she played "Old Maid" with me – it was great fun.)

John Lithgow's strict preacher character in the movie, *Footloose* (1984) exuded the "holiness hang-up" – kids shouldn't go *footloose!* Of course, Kevin Bacon demonstrated otherwise. Kid's "got to go footloose!" Despite Hollywood's derision of such "holy convictions," we still must ask ourselves in the twenty-first century, "Doesn't the LORD call us to live holy lives?" The answer should be obvious to readers. But how do we obtain it?

Literature about the processes of sanctification and glorification is scarce. What does exist, with only one or two exceptions, was published at least 20 years ago. There are no popular books on these subjects nowadays, because the subject isn't popular by all counts even among enthusiastic prophecy buffs. And yet, one would think the incredible prophetic prospect of sharing the glory of God would be a captivating topic for all earnest believers and especially those who hold prophecy out as one of their favorite subjects to study. We acknowledge a supernatural worldview and we believe that God is active in our everyday world. But the most supernatural event of all, our resurrection or rapture culminating in a new, glorious body free from sickness and sin, isn't a "hot topic."

Indeed, the wondrous promise of partaking in the divine nature remains easily overridden by topics that focus on apologetics or simply titillate the imagination. It is incumbent upon us to realize that *defenses for the faith* do NOT really target unbelievers. Proofs for the Bible are popular because *they strengthen the faith of the already faithful.* What this says about us isn't very hard to pin down. Simply stated, we would rather entertain topics that encourage our faith instead of hearing a sermon or reading a book dedicated to the process of "growing in holiness." We would much prefer to be "wowed" by an astonishing discovery on the Nephilim more than learning what the future life of believers will be like. Why is this so? One is hard to swallow (it demands the elimination of sin in our lives), while the other is incredulous ("We partake of the *divine nature* – are you serious?"). Both doctrines challenge our mindset and lifestyle. They require we reset our priorities. Our routines ought to require spiritual workouts and finding ways to spike our interest in future glory.

Going one step further: there are three baptisms, water, the Spirit, and *fire* (Matthew 3:11). Christians, even the more spiritual among us, avoid the baptism of fire like the plague. But Huffman insists we face the fiery furnace. Concerning the baptism of fire, his instruction constitutes an inspired and hopeful perspective acquired through his many years of personally living out the life of Christ. His words encourage us while still adhering to the uncompromising plain talk of scripture. The Word always yields the fruit of the spirit (Galatians 5:22-24) which develops in the life of the believer as a result of the Spirit's work and through "the crucifixion of the flesh" (overcoming the power of sin in the flesh). *"Knowing this, that our old man is crucified with him, that the body of sin might be destroyed, that henceforth we should not serve sin."* (Romans 6:6, KJV)

PUTTING FIRST THINGS FIRST

Regardless of the topics chosen by most Christian writers and teachers, we believe it is obvious that subjects which occupy first place in the teachings of the Apostles *should be priority for us as students of the Word*. Biblical prophecy, for those who study eschatology, stands out as one of those teachings. However, learning about "what is the hope of His calling" and "the glory of the inheritance in the saints" (Ephesians 1:18) is a positive, wonderful promise of Bible prophecy that deserves greater emphasis – even though it seldom finds its way into sermons, serious bible studies, or best-selling books. I find this lapse especially disconcerting. It has caused me to rethink my writing subject matter. And I therefore recommend that students of eschatology balance what they study.

One such priority that must be underscored to make our way to our "future state," consists of the essentials of salvation. Here typology helps. Huffman explains that the pattern God has established through His "Tabernacle in the Wilderness" reinforces the stages of salvation. The Tabernacle confirms and illustrates justification, sanctification, and finally, glorification. When finally considered, we realize how all three stages combine into one seamless package. We see this plainly in one paragraph from the book that also highlights the insights in store for the reader:

Sanctification blossoms through internalizing the Word of God, taking it into our hearts and feeding upon it daily. We grow progressively as we "absorb" the knowledge of God's Word, and actively practice its teachings. And it is the Spirit that is the catalyzing agent, taking God's Word and applying it to our "hearts and minds." We develop in what was once called, "the Deeper Life" through the dual action of the Living Word and the Divine Spirit. Obedience to *the Word and the Spirit* is the "warp and woof" of how *we grow in our faith, experience the life of Christ living in and through us, conquer sin, begin our progression toward holiness, and carry out our mission as Christians.* Furthermore, as it relates to the subject of this book, this process constitutes the doorway through which we must pass to ultimately obtain glory. *"The Revealing" commences in our earthly life NOW, and will be completed to the fullness of the measure of Christ, at the Day of Christ.* However, and this is vital, if we do not commence the process of sanctification now, we have reason to doubt we will see our salvation completed later. Our salvation is **not** *made sure* unless we progress into the inner sections of the Tabernacle.

This book's goal might be summarized in this one verse, *"(That) the eyes of your understanding being enlightened; that ye may know what is the hope of His calling and what (are) the riches of the glory of His inheritance in the saints"* (Ephesians 1:18). Nonetheless, you will be astonished how this theme exists throughout Scripture and constitutes the *pinnacle of the plan* for the Body of Christ and its members.

I would be amiss if I didn't point out that the claims made in this book demand strong scriptural support. Happily, I can boast that seldom has a book paid more attention to providing biblical evidence of what it teaches. You will benefit greatly by working through the many scriptures provided here, topic by topic, a good portion of which the reader may not have understood before now. Because of the plentiful presentation of scripture in the pages ahead, we offer this book hoping it becomes a useful resource to "recharge your batteries" and "realign your wheels."

ITS ABOUT THE AFTERLIFE, AFTER ALL

Almost all religions speak of an afterlife. Perhaps the exception would be those teachings that advocate reincarnation, a continuous process of jumping from one imperfect life to another in pursuit of purification – someday – but only if you perform *enough good works to earn it.* But for most other religions, the afterlife is viewed as a *destination.* This is where the teaching of the Bible is so different from all other religions. In effect, Christianity comprises the opposite of reincarnation. To be more specific, Karma means "getting what you deserve" while *the gift of glory,* what God promises those that trust in Him, "is getting what you don't." *"For by grace you have been saved through faith. And this is not your own doing; it is the gift of God."* (Ephesians 2:8) Our "next life" unlike the teaching of other religions, centers on a perfected corporeal nature – a tangible, powerful, almost "superhero" body. And that body is no longer subjected to corruption. That leads me to ask the question, "How much more would we look forward to the next life if we were promised living in a body like Superman?" Guess what? The promise of the Christian's future life is nearly that – without the Kryptonite. And It's even better than looking forward to the company of 72 virgins which Islamic extremists contemplate. [Has anyone ever noticed how sexist that view of the afterlife is?] In Christianity, *both men and women* – there is no distinction – will be glorified at our resurrection or the Rapture.

Marx said that religion is the opiate of the people. Some critics describe the Christian faith as "Pie in the sky, by and by." Others have slammed believers by saying, that we are "so heavenly minded, we are no earthly good." Well, we are here to say it's high time we get ourselves focused on the promise of the glory of God which will soon be imparted to each of us who eagerly await the return of Jesus. Day by day, our translation, our being "caught up" to be with one another and with our LORD comes closer (Romans 13:11). We should always affirm that our transition to the next life may be only days, weeks, or months away. We must make the most of our time for the days are evil (Ephesians 5:16). And as the Psalmists says, "So teach us to number our days, that we may apply our hearts unto wisdom." (Psalm 90:12 KJV)

DIVING INTO THE DEEP WATER

In addition to providing a readable narrative from cover to cover, our book employs a technique called the "Deep Dive," invented in my very first book seven years ago (*Are We Living in the Last Days?*) Together, we employ it to appeal to authorities, highly regarded scholars (and a few from a writer like me), with evangelical backgrounds committed to the infallibility and inspiration of the Bible. What they teach adds significant depth to the book's thesis. No surprise many of them lived long ago.

In some cases, the reader may feel the guidance provided hovers a bit "over their heads." I would request that the reader recognize that those who pick up this volume have varied backgrounds and differing levels of Bible knowledge under their belts. For those more studied, the *Deep Dives* don't hold back in supplying solid scholarship, including reference to Hebrew and Greek. Ultimately, we hope that everyone will gather a good measure of value from them. In contrast, for those readers who are more skeptical, we hope that having a cadre of other teachers sharing their understanding on these topics helps to confirm our own.

Most points made in this book, Evangelical readers will find acceptable. But some points Huffman and I make will no doubt challenge readers to "search the scriptures to see if these things be so." (Acts 17:11) Additionally, we attempt to differentiate between what is speculation and what we believe the Bible presents without much (if any) debate. We avoid being dogmatic on most topics. Where we are, we don't expect "push back" from the reader. Nevertheless, the arguments are developed carefully and thoroughly to avoid as many anticipated counter-arguments and challenges as possible.

FINAL THOUGHTS

Now, I should explain my involvement in this effort. First, I contribute as a heavily involved editor and to a lesser extent, a co-author, offering some clarification from my learning along the way. Gary and I have met many times and exchanged too many emails to mention. We took these opportunities to discuss the more controversial issues I confronted when reading his manuscript. It wasn't always easy for Gary to convince me he was right about what he had written. Nevertheless, we accomplished this meeting of the minds through a number of long distance phone calls over Skype (Gary lives in Montana and I in Oklahoma). Additionally, we did have the pleasure of meeting once face to face at my daughter's apartment in Seattle when I was visiting and Gary was driving back to Montana from a vacation he just completed in Washington State. Consequently, while I'd like to share only in the accolades this book might garner, I deserve more than equal blame for any mistakes and errors contained herein. Performing the work of a contributing author, its editor and its publisher demands I receive the lion's share of blame for where we go awry.

On that count, to those that have followed Faith Happens, this book is the first officially published by me under the new corporate title, FAITH HAPPENS BOOKS LLC. I hope many other books will follow under this banner. I certainly have no lack of ideas myself for more books, and hope to work with other authors who have great ideas to share. I just hope they share the work ethic of a Gary Huffman.

If you appreciate what we have presented here, do share with your friends, and show your gratitude by offering up a sacrifice of writing a short review on one of the various on-line services where book reviews are encouraged. It's a big help. It might even be rewarded by our Heavenly Father for blessing us with your important contribution to spread the word! Now on to the study while the LORD still tarries.

S. Douglas Woodward
Oklahoma City, Oklahoma   May 2017

1: GOD'S PATTERN FOR RESTORATION

ONE SHINY PENNY

Ever since the resurrection of Jesus, born-again believers who have died, have gone to heaven to be with the Lord. One day, those "sleeping" believers and the one generation of believers living on the earth at that time, will have their bodies changed. They will return to rule the earth in the authority of Jesus Christ and manifest His glory over all the earth. Some Christians will have been in heaven for (plus or minus) 2000 years – and some will have been there only a year, a month, or a day![ii] The ones who are raptured, or taken up alive, may barely see "heaven"!

Even if they are taken up before the last seven years before Christ's visible return (Daniel's 70th Week), they will return right before or within the seven years to rule with Christ (the specific timing depends on your brand of eschatology). So, the maximum time in heaven for these saints could be seven years! If so, it seems heaven alone cannot be the reward that God has for those that love Him. God is just and His grace extends beyond our imaginings. What could the true reward be for those who believe in Him? Seven years isn't enough. In this book, we argue *His greatest gift is His glory in which we shall share.*

[ii] We will discuss later that the Old Testament believers may have been taken to be with Christ to dwell in Heaven when He ascended (Acts 1). If they were resurrected (see Matthew 27:52-53), they were not glorified at that time, but their spirits "in Abraham's Bosom," might have ascended with Christ when he "led captivity captive." (Ephesians 4:8)

Mat 20:1-16: [1]"For the kingdom of heaven is like a landowner who went out early in the morning to hire laborers for his vineyard. [2]Now when he had agreed with the laborers for a denarius a day, he sent them into his vineyard. [3]And he went out about the third hour and saw others standing idle in the marketplace, [4]and said to them, 'You also go into the vineyard, and whatever is right I will give you.' So they went. [5]Again he went out about the sixth and the ninth hour, and did likewise. [6]And about the eleventh hour he went out and found others standing idle, and said to them, 'Why have you been standing here idle all day?' [7]They said to him, 'Because no one hired us.' He said to them, 'You also go into the vineyard, and whatever is right you will receive.' [8]"So when evening had come, the owner of the vineyard said to his steward, 'Call the laborers and give them *their* wages, beginning with the last to the first.' [9]And when those came who *were hired* about the eleventh hour, they each received a denarius. [10]But when the first came, they supposed that they would receive more; and they likewise received each a denarius. [11]And when they had received *it,* they complained against the landowner, [12]saying, 'These last *men* have worked *only* one hour, and you made them equal to us who have borne the burden and the heat of the day.' [13]But he answered one of them and said, 'Friend, I am doing you no wrong. Did you not agree with me for a denarius? [14]Take *what is* yours and go your way. I wish to give to this last man *the same* as to you. [15]*Is it not lawful for me to do what I wish with my own things? Or is your eye evil because I am good?'* [16]*So the last will be first, and the first last. For many are called, but few chosen."*

Jesus tells us about a man who hired laborers for his vineyard. The laborers hired at the eleventh hour were paid the same as the laborers hired the first hour – one penny. This tells us, indirectly, that heaven is not our reward but is "a wonderful waiting room" until all laborers are paid the same wages on the same day. We believe scripture teaches that our wages, our reward, begins at the resurrection when the glorification of each believer takes place. This, we believe, is *the one shiny penny.*

HEAVEN IS NOT OUR REWARD

Jesus taught us to pray, "thy kingdom come, thy will be done, on earth as it is in Heaven" – *this prayer will be answered* because it is the heart of God. God will bring His Heavenly Kingdom to this earth. The fullness of our inheritance is yet to come, even though we have already "legally" received all things in Christ (As far as the Most High God is concerned, it is settled – a "done deal"). Comprehending this fact constitutes our *ultimate motivation* to persevere until we finish the race and win the "prize of the High Calling of God in Christ Jesus."

A quick study about heaven might help answer some reasonable questions the reader has about our final reward. We begin in Hebrews:

> **Heb 12:18-24** [18]For you have not come to the mountain that may be touched and that burned with fire, and to blackness and darkness and tempest, [19]and the sound of a trumpet and the voice of words, so that those who heard *it* begged that the word should not be spoken to them anymore. [20](For they could not endure what was commanded: *"And if so much as a beast touches the mountain, it shall be stoned or shot with an arrow."* [21]And so terrifying was the sight *that* Moses said, *"I am exceedingly afraid and trembling."*) [22]*But you have come to Mount Zion and to the city of the living God, the heavenly Jerusalem,* to an innumerable company of angels, [23]to the general assembly and Church of the firstborn *who are* registered in heaven, to God the Judge of all, to the spirits of just men made perfect, [24]to Jesus the Mediator of the new covenant, and to the blood of sprinkling that speaks better things than *that of* Abel.

The writer of Hebrews says that we believers have come to Mount Zion, also calling it the City of the Living God, the Heavenly Jerusalem, and the Church of the Firstborn. These are all terms for the Church... for believers... those that call upon the name of Jesus Christ! This does not consist in merely the location in the sky to which we will someday go. Heaven is a place. However, the reward goes beyond living in the "sweet by-and-by." The reward is found among *the assembly of who we are, the Church*, as it is meant to be, even *today*.

Abraham waited for this city (the Assembly – not heavenly bliss):

Heb 11:10 for he waited for the city which has foundations, whose builder and maker *is* God.

Abraham's offspring waited for this city:

Heb 11:16 But now they desire a better, that is, a heavenly *country*. Therefore, God is not ashamed to be called their God, for He has prepared a city for them.

Even we are waiting until the completion of this city:

Heb 13:14 For here we have no continuing city, but we seek the one to come.

Even now, the Church is not yet built into that complete city. God continues in the process of building it. When the Church receives her inheritance, she will be that permanent city. Jerusalem is that city. *But that city comprises believers from all time who become glorified – that they may dwell there.* **Jerusalem isn't just a place, it is a people!**

Gal 4:26 Jerusalem above is free, *which is the mother of us all.*

Here in Galatians, Paul refers to "Sarah" which represents the heavenly city of Jerusalem – which we see consists of those who believe in Christ.

Rev 3:12 He who overcomes, I will make him a pillar in the temple of My God, and he shall go out no more. *I will write on him the name of My God and* **the name of the city of My God, the New Jerusalem,**

which comes down out of heaven from My God. And *I will write on him My new name.*

Rev 21:2-3 [2]Then I, John, saw *the holy city, New Jerusalem, coming down out of heaven from God, prepared* **as a bride adorned for her husband.** [3]And I heard a loud voice from heaven saying, "Behold, *the tabernacle of God is with men,* and He will dwell with them, and they shall be His people. God Himself will be with them *and be* their God.

Rev 21:9-14 [9]Then one of the seven angels who had the seven bowls filled with the seven last plagues came to me and talked with me, saying, "Come, I will show you **the bride, the Lamb's wife.**" [10]And he carried me away in the Spirit to a great and high mountain, and showed me the great city, the holy Jerusalem, descending out of heaven from God, [11]**having the glory of God.** Her light *was* like a most precious stone, like a jasper stone, clear as crystal. [12]Also she had a great and high wall with twelve gates, and twelve angels at the gates, and names written on them, which are the names of the twelve tribes of the children of Israel: [13]three gates on the east, three gates on the north, three gates on the south, and three gates on the west. [14]Now the wall of the city had twelve foundations, and on them were the *names of the twelve apostles of the Lamb.*

In fact, God plans to bring Heaven to Earth, restoring Eden to the entire earth for us to tend. This was Adam's original job – a job at which he failed miserably. (We explore the concept of this restoration of Eden later in Chapter 8 for it is core truth, being much more than a metaphor.)

So how does God intend to do this? By manifesting His Kingdom through His Church to the earth! This is the New Jerusalem coming down from heaven to earth. "Thy kingdom come, thy will be done, on earth as it is in heaven". One day *all believers* will be included in this throng. But our focus in this book is the **Church of Jesus Christ** – the people called out for His name. (Acts 15:13-15). We read about this parenthetical process, known by God from the beginning:

> **Acts 15:12-18** [12] Then all the multitude kept silence, and gave audience to Barnabas and Paul, declaring what miracles and wonders God had wrought among the Gentiles by them. [13] And after they had held their peace, James answered, saying, Men and brethren, hearken unto me: [14] Simeon hath declared how God at the first *did visit the Gentiles, to take out of them a people for his name.* [15] And to this agree the words of the prophets; as it is written,
>
> > [16] *After this I will return, and will build again the tabernacle of David, which is fallen down; and I will build again the ruins thereof, and I will set it up:* [17]*That the residue of men might seek after the Lord, and all the Gentiles, upon whom my name is called, saith the Lord, who doeth all these things.*
>
> [18] Known unto God are all his works from the beginning of the world.

These verses all speak of the Church, but are commonly mistaken for descriptions of Heaven. Notice the New Jerusalem is prepared as "a bride for her husband" in Revelation 21. In verse 9, the angel says he will show John "the bride, the Lamb's wife." What does he show John as the bride? *The great city, the Holy Jerusalem, descending out of heaven from God, having the glory of God.* This is not heaven, *but rather comes down from heaven, and dwells on* or exceedingly close *to earth*. **The great city, the New Jerusalem is the bride of Christ.** When Jesus returns to the earth with *His holy ones in glory* (remember *saints* means "holy ones" and that includes *all believers*), that is a *partial fulfillment of the New Jerusalem coming down from heaven to the earth.*

There have been many false distinctions made between the "place" of heaven, the New Jerusalem, and finally, of where and what believers consist. First off, a common mistake asserts heaven is the residence of all believers. Not so. Heaven can mean many things in the Bible, but we must not mistake it for the New Jerusalem which actually is the residence of all believers. (Be mindful that ultimately no differentiation in eternity (after the Millennium) exists between the Church and believers from all ages).

Next, the usual perspective separates **the place from the people** *that comprise the New Jerusalem. The Scripture equates the two.* It is not an easy concept for us to grasp – that the glorified believers and the city itself are identified as essentially "one and the same." Certainly, we can reckon that glorified believers would make the city gleam. But the connection is more than that. *This composition of the city as the glorified believers and not just the "pearly gates" is what Scripture teaches and is a cornerstone of the book you are reading.* (See the "Deep Dive" at the end of chapter 9, *The New Jerusalem*, for a detailed explanation of the "city").

GOD'S ETERNAL PURPOSE: THE ULTIMATE MOTIVATION

Heb 1:1-3 [1]God, who at various times and in various ways spoke in time past to the fathers by the prophets, [2]has in these last days spoken to us by *His* Son, whom He has appointed heir of all things, through whom also He made the worlds; [3]who being the brightness of *His* glory and the express image of His person, and upholding all things by the word of His power, when He had by Himself purged our sins, sat down at the right hand of the Majesty on high.

Jesus, the only begotten Son of God, is the "brightness of His (God's) glory." No one else now or in eternity will alter that truth. But God has a plan for this earth and His Church that transcends what we see and hear and touch, and it includes His glory. God wants us to comprehend His plan for the Church – all of us – because this is the *ultimate motivation* to "fight the good fight of faith." Jesus, as the "heir" of all things, *has shared His inheritance with us, His Bride and His Body.*

Heb 12:2 Looking unto Jesus, the author and finisher of *our* faith, *who for the joy that was set before Him* endured the cross, despising the shame, and has sat down at the right hand of the throne of God.

Apparently, so we are told, even the Son of God needed motivation to fulfill His mission on the earth. His Father had revealed to Him that there was a joy waiting for Him at the end of the cross that He had never known. Jesus was not only looking forward to the joy of being back with His Father, but bringing many with Him to exhibit them to the Father – so that the Father and the Son might enjoy the presence of these glorified sons and daughters, while they enjoy the presence of the LORD.

1 Thes 1:9b-10 And how you turned to God from idols to serve the living and true God, [10] and *to wait for his Son from heaven*, whom he raised from the dead, *Jesus who delivers us from the wrath to come*. (ESV)

Acts 7:54-60 [54]When they heard these things they were cut to the heart, and they gnashed at him with *their* teeth. [55]But he, being full of the Holy Spirit, gazed into heaven and saw the glory of God, and Jesus standing at the right hand of God, [56]and said, "Look! I see the heavens opened and the Son of Man standing at the right hand of God!" [57]Then they cried out with a loud voice, stopped their ears, and ran at him with one accord; [58]and they cast *him* out of the city and stoned *him*. And the witnesses laid down their clothes at the feet of a young man named Saul. [59]And they stoned Stephen as he was calling on *God* and saying, "Lord Jesus, receive my spirit." [60]Then he knelt down and cried out with a loud voice, "Lord, do not charge them with this sin." And when he had said this, he fell asleep.

God gave Stephen *a vision to give him strength* just as Jesus needed a vision or revelation to strengthen Him to endure the cross. His vision included Jesus standing at the right hand of God (the place of honor and authority), and *the visible glory of God in the open heavens*. Meditating on the glory of God strengthens us. Realizing that we will share that glory incentivizes us to endure hardship, persecution, and even martyrdom. It is vital to understand how important this doctrine is.

THE HOPE OF GLORY

Oftentimes, Christians aren't clear regarding what their motivation should be to "make it through the pearly gates", or how our lives can exemplify the life of Christ right now. However, the proper motivation should not be confusing nor fail to fully inspire us. Paul teaches:

> **Col 1:26-27** [26]*The mystery which has been hidden from ages and from generations, but now has been revealed to His saints.* [27]To them God willed to make known what are the riches of the glory of this mystery among the Gentiles: *which is Christ in you, the hope of glory.*

Paul's letter to the Colossians is most clear: *Glory is our hope* – we typically think of this "glory" as living in heaven ("Lord Build Me A Cabin in Gloryland" or "take me to my mansion in the sky"). However, it is much more than that. *"Christ formed in you"* brings this glorious fulfillment. The word translated "in" also means "among" *which carries with it the idea that Christ is to be formed in the many-membered Body of Christ.* In this book, we will examine at least some of the many riches of God's glory to which Paul refers. In this regard, consider this passage chock full of meaning:

> **Heb 2:9-10** [9]But we see Jesus, who was made a little lower than the angels, for the suffering of death crowned with glory and honor, that He, by the grace of God, might taste death for everyone. [10]For it was fitting for Him, for whom *are* all things and by whom *are* all things, *in bringing many sons to glory*, to make the captain of their salvation *perfect through sufferings.*

It is the riches of glory, not the hope of heaven, that we should seek. Understand God has a father's heart – He wants His sons and daughters to be secure, but he also wants them to succeed, to complete their mission. And success in God's eyes is maturing to a glorious destiny – receiving the promised inheritance – coming unto glory (*experiencing* God's manifest presence) and expressing it on this earth. We should show forth His glory

21

in our lives – now in part - and at the Parousia (His coming) in fullness. Escaping trials and tribulation is not the primary directive for the Church.[iii] Fellowship through suffering is (Phil 3:10). Glory grows through tribulation.

Eph 3:8-11 [8]To me, who am less than the least of all the saints, this grace was given, that I should preach among the Gentiles the unsearchable riches of Christ, [9]and to make all see what *is the fellowship of the mystery, which from the beginning of the ages has been hidden in God* who created all things through Jesus Christ; [10]to the intent that now the *manifold wisdom of God might be made known by the Church* to the principalities and powers in the heavenly *places,* [11]according to the eternal purpose which He accomplished in Christ Jesus our Lord, [12]in whom we have boldness and access with confidence through faith in Him. [13]Therefore I ask that you do not lose heart *at my tribulations for you, which is your glory.*

Scholars teach that Satan was jealous of Adam's authority and even more that Adam should possess even a modicum of God's glory. As Lucifer, (or Light-Bearer), he held the responsibility of leading the heavenly worship of God. As the most exalted angel and perhaps the high priest of heaven, apparently, he had the privilege of exhibiting a large measure of glory that ultimately belonged to God. However, Satan lost God's glory through his rebellion. Since then, he seeks to establish his own glory. Furthermore, by usurping the dominion God gave Adam he hopes to deny the measure of God's glory destined for humanity.

God does have a plan to reveal His manifold wisdom *through the Church to the principalities and powers in heavenly places.* This will include a "panoramic" exhibition of God's authority directed at Satan, his angels, as well as the antichrist and false prophet. More to the point, God intends to display His glory through the Church – the body of Christ – which will be

---

[iii] This statement has nothing to do with the timing of the Rapture. Or the necessity that the Body of Christ "go through the Tribulation."

fully infused with the glory of God. God's strategy, at its very least, consists of a restoration of humankind to its Edenic state on this earth. The Church is His mechanism, the means, for accomplishing this goal.[iv] But we will discuss a greater goal in a moment.

Gen 1:26 Then God said, "Let Us make man in Our image, according to Our likeness; let them have dominion over the fish of the sea, over the birds of the air, and over the cattle, over all the earth and over every creeping thing that creeps on the earth."

Humanity was given dominion over God's creation, but in Genesis, chapter three, Adam relinquished his dominion. By his disobedience to God's command, he gave over his dominion to the usurper, Satan. Adam had been given special abilities necessary to rule the entire planet. But believing there was more for humanity to gain if he listened to the serpent, Adam lost this dominion. Instead, principalities and powers who desired that rule took it from him. Humanity forfeited the right to rule this earth (and possibly the entire cosmos). Thus, we reap thorns and thistles.

Gen 3:18-19 [18]Both thorns and thistles it shall bring forth for you. And you shall eat the herb of the field. [19]In the sweat of your face you shall eat bread, till you return to the ground. For out of it you were taken; for dust you *are,* and to dust you shall return."

Rom 3:23 For all have sinned and fall short of the glory of God.

[iv] Israel was established to be the light unto the Gentiles. (Isaiah 42:6, 49:6) However, Israel and Judah failed in their duty and God, turned to the Church to complete His plan for saving humanity and restoring God's plan for humankind. This does not mean that God has rejected Israel. Israel's rejection opened the door to Gentiles that they may be the means to advance God's plan. (Romans 11:11,12) God has not forsaken Israel. (Romans 11:1) Of course, this is an enormous controversy within the Evangelical church, so it is not easily demonstrated. There is also the view of Dr. Michael S. Heiser (who we will liberally reference) who sees the 10 lost tribes of Israel signifying "the nations" and the Gentile believers in whom they were mixed. Therefore, in Heiser's view, it is as if the dispersion of the 10 lost tribes infused of all humanity with the possibility to be saved by the God of Israel, Yahweh. See Michael S. Heiser, *Reversing Hermon,* Defender Books, Crane, Mo.

Adam came short of God's glory. Indeed, so do we. Literally, Adam desired "soul food" over spirit food. As his spirit died because his soul became dominant, he lost the measure of God's glory given to him at creation. This glory had been his clothing. He was naked in an "ultimate sense." He hadn't experienced life without this sheathing. We could say, "He lost his *glory* shirt" in his deal with the devil. Was this glory the glory of God? It was one kind of glory. And there are different kinds of glory. "There is one glory of the sun, another glory of the moon and another glory of the stars, for one star differs from another star in glory." (1 Corinthians 15:41) After he sinned, Adam's glory was lost. He was in this spiritual sense, "naked." Therefore, he hid from God. His glory was missing. This wasn't just about being "in the altogether."

Moreover, it was by this presence of God that Adam was meant to have dominion over creation. After he lost his glory, Adam lost the ability to exercise dominion. It has always been God's plan (as a wise father) that *humanity must be the one to gain that dominion back.* God could have said (as many of us do as mothers and fathers) "you messed up, I'm going to do it myself." However, through Christ, who became man, God did accomplish salvation on our behalf. As we will address in detail in this book, that salvation is not just justification, it is also sanctification and glorification. One day, in the Millennial Kingdom, humanity will take dominion back from Satan and his henchmen. As Milton put it, we will see "Paradise restored."

But allow us to put forth this premise: We will acquire *some* facets of "gaining back dominion" before the Kingdom comes in full. We witness this in all manner of spiritual warfare. ("On this rock, I will build my Church and the gates of hell shall not prevail against it" Matthew 16:18). To the extent the Church influences society positively and permanently, dominion is restored. On the other hand, in this life before Christ returns, complete dominion (as preached in "Dominionist" theology) will not be achieved by the Church. The Body of Christ, during this age, is to be characterized more *by persecution and martyrdom, than by acquiring and exercising dominion.*

Still, we are to engage in alleviating suffering and in championing justice, in a biblical sense, even though our efforts will never achieve the status of "mission accomplished." Human government, even inspired by God's Law, will not bring true unity and justice, for humanity remains flawed. Finally, we should not mistake the ultimate purpose of God's plan. Instead of "dominion" or restoring Eden, what God has had in mind even before the world was, his "ultimate intention," was hidden from God's people and His prophets, until it was revealed to the Apostle Paul. It is known as "the Mystery". We pause here for a Deep Dive on "the Mystery" by examining the words of the great teacher, T. (Theodore) Austin-Sparks (1888 – 1971), from his book, *The Stewardship of the Mystery, Volume 2.* This teaching is foundational to our argument in this study.

DEEP DIVE: *THE REVEALING* OF THE MYSTERY IN PAUL

T. Austin-Sparks

In his last Letters, Paul gave a strong place (from which to view) this conflict of the ages... In "Colossians" it is obvious (see 1:13,20; 2:15), but in "Philippians" it is more by inference and allusion. We believe that when Paul, writing of the self-emptying of the Son of God, said that "although He was equal with God, He thought it not something to be grasped (held on to) to be equal with God, but emptied Himself" (2:6), the Apostle was alluding to the ambitious pride of "Lucifer" to be like the Most High (Isa. 14:14; Luke 10:18). If this is a right interpretation (cf. 2 Pet. 2:4 and Jude 6), then the scene in Philippians two, in keeping with so much other teaching in the New Testament, is that of the Son of God becoming the Son of Man, taking man-form to fight out this battle with the usurper. "A final Adam to the fight and to the rescue came." And Paul, a "good soldier of Jesus Christ," in the same letter (Phil. 3) goes on to show that the way of victory is the way of "counting all things as loss." Let us sum up. "Before the foundation of the world" Divine counsels took place which are called "The good pleasure of His will," "The mystery of His will," "The purpose of Him Who worketh all things according to His will..."[v]

We have also seen that the heart of this whole matter is reached and touched by one phrase which sums up the purpose of God at the end. That phrase is: "Unto a dispensation of the fulness of the times, to sum up (reunite) all things in Christ, the things in the heavens, and the things upon the earth; in Him, I say..." (Eph. 1:10). But, while we may embrace that as the end, beyond this age, our concern is for this age. Is there no way or hope for at least an approximation to that now? The Letter would surely leave us in our dilemma if it only pointed to a future age and had no answer to the present tragedy. But it has the answer. This answer is given by several means and ways. Perhaps the simplest, most direct, and most helpful way will be to let Paul himself be the answer. Seeing that the Apostle makes such strong and categorical claims as to his own personal revelation, it will be best to examine that revelation, and what it did in this man's life. We noted at the end of chapter four that the personal name of Jesus Christ is mentioned some forty times in this short letter, plus all the pronouns "He," "Him," "His," "Whom." This, in itself, is the strong clue. In his Letter to the Galatians, Paul made the statement in these words: "An apostle (not from men, neither through man, but through Jesus Christ, and God the Father...)"; "Neither did I receive it from man... but through revelation of Jesus Christ"; "It was the good pleasure of God... to reveal His Son in me" (Gal. 1:1,12,15,16).[vi]

The next thing that we must take account of in this connection is Paul's particular viewpoint. It is from above. Five times in this Letter to the Ephesians he uses the phrase "in the heavenlies" (1:3,20; 2:6; 3:10; 6:12) and in that form it is found nowhere else. This is one of the most difficult of Paul's phrases for any of us to understand. We are not altogether helped by other phrases referring to heaven, such as "every knee should bow, of things in heaven..." (Phil. 2:10). The translation "in the heavenly places" is not too fortunate. But let us look at the various references. 1. The present realm and

---

[v] Austin-Sparks, T. The Stewardship of the Mystery - Volume 2 (Kindle Locations 385-395). Austin-Sparks.Net. Kindle Edition.
[vi] Ibid. (Kindle Locations 526-537).

nature of the believer's blessings is in the heavenlies. 1:3. 2. Christ is now seated in the heavenlies "above all rule, and authority, and power, and dominion, and every name..." 1:20,21. 3. The position of Christ is said to be that also of the Church. 2:6. 4. There are principalities and powers in the heavenlies which are having made known unto them, through the Church, the manifold wisdom of God. 3:10. 5. The warfare of the Church is not now in the realm of flesh and blood, but in the heavenlies with principalities and powers, etc. 6:12...[vii]

We must return to the great matter of the "Mystery," for there are things related thereto in (Ephesians) which need clarifying. In all his Letters Paul uses this word some twenty times [some are duplicated in this list]:

1. The mystery (secret) of the blindness which has happened to Israel. Rom. 11:25.
2. The mystery of the wisdom of God. 1 Cor. 2:7.
3. The mysteries of God. 1 Cor. 4:1.
4. The mysteries in speaking in tongues. 1 Cor. 14:2.
5. The mystery of the Rapture and change of body. 1 Cor. 15:51.
6. "The mystery of His will." Eph. 1:9.
7. The mystery made known to Paul. Eph. 3:3,4.
8. The fellowship of the mystery. Eph. 3:9.
9. The mystery of the union between Christ and the Church. Eph. 5:32.
10. The mystery of the Gospel. Eph. 6:19.
11. The mystery which hath been hid. Col. 1:26.
12. The mystery of Christ within or in the midst. Col. 1:27.
13. The mystery of God—Christ. Col. 2:2; 4:3.
14. The mystery of iniquity. 2 Thess. 2:7.
15. The mystery of the faith. 1 Tim. 3:9.
16. The mystery of Godliness. 1 Tim. 3:16. (Some of the above are duplicated.)[viii]

T. Austin-Sparks, *The Stewardship of the Mystery, Volume 2*, Austin-Sparks.Net, Kindle Edition

The mystery has many aspects as Austin-Sparks lays out. But the crux of the mystery boils down to this: *Christ in us, the hope of glory* (Col

---

[vii] Ibid., (Kindle Locations 610-619).
[viii] Ibid. (Kindle Locations 599-607).

1:27) and the mystery of *the union between Christ and the Church* (Ephesians 5:32). We will continue to explore these throughout our book.

However, one of the great points of divergence between Pre-Millennial Theology and Post-Millennial Theology has to do with the impact of the Church during this current dispensation.[ix] Catholic Theology is Post-Millennial, asserting that the Church will continue to improve society until Christ returns. Pre-Millennial Theology believes the Church of Jesus Christ will not bring the Kingdom of God to this earth. Nevertheless, we are to model the Kingdom, through the power of the Holy Spirit, providing witness and with attesting signs (as God wills) that a great change is coming – *a great reversal of fortune awaits.* As our lives are changed, we supply greater testimony to the coming Kingdom. And recall: Paul tells us we were saved *for good works* (not saved *by good works*), that we should *walk in them.*

> **Eph 2:8-10** [8]For by grace you have been saved through faith; and that not of yourselves, *it is* the gift of God; [9]not as a result of works, so that no one may boast. [10]For we are His workmanship, *created in Christ Jesus for good works,* which God prepared beforehand *so that we would walk in them.*

THE GLORY OF GOD

GLORY as defined in Webster's New Collegiate Dictionary:
1. Praise, honor. 2. Something that secures praise and honor.
3. Resplendence, magnificence.

The Glory of which we speak comprises the second and third meanings listed above. The first meaning speaks of our praise and honor unto God, while the second and third relate to something that emanates

---

[ix] For the record, the authors hold to the dispensational framework to understand the cosmos and the salvific events of the Bible. We are not dogmatic about this however. We recognize others whom we cite may be Covenantal or Wesleyan. Still, their points of view are worthy for review within the scope of this book to the extent they speak on this topic.

from God – His magnificence. Glory is the manifestation of the presence of God – manifested to us in a very real and often physical way. At times His presence is felt, heard, seen, and even smelled. Healings and other physical miracles are our most common example today of the manifest presence, or glory of God. To the Jews of Moses' and Solomon's time, the Shekinah Glory of God was the pillar of fire by night and the cloud of glory by day. It guided them through the wilderness, appeared in the tabernacle and temple, and *was a sign to all other nations that the God of Abraham, Isaac and Jacob was with them*. In later chapters, we will expand on the Glory of God and the Jewish Exodus experience. What will be a central proposition of this book is that *the "pillar and the cloud" will appear again in the last days. And the Church will be right in the middle of it.*

One of the greatest problems of the Church today is that we do not understand God's glory. Sharing His glory doesn't excite us. We would much rather *seek the riches of this world than the riches of His glory.* But Peter teaches that it is an unfathomable gift, a precious gift, to become partakers of God's glory (2 Peter 1:4).

2 Pet 1:4 By which *He has granted to us his precious and very great promises,* so that through them *you may become partakers of the divine nature*, having escaped from the corruption that is in the world because of sinful desire. (ESV)

DEEP DIVE: THE GLORY OF GOD

The basic idea of the Hebrew *kabod [which is often replaced by the word, Shekinah]* is that of **weightiness**. People become 'weighty' through riches. "Abraham became very weighty in livestock, in silver, and in gold" (Gen 13:2).

God's 'glory' is to be perceived in His works, i.e.., the world, human beings, and historical events (Num 14:21-22; Ps 8:5; 57:6.12; Isa 6:3). In the age to come it will be revealed so that all flesh will see it (Isa 40:5; Hab 2:14). This revelation of divine glory can be connected with the restoration of Israel (Isa

42:8; 43:6-7; 48:10-11; 58:8; 60: 1-3) and/or God's judgement (Isa 59: 19; Ezek 28:22; 39: 13.21). In some texts belonging to the Priestly Document (P), one of the sources of the Pentateuch, the Glory is associated with the Pillar of Cloud and fire, which according to older sources, encompassed Yahweh leading the People through the desert and indicated God's presence at the Tabernacle: "... the Glory of Yahweh appeared in the Cloud" (Exod 16: 10): "The Glory of Yahweh rested on Mount Sinai, and the cloud covered it ... the Glory of Yahweh looked ... like a devouring flame on the top of the mount" (Exod 24: 16-17: ef. 40:38: at night, there was fire in the Cloud); "The Cloud covered it [the Tabernacle), and the Glory of Yahweh appeared" (Num 17:7: cf. Exod 24:43-44).

In Ezekiel, the prophet recounts that he once had a vision of a throne-chariot in heaven. Seated upon the throne was a "Likeness as the appearance of a man *(Adam)*" (v 26). Ezekiel describes the body of this figure: "His torso was like gleaming metallic substance, and his lower body was like fire." The prophet concludes: "This was the appearance of the likeness of the Glory of Yahweh" (v 28).

In Ezekiel 9:3-4, Yahweh and the Glory even appear as interchangeable, as is the case with God and the Angel of Yahweh in Genesis, Exodus and Judges: "Now the Glory of the God of Israel had gone up from the cherubim on which He rested to the threshold of the house and called to the man in linen ... and Yahweh said to him ..." However, the Glory has a radiant body and is accompanied by phenomena similar to those associated with the Glory in the P source and the texts influenced by it: When the Glory rose from the cherubim, the Temple was "filled with the Cloud, and the court was full of the brightness of the Glory of Yahweh" (9:4). The NT continues the usage of the LXX; *doxa* in the NT should often be seen as a technical term loaded with the Jewish understanding of "glory". *Doxa* is a phenomenon of light characteristic of angelophanies, theophanies, and Christophanies (Luke 2:9: 9:31-32; Acts 7:55; 2 Pet 1: 17). The Son of Man will come in or with God's glory (Mark 8:38 [cf. 2 Thess 1:7]: 13:26; cf. 10:37: Malt 19:28).

The Gospel of John speaks of "seeing" the glory of God (11 :40) or the glory of the Son (1:14: 12:41; 17:24; cf. 2:11). In 1:14 ("we saw his glory"), the background may be the vision of the Glory described in Exod 33: 18-34:8 (HANSON 1977:90-100); it is thus possible that John regards the Son not only as the one who manifests the divine presence and power through his words and works, but as the personified Glory. It is noteworthy that the phrase "saw his glory" is repeated in 12:41: "he [Isaiah] saw his [Christ's] glory". Isa 6:1, however, reads "I saw the Lord seated upon a high and lofty throne... " *Tg. Isa.* 6: 1 reads, "*yeqara* of the Lord", but *Tg. Isa.* 6:5 says that the prophet saw "the glory (*yeqara*) of the Shekinah of the King of the Worlds". While *sekina* in the Targums is generally regarded as a buffer word meant to safeguard God from coming into too close contact with the world, the Merkabah mystics used it as an alternative term for the Kabod. Thus, *Ma'aseh Merkabah* contains the statement, "I gazed upon the Shekinah and saw everything that they do before his Throne of Glory *(kabod)*" (SCHAFER 1981:§592). When it is said that Isaiah saw the glory of Christ, it is implied that the Son is the divine manifestation upon the heavenly throne, even the Glory.

There are other NT texts; where Jesus may be seen as the Glory. The conjunction *kai* ('and') in Acts 7:55 may be epexegetical: "... he saw the Glory of God, namely *(kai)* Jesus standing at the right hand of God" (MARTIN 1967:312). The idea of Jesus being seated at the right hand of the "Power" (Mark 14:62 [Luke 22:69: "Power of God"]). however, may be taken to imply that he was enthroned alongside the Glory, since the mystical texts use "Power" as a synonym of "Glory" (FOSSUM 1989:191-193).

The Christological hymn in Phil 2 says that Christ was "existing in the form *(morphe)* of God" (v 6). This description corresponds to the subsequent incarnational phrases, "taking the form of a slave", "becoming in the likeness of men", and "being found in the fashion as a man" (vv 7-8). Given the OT evidence that God's visible form is the man-like form of the Glory, Phil 2:6 would seem to say that Christ is the divine Glory. The same idea is expressed by the title, "image of the invisible God", in the beginning of the hymn on Christ in Col I: 15-20 (FOSSUM 1989:185-190). In Biblical terminology, "image" (and "likeness"), "form", and "glory" are interchangeable (FOSSUM 1985:269-270.284).

In Ephesians I: 17, we find the phrase, "the God of our Lord Jesus Christ. the Father of the Glory". The parallelism suggests; that "our Lord Jesus Christ" is "the Glory". Tit 2: 13 may be translated, "the Glory of our great God and Savior, Christ Jesus". Here Christ Jesus may be the Glory of "our great God and Savior". Jas 2: I, a notoriously difficult verse to translate, may in effect say, "our Lord Jesus Christ, the Glory". 1 Pet 4:14 says, " ... the Spirit of the Glory and of God rests upon you." Here, too. the Glory may be the Son.

Phil 3:21 speaks of Christ's "body of glory" to which the body of the believers will be conformed. The term may reflect that of *gup hakkabod* or *gup hasekina* found in the Jewish mystical texts (SCHOLEM 1991:278 n. 19). The idea that one who ascended to heaven was transformed, often as a result of the vision of God (or his garment) or the divine Glory, is found in several texts (MORRAY-JONES 1992:11.14.22-26). In 2 Cor 3:18, Paul says that the Christians, "gazing with unveiled face on the Glory of God, are being transformed into the same image, from glory to glory." Here mystical terminology has been adapted *to describe what goes on when the Christians are reading the Scriptures.* In contrast to the Jews (cf. vv 13-16; 4:4), the Christians see the Glory of God. Moreover, they are transformed into the "same image", obviously, that which they behold. A few verses later, it is said that Christ is the "image of God" (4:4). The Glory obviously is Christ.

Romans 8:29-30 says that the elect will be "conformed to the image of His Son" and be "glorified" (cf. vv 17-18; Col 3:4; 1 John 3:2). The same eschatological adaptation of this thought is found in 1 Cor 15:49, "... we shall bear the image of the heavenly man." Paul can even say that the Christian male *is* the "image and glory of God" (I Cor 11:7). The statement alludes to Gen 1:26 and presupposes that Christ is the heavenly Adam, the Glory, after whose image and likeness man was created (cf. 4Q504. frag. 8, "You have fashioned Adam, our Father, in the image of [Your] Glory").

From the *Dictionary of Deities and Demons in The Bible* (excerpts, pp. 348-352):

THE PATTERN

This book is based in no small part on the *typology* of the Old Testament and the prophetic implications. *Understanding what is meant by typology is important.* While we cite Scripture explicitly to demonstrate our argument's biblical basis (no one can accuse us of failure to cite Bible passages), the *typology and foreshadowing* contained in the Old Testament comprises a crucial element of our approach. Therefore, we offer the following citation from *The International Standard Bible Encyclopedia:*

DEEP DIVE: TYPOLOGY

The word "type" is derived from a Greek term *tupo (tupos)*, which occurs 16 times in the New Testament. It is variously translated in the King James Version, e.g. twice "print" (John 20:25); twice "figure" (Acts 7:43; Romans 5:14); twice "pattern" (Titus 2:7; Hebrews 8:5); once "fashion" (Acts 7:44); once "manner" (Acts 23:25); once "form" (Romans 6:17); and seven times "example" (1 Corinthians 10:6,11; Philippians 3:17; 1 Thessalonians 1:7; 2 Thessalonians 3:9; 1 Timothy 4:12; 1 Peter 5:3). It is clear from these texts that the New Testament writers use the word "type" with some degree of latitude; yet one general idea is common to all, namely, "likeness." A person, event or thing is so fashioned or appointed as to resemble another; the one is made to answer to the other in some essential feature; in some particulars, the one matches the other. The two are called type and antitype; and the link which binds them together is the correspondence, the similarity, of the one with the other.

Three other words in the New Testament express the same general idea. One is "shadow" (*skia, skia*, Hebrews 10:1), "For the law having a shadow of the good things to come"--as if the substance or reality that was still future cast its shadow backward into the old economy. "Shadow" implies dimness and transitoriness; but it also implies a measure of resemblance between the one and the other.

The second term is "parable" (*parabolh, parabole*, Hebrews 9:9); the tabernacle with its services was an acted parable for the time then present, adumbrating [predicting] thus the blessed reality which was to come. The third term is "copy" or "pattern" (*upodeigma, hupodeigma*), a word that denotes a sketch or draft of something future, invisible (Hebrews 9:23); the tabernacle and its furniture and services were copies, outlines of heavenly things.

Types are pictures, object-lessons, by which God taught His people concerning His grace and saving power. The Mosaic system was a sort of kindergarten in which God's people were trained in divine things, by which also they were led to look for better things to come. An old writer thus expresses it: "God in the types of the last dispensation was teaching His children their letters. In this dispensation, He is teaching them to put the letters together, and they find that the letters, arrange them as they will, spell Christ, and nothing but Christ."

In creation, the Lord uses one thing for many purposes. One simple instrument meets many ends. For how many ends does water serve! And the atmosphere: it supplies the lungs, conveys sound, diffuses odors, drives ships, supports fire, gives rain, fulfills besides one knows not how many other purposes. And God's Word is like His work, is His work, and, like creation, is inexhaustible. Whatever God touches, be it a mighty sun or an insect's wing, a vast prophecy or a little type, He perfects for the place and the purpose He has in mind.

From William G. Moorehead, *The International Standard Bible Encyclopedia*, ed. James Orr (Chicago: Howard-Severance Co., 1930), vol. 5, pp. 3029-3030. See http://www.bible-researcher.com/type.html.

JESUS CHRIST: GOD'S PATTERN FOR RESTORATION

Now we will look at God's Pattern for Restoration – JESUS CHRIST.

The Old Testament typological patterns point to JESUS CHRIST the LORD and that is the basic premise upon which our study will be based. We know that God's eternal plan has always been summed up in Jesus Christ:

Eph 3:11 According to the eternal purpose which He accomplished in Christ Jesus our Lord.

We find that a closer look at the meaning of His *name, title, and office* will give us an insight into God's plan to restore His Church and complete the work He has started:

Eph 1:10 That in the dispensation of the fullness of the times He might gather together in one all things in Christ, both which are in heaven and which are on earth – in Him.

The name, **Jesus**, means "savior" – which speaks of salvation – to which our initial "born-again" experience opens us. This is "the way" spoken of by Jesus in John 14:6:

John 14:6 Jesus said to him, "I am the way, the truth, and the life. No one comes to the Father except through Me.

Jesus is the new and living way to the Father by His sacrificial death:

Heb 10:20 By a new and living way which He consecrated for us, through the veil, that is, His flesh.

Jesus is *the way* (and the only way) to the Father by the Spirit:

Eph 2:18 For through Him we both have access by one Spirit to the Father.

He is the **door** (way) of the sheep into the sheepfold.

John 10:7 Then Jesus said to them again, "Most assuredly, I say to you, I am the door of the sheep.

The door speaks of God, the Son, justification by faith in Jesus (Romans 5:1), and the regeneration of the spirit of the believer, bringing to life, or salvation of the believer's spirit (Romans 8:10). Salvation here means *deliverance of the believer's spirit* or salvation from spiritual death.

Next, His **title**, "Christ," means "anointed one" – which speaks of the anointing of the Holy Spirit – to which our experience of being baptized in (or being "filled with") the Holy Spirit opens us. (Ephesians 5:18) This is the "truth" spoken of by Jesus in John 14:6.

John 14:6a Jesus said to him, "*I am the way, the truth, and the life.*

John 16:13 However, when He, the Spirit of truth, has come, He will guide you into all truth; for He will not speak on His own *authority,* but whatever He hears He will speak; and He will tell you things to come.

1 John 5:6 This is He who came by water and blood – Jesus Christ; not only by water, but by water and blood. And it is the Spirit who bears witness, because the Spirit is truth.

These passages present God, the Holy Spirit, and sanctification of the believer's soul by the Spirit of Truth. *This encompasses deliverance or salvation of the soul* (1 Peter 1:9).

Third, and finally, Christ's **office**, "Lord," means "supreme in authority," or controller. This speaks of Jesus as Master and King over His Kingdom. He is our King and we are His subjects. Our obedience is implied. Brought by the Holy Spirit, the Kingdom brings life and *ultimately the manifest presence of the Father into our lives*. This is the "life" spoken of by Jesus in John 14:6. As we proceed, you will see that this glory is directly connected with the glorification of the believer at our *resurrection and deliverance from the corruption present in our body*.

John 14:6a Jesus said to him, "I am the way, the truth, and *the life.*

John 1:4 In Him *was life*, and the life was the light of men.

Rev 22:1 And he showed me a pure river of *water of life,* clear as crystal, proceeding from the throne of God and of the Lamb.

1 John 1:2 *The life* was manifested, and we have seen, and bear witness, and declare to you that *eternal life* which was with the Father and was manifested to us.

John 5:26 For as the Father *has life* in Himself, so He has granted the Son to *have life* in Himself,

Mat 19:17 So He said to him, "Why do you call Me good? No one *is* good but One, *that is,* God. But if you want to enter *into life,* keep the commandments."

This speaks of *God the Father* – His rule or Shepherding of His family, the Church, through His Son Jesus Christ. This prepares us for the glorification of the Church to come.

THE TRIPARTITE NATURE OF SALVATION FOR HUMANKIND

In the next passage, we discover substantial biblical evidence of the pattern in the *threefold nature of human beings* as the creation of God:

1 Th 5:23 *Now may the God of peace Himself sanctify you completely;* and may your whole *spirit, soul, and body* be preserved blameless at the coming of our Lord Jesus Christ.

In this verse, Paul mentions the *spirit, soul, and body* – the three parts of humanity – in the order of our deliverance. Even if your view of our human nature is "Freudian" and doesn't accept the biblical teaching of our tripartite (threefold person), Paul uses the concept here to imply *the whole person,* and the expression just happens *to fit the Biblical Pattern of salvation.* Delivering us from sin comprises regeneration of the spirit, sanctification of the soul, and glorification of the body. These three parts of the Pattern overlap because they all are constituent portions of our *complete salvation.* In a few words, salvation can be summarized as follows:

1. *Regeneration* (Titus 3:3-7) is the salvation or *deliverance of the spirit.*
2. *Sanctification* (Romans 6:22) is the salvation or *deliverance of the soul.*
3. *Glorification* (Colossians 1:27) is the salvation or *deliverance of the body.*

First, we see salvation or deliverance of the spirit (regeneration):

Tit 3:4-6 [4]But when the kindness and the love of God our Savior toward man appeared, [5]not by works of righteousness which we have done, but according to His mercy He saved us, through the washing of regeneration and renewing of the Holy Spirit, [6]whom He poured out on us abundantly through Jesus Christ our Savior.

Secondly, the next two verses both speak of the second phase of salvation, or *deliverance of the believer's soul* (sanctification):

Phil 2:12 Therefore, my beloved, as you have always obeyed, not as in my presence only, but now much more in my absence, work out your own salvation with fear and trembling;

1 Pet 1:9 Receiving the end of your faith – the salvation of *your* souls.

The New Testament teaches that sanctification is an ongoing process. However, Paul and Peter appear to speak as if sanctification can be achieved in this life. While the issue of "complete sanctification" is a subject we don't wish to explore in depth, arguing for or against it, what is crystal clear is that *we are to set our eyes on sanctification as if it can be achieved fully in this life. We are **not** to have a "defeatist" attitude:* "Nobody's perfect, especially me." We are to look upon Christ through His word. As we learn of Him, as we follow this pattern, we are transformed from "glory to glory." This is the most essential mission of the Holy Spirit – to make us like Christ.

2 Cor 3:17-18 [17]Now the Lord is that Spirit: and where the Spirit of the Lord is, there is liberty. [18]But we all, with open face beholding as in a *glass the glory of the Lord*, are *changed into the same image* from *glory to glory*, even as by the Spirit of the Lord. (KJV)

Thirdly, we read of salvation or deliverance of the body (glorification):

Rom 8:20-23 [20]For the creation was subjected to futility, not willingly, but because of Him who subjected *it* in hope; [21]because the creation itself also will be delivered from the bondage of corruption into the glorious liberty of the children of God. [22]For we know that the whole creation groans and labors with birth pangs together until now. [23]Not only *that,* but we also who have the firstfruits of the Spirit, even we ourselves groan within ourselves, eagerly waiting for the adoption, the redemption of our body.

One of the greatest shortcomings in the Church today is this: *The lack of teaching on sanctification and its connection to glorification.* Christians do not know how the two fit together. We hope to remedy that shortcoming through the teaching presented in this book.

- **The Pattern in The Church:**

This Divine Pattern seen in the believer's life above, is also present in God's provision for the Church. Jesus was crucified and became our way of regeneration and justification. The Holy Spirit was sent and became our way of sanctification. And the Spirit created the Church. Furthermore, from time to time, the power of revival comes upon the Church and, in America, we witnessed this in the so-called Great Awakenings.[x] In the last days, revival (in terms of the powerful working of the Spirit of God in us and through us), will become more and more "standard operating procedure." The signs of the Spirit will be manifested in greater measure. If they aren't being manifested, it could be argued that the Church is obviously not yet ready to receive the final gift of glorification. [xi]

---

[x] See https://en.wikipedia.org/wiki/Great_Awakening.

[xi] The imminence of the Rapture is a core doctrine of the dispensational point of view. According to it, no sign is required before the Church is raptured. However, the Church is likely to be tried by fire "until we all attain to the unity of the faith and of the knowledge of the Son of God, to mature manhood, to the measure of the stature of the fullness of Christ" (Ephesians 4:13, ESV). This aspect of the rapture, to these

John 14:12 Verily, verily, I say unto you, He that believeth on me, the works that I do shall he do also; *and greater works than these shall he do;* because I go unto my Father. (KJV)

- ## **The Pattern in Church History:**

This Divine Pattern is also seen in the recent history of the Church as God began His restoration process. The 1500s brought Martin Luther's Reformation and the emphasis on salvation by grace. This is a revelation of God, the Son, and began to restore the truth of salvation to the Church. The 1900s brought the Pentecostal revival and the emphasis on the baptism of the Holy Spirit. God moved afresh and began to restore understanding of the Holy Spirit and its importance in the daily lives of believers who were filled with the Spirit (Ephesians 5:18). The present and continuing move of God demonstrates His Lordship. We are to follow Him as obedient children.

During the 1960s and 1970s (perhaps the fourth "Great Awakening" in America), the powerful action of the Holy Spirit became apparent to millions in the Church. The popular magazine, *Charisma*, is a prime example of a fresh perspective on the presence and power of Christ's Spirit in our personal lives. Many new organizations were formed that emphasized the power of the Holy Spirit.

We still see the impact of this work of the Spirit, especially in Christian media, most of which was a byproduct of this movement of God. But what is key today being this: *Christ dwells in us.* This empowerment lies "latent" within us. We must learn how to allow the power of the Holy Spirit to awaken us and work through us. It is the same Spirit who did great miracles in times past. He will do them

---

authors, becomes increasingly less relevant as we move closer to the very last of the last days. Jesus taught us to "watch always" – and that is a commandment for us all.

again through His people in the Church as the situation demands and in accordance with His providence. *But **our work now** is to continue to be transformed more and more into His image through the **work of the Spirit.***

- ### The Pattern in the Maturing of the Believer from Child to mature Son:

The first part of the Pattern <u>introduces new believers into the Kingdom:</u>

1 John 3:1-2 Behold what manner of love the Father has bestowed on us, that we should be called children of God! Therefore, the world does not know us, because it did not know Him. [2]Beloved, now we are children of God; and it has not yet been revealed what we shall be, *but we know that when He is revealed, we shall be like Him*, for we shall see Him as He is. (Note: This NKJV translation rings true, because we are now children of God, growing up to be mature sons of God).

The second part of the Pattern <u>gives us the Spirit of adoption:</u>

Rom 8:15 For you did not receive the spirit of bondage again to fear, but you received the Spirit of adoption by whom we cry out, "Abba, Father."

The third part of the Pattern will <u>culminate in the adoption as sons...</u>

Rom 8:17-25 [17]And if children, then heirs – heirs of God and joint heirs with Christ, if indeed we suffer with *Him, that we may also be glorified together.* [18]For I consider that the sufferings of this present time are not worthy *to be compared **with the glory which shall be revealed in us.*** [19]For the earnest expectation of the creation eagerly waits *for the revealing of the sons of God.* [20]For the creation was subjected to futility, not willingly, but because of Him who subjected *it* in hope; [21]because the creation itself also will be delivered from

41

the bondage of corruption into the *glorious liberty of the children of God.* ²²For we know that the whole creation groans and labors with birth pangs together until now. ²³Not only *that,* but we also who have the firstfruits of the Spirit, even we ourselves groan within ourselves, *eagerly waiting for the adoption, the redemption of our body.* ²⁴For we were saved in this hope, but hope that is seen is not hope; for why does one still hope for what he sees? ²⁵But if we hope for what we do not see, we eagerly wait for *it* with perseverance.

Paul asserts that we do not see the adoption of sons yet – therefore we hope and wait for it. The death that grips not only humankind, but since the fall of Adam, *all of creation*, will one day be stamped out. This "curse" to which the creation was subjected will be overcome when the Children of God are manifested in glory ("the redemption of our body").[xii] The three baptisms mentioned by John the Baptist in Matt 3:11 are also a reference to the same Pattern:

> **Mat 3:11** I indeed *baptize you with water* unto repentance, but He who is coming after me is mightier than I, whose sandals I am not worthy to carry. He will baptize you *with the Holy Spirit* and *fire*.

Simply put, baptism means to "dunk or immerse in." Baptism with water speaks of the initial born again experience. Baptism in the Holy Spirit remains controversial to this day. But being baptized in the Spirit should mean to all Christians that we are suffused (inundated) by the power of God. *Baptism in fire* speaks of the fire of purification, administered by the Holy Spirit (Spirit of adoption), to make believers ready for God's glory. We generally omit the third and final baptism from our theology today. If that statement offends you, perhaps you are someone for whom that word is intended.

[xii] This law of death is called by science the *Second Law of Thermodynamics*, or the *Law of Entropy*. This states that the whole universe tends to disorder, and is winding down. Only the manifest presence of God can reverse and even supersede this law. God will reverse this trend through the same power by which He glorifies the saints! Believers stand at the crossroads or a tremendous act of re-creation!

JESUS CHRIST: GOD'S PATTERN FOR RESTORATION

JESUS ▪	CHRIST ▪▪	the LORD ▪▪▪
Son	Holy Spirit	Father
Way	Truth	Life
"Savior"	"Messiah" – "Anointed One"	"King"
Salvation	Holy Spirit Baptism	Kingdom
Justification	Sanctification	Glorification
Spirit	Soul	Body
1500's	**1900's**	**Present**
Reformation: Salvation by Grace	**Spirit Renewal:** Baptism of Spirit	**Lordship:** Obedience
Revelation of: God, the Son	**Revelation of:** God, the Holy Spirit	**Revelation of:** God, the Father
Baptism of Water	Baptism of Spirit	Baptism of Fire
Children of God I John 3:1-2	Spirit of Adoption Rom 8:15	Adopted as Sons Rom 8:17-25
Tabernacle in the Wilderness		
Outer Court	Holy Place	Holy of Holies
Feasts of Israel		
Feast of Passover	Feast of Pentecost	Feast of Tabernacles
Mount Sinai		
Base of Sinai: Camp of Israel	1/2 Way Point: 70 Elders eat with God	Summit of Sinai: Moses in Glory of God
Eden		
Eden	Garden of Eden	Tree of Life
The Heavenly Tabernacle		
Earth/Air	Sky	Heavenlies

TABLE 1 - JESUS CHRIST THE LORD: GOD'S PATTERN FOR RESTORATION

Nevertheless, two issues remain: "Does the Bible teach this to be so?" and "Are we willing to be baptized with fire that we may attain to the glory of God and be partakers of the divine nature?" Note: Every key word in this proverb fits into the right-hand column on the Pattern Chart above: "*In the light of the king's face is life. And his favor is like a cloud of the latter rain.*" (Proverbs 16:15) "For through Him we both have access by one Spirit to the Father."[xiii] Ephesians 2:18.

Through Him (Jesus, the Way) we have access by the Spirit (of Truth) to the Father (of Life). This is the complete pattern of the glory that comes to us through Jesus Christ, our Lord. Please study the following chart to make it clearer (a picture is worth a thousand words!) and read the following Deep Dive from Woodward's previous book, *Blood Moon*, who offers several useful contributions to this topic:

DEEP DIVE: THE LEAST UNDERSTOOD PHASE OF SALVATION – GLORIFICATION

More often than not, those rejecting the Christian gospel do so because they have not heard the gospel presented in a biblical way. What they reject is not necessarily 'the gospel truth' but their misconception of it. In a similar way, too often the sound bites we throw out concerning how to *become* a Christian as well as what it means to *be* one, fall on deaf ears. To many, our oft-repeated phrases regarding 'accepting Christ' have become meaningless clichés. In effect, our pearls have been trampled in the dust.

Because our easy summations are meager and hollow sayings in the minds of many people, the meaning of 'receiving Christ' is not obvious to all those outside the circle of faith. We who attempt to share our faith (and that should include all who call themselves Christian), now must work harder than ever to explain what it means to come to an authentic, saving faith in Jesus Christ.

[xiii] Note: Credit to Bill Britton (Latter Rain teacher) for aspects of this chart. See Bill Britton, *Sons of God - Awake!* p. 24, Springfield. Note: we do not subscribe to *Latter Rain* teachings.

Likewise, when it comes to, if you will, explaining the essence of salvation, our notions seem rather abbreviated. Salvation comprises much more than most of us realize. We understand we are forgiven of our sins. When Jesus died at Golgotha outside Jerusalem, He took our sins to the cross with Him. *"He who knew no sin became sin on our behalf that we might become the righteousness of God in Him."* (2 Corinthians 5:21, paraphrased). We also know that *"While we were yet sinners, Christ died for us"* (Romans 5:8). This is indeed wonderful news. The whole story, however, involves far more that should be communicated.

Evangelicals readily acknowledge *being saved* enables us to 'go to heaven.' We recall the famous passage that shrinks the essence of the gospel down to a single verse – John 3:16: *"For God so loved the world that He gave His only begotten Son, that whosoever believeth in Him should not perish, but have everlasting life."* Nevertheless, the culmination of Christian salvation constitutes *one of our best kept secrets.* So much more remains to be said about the afterlife than we have typically been taught. And this lack of understanding constitutes *a big chink in our armor.* Our failure to fully appreciate what lies before us could be our undoing as we enter into these increasingly perilous times where we face persecution and all manner of difficulty. We do well to remember the epistles of the Apostles were written to their churches during times of turmoil. Being a follower of 'the Way' was not an easy task. The leaders of the early church armed the flock with a deep understanding of what was at stake. As we say today, their notion was truly a 'big idea.' For the most part, the early church stood up to the opposition even when it meant martyrdom. *We can be assured what they believed about the afterlife was a major factor energizing their amazing courage.*

That is why Paul prayed for his church at Ephesus with such intensity: he strove earnestly that they might fully realize what the salvation of God through Jesus Christ meant. He prayed that: *"The eyes of your understanding being enlightened; that ye may know what is the hope of His calling and what the riches of the glory of His inheritance in the saints"* (Ephesians 1:18). He also prayed the same for the church at Colossae: *"To whom God would make known what [is] the riches of the glory of this mystery among the Gentiles; which is Christ in you, the hope of glory."* (Colossians 1:27).

Today, more than ever, this astonishing truth is crucial to our Christian perspective: Not only are we made righteous in the eyes of God; but *the glory of God* awaits those who are adopted as His children. It comprises a wonderful and remarkable gift to have 'right standing with God' – but it stands as quite another matter altogether to partake in the *the glory of Christ.*

"The glory of God" – what does that mean? Are we really destined to be glorious like God? Will we really share in His glory? This seems incredible – to some perhaps even heretical. Does the Bible really say such a future awaits us?

Most everyone has at least a vague concept of eternal life. But the truth of the matter goes beyond clarifying that Christians (and orthodox Jews) believe in a bodily, physical resurrection. The historical Judeo-Christian view of heaven begins with an appreciation of our *corporeal* nature there. Jews and Christians believe 'having a body' is a good thing. This stands in contrast to (1) the classic view of the Greeks, and (2) the original Gnostics (familiar to us today through the publication of the Gnostic gospels of Thomas, Judas, and Mary Magdalene), as well as (3) today's variants to Gnosticism—occultists, theosophists, and advocates for the New Age.

All of these religions, whether ancient or current, believe the afterlife implies existence as little more than a *ghost*—a spirit being that passes between 'this side and *the other side.'* They disparage the bodily resurrection because at the core of this universal pagan religion are these beliefs: (1) matter is tainted with evil; and therefore (2) requires a less-than-pure being to handle matter; consequently, (3) the creation was formed by an imperfect 'middle-man' (be it the ancient notion of a *demiurge* or today's new idol implied in 'smart matter' or 'lively matter' as depicted in modern physics – a 'fantastic reality' allegedly explaining miracles and the supernatural). This worldview (or cosmology) provides an explanation for *why evil exists* despite its assumption that 'God is good.' It also provides a defense for God's goodness – known as a *theodicy* – that is, the classic (i.e., ages old) explanation for *why evil exists in the world when God is good.*[xiv] But the point is that, unlike these

---

[xiv] See Woodward's introduction at the beginning of the recent book, *Revising Reality: A Biblical Look at the Cosmos, Volume 1,* for a deeper discussion on Christian theodicy, and the nature of the Cosmos.

other religions, the body in the life after this one, will be glorified. We will share in the glory of God and no longer be corrupted. Nor will the creation. *That is salvation.*

S. Douglas Woodward, *Blood Moon: Biblical Signs of the Coming Apocalypse*, (2014), Oklahoma City: Faith Happens Books, pp. 271-274.

2: THE TABERNACLE IN THE WILDERNESS

THE RELIGION JESUS BROUGHT TO US

In a very definite sense, Jesus Christ did not found a new religion. His mission was to fulfill the old. The Gospels make this plain. For instance, we read in chapter 24 of Luke's "good news:"

Luke 24:27 And beginning at Moses and all the Prophets, He expounded to them *in all the Scriptures the things concerning Himself.*

Luke 24:44 Then He said to them, "These *are* the words which I spoke to you while I was still with you, that all things must be fulfilled which *were written in the Law of Moses and the Prophets and the Psalms concerning Me."*

The law, the prophets, the Psalms, and indeed "all the Scriptures" speak of Jesus. For instance, God gave us *50 chapters* of the Bible that tell us every detail of the Tabernacle in the wilderness. God does not emphasize something without a deeper purpose.

Now, there are many fine books written on the Tabernacle and the symbolism represented by its structure. We will, however, concern ourselves with *its basic pattern* and *unusual furniture.* We do this because Jesus Christ is revealed there *and so is our future life.*

The three basic rooms of the tabernacle were the *Outer Court*, the *Holy Place*, and the *Holiest Place aka Holy of Holies*. There was no shortcut from one to the other. One door opened to the Outer Court. From the Outer Court, there was one way to the Holy Place, and one way to the Holy of Holies. The entrant passed by each piece of furniture in its special order. As we learn why each room and piece of furniture are symbolic of phases of the individual Christian life, and of the Church as a unified body, our advance through the Tabernacle implies a progression *from justification to sanctification to glory*. As we move with our imaginations through the Tabernacle, remember the crucial typological Divine Pattern we have already seen: Jesus Christ our Lord.

(Now please refer to the picture of the Tabernacle on page 64.)

THE OUTER COURT

In the Outer Court are two pieces of furniture – *the Brazen Altar* (Exodus 27:1) and *the Laver*.

> This bronze altar "received" (i.e., on God's behalf) the offerings of the Israelite. God met the Israelite where the Israelite was – in the courtyard – rather than where God was, within the veil. Nevertheless, the Israelite was called to make a special effort to approach God, by entering the courtyard to present his offering (cf. 2 Cor. 5:18-20). (*Constable's Notes*, Exodus, p. 163)

The altar was where the sacrifice was laid out and burnt. It symbolizes the sacrifice of Jesus. To give you an idea of the detail of the symbolism in the tabernacle, the altar was made of brass on wood. Brass is the symbol of judgment and wood is the symbol of human weakness and sin. The wood overlaid with brass symbolizes divine judgment upon sin – the blood of the sacrifice spilled over and covered both. This comprises a picture of Christ's work on the Cross for our redemption as the sacrificial Lamb:

John 1:29 The next day John saw Jesus coming toward him, and said, "Behold! The Lamb of God who takes away the sin of the world!

Rev 13:8 All who dwell on the earth will worship him, whose names have not been written in the Book of Life of the Lamb slain from the foundation of the world.

The Tabernacle is filled with rich symbolism like this. The Brazen Altar is only the first piece of furniture we encounter. Next was *the Laver* (Exodus 30:17-20). "It stood between the brazen altar and the sanctuary. Its presence in that position symbolized the fact that cleansing is necessary after the making of atonement, but before the enjoyment of fellowship with God." (*Constable's Notes, Exodus,* p. 173). The legs of the sacrifice animal were washed below it and the hands of the priest in the bowl upon it. *This symbolized water baptism (justification) and the beginning of sanctification.*

Make note that while the Holy Spirit enters the believer at regeneration, the moment we believe and are justified, our sanctification progresses with the overflowing (aka immersion or baptism) of the Holy Spirit. It is the Spirit of God that enables us to live a holy life and personify (or "image") the glory of God. Consequently, we shouldn't demand that any particular gift of the Spirit evidences our being filled by the Spirit of Christ (historically, this has been a point of dissension and division). After all, recall the gift of tongues, the typical gift emphasized in Pentecostal teaching, has a dual purpose. While equated with *being baptized in the Spirit* (as the believer first speaks in tongues), Paul teaches that speaking in tongues was *also* a "sign" of judgment. Its display in Acts chapter 2 fulfilled a prophecy condemning the Jews for their unbelief.[*] (1 Corinthians 1:22, 14:22) and it fulfilled the prophecy of Isaiah 28:11:

---

[*] "In the very same chapter that we find Paul making the statement that tongues are for unbelievers, he also makes several statements which clearly indicate that tongues are for believers: tongues and interpretation serve to edify the church (I Corinthians 14:27-28); the individual who speaks in tongues edifies himself (14:4); Paul, a believer, prayed and sang in

Isa 28:11 "*By people with strange tongues and by the lips of strangers I will speak to this people, yet not even in this way will they listen to me.*"

Recall the judgment at Babel was "confusion of tongues." God divided the nations of the world through forcing humanity to separate by nation and by tongue. And yet, in Acts 2, the descendants of Israelites, dispersed through the previous millennia, had come together in Jerusalem. Foreign tongues were manifested as the Spirit "gave their utterance." And the massing of Jews in Jerusalem, gathered from the diaspora for Pentecost, literally heard the gospel proclaimed to them miraculously, in their own distinctive languages, replete with the "accent" of each respective dialect. There are a number of meanings to this amazing event. But one meaning often overlooked: the division of humanity begun at Babel would one day be reversed. *The judgment at Babel was now terminated.* Peter testifies that this fulfilled (a portion) of Joel's ancient prophecy:

Joel 2:28-29 [28]And it shall come to pass afterward, that I will pour out *my spirit upon all flesh*; and your sons and your daughters shall prophesy, your old men shall dream dreams, your young men shall see visions: [29]And also upon the servants and upon the handmaids in those days will I pour out my spirit. (KJV)

While there is general consensus that water baptism comprises the first step of obedience – signifying the new life we have in Christ upon receiving Him – that is, inviting Him into our lives, most experienced teachers of God's Word believe that the experience commonly called "baptism of the Spirit" may be manifested in more than one way. However

---

tongues (14:15); to give thanks in tongues is to give thanks well (14:17); Paul thanked God he spoke in tongues more than the Corinthians (14:18); tongues should not be forbidden among the church (14:39). All these verses describe the tongues of believers. If tongues were not for believers, but only unbelievers, then most of 1 Corinthians 14 would be in error." (Retrieved February 17, 2017 from http://www.onenesspentecostal.com/tonguesunbelievers.htm). Note once again that in referring to this source, I (Huffman) am not implying I accept *all* of their theology.

it manifests in our personal experience, the infilling of the Holy Spirit signals "a next step." It underscores that our growth in the Spirit should have *outward and visible evidence* just as the tongues spoken by the early Christians at Pentecost demonstrated a miraculous evidence of the outpouring of the Spirit of Christ "in the visible world." This outward evidence of the inward change constitutes a crucial aspect of *sanctification.*

Sanctification blossoms through internalizing the Word of God, taking it into our hearts and feeding upon it daily. We grow progressively as we "absorb" the knowledge of God's word, and actively practice its teachings. And it is the Spirit that is the catalyzing agent, taking God's Word and applying it to our "hearts and minds." We develop in what was once called, "the Deeper Life" through the dual action of the Living Word and the Divine Spirit. Obedience to *the Word and the Spirit* is the "warp and woof" of how *we grow in our faith, experience the life of Christ living in and through us, conquer sin, begin our progression toward holiness, and carry out our mission as Christians.* Furthermore, as it relates to the subject of this book, this process constitutes the doorway through which we must pass to ultimately obtain glory. *"The Revealing" commences in our earthly life NOW, and will be completed to the fullness of the measure of Christ, at the Day of Christ.* However, and this is vital, if we do not commence the process of sanctification now, we have reason to doubt we will see it completed later. Our salvation is **not** *made sure* unless we progress into the inner sections of the Tabernacle.

1 Th 4:7 For God hath not called us unto uncleanness, but unto holiness.

2 Th 2:10-13 [10] When he shall come to be *glorified in his saints*, and to be admired in all them that believe (because our testimony among you was believed) in that day. [11] Wherefore also we pray always for you, *that our God would count you worthy of this calling,* and fulfil all the good pleasure of *his* goodness, and the work of faith with power: [12]That the name of our Lord Jesus Christ may be glorified in you, *and ye in him,* according to the grace of our God and the Lord Jesus Christ. [13] But we are bound to give thanks to God always for you, brethren beloved by the Lord, because God from the beginning *chose you for salvation through sanctification* by [1] the Spirit and [2] belief in the truth.

1 Pet 1:2 (We are the) elect according to the foreknowledge of God the Father, in sanctification of the Spirit, for obedience and sprinkling of the blood of Jesus Christ.

Eph 5:26-27 [26]that He might sanctify and cleanse her with the washing of water by the word, [27]that He might present her to Himself *a glorious Church, not having spot or wrinkle or any such thing, but that she should be holy and without blemish.*

John 17:17 Sanctify them by Your truth. *Your word is truth.*

Sanctification (that is, the ongoing saving effect of Y'shua) comes from truth and truth from God's Word (Romans 10:17), working through the Holy Spirit.

Thus, the outer court symbolizes our redemption through Christ's sacrifice and the initial cleansing that takes place. This is the "born again" experience. However, we must not stop at the *altar* but go beyond, all the way to the *laver,* and finally into the *Holy Place.* To be sure, this requires *dedication and progression. Walking daily in the light and love of Jesus is the passageway to progress to these inward levels where only those made **holy** (set apart, sanctified) can go.* Once again, we emphasize, if we do not move forward and progress the Scripture warns us that our salvation is "questionable". It has been "made more sure" as we grow sanctified. You must commit to making progress, not absolute perfection, although Jesus and Paul proclaim, "Be ye therefore perfect as your Heavenly Father is perfect." (Matthew 5:48)

THE HOLY PLACE

Thus, we come to the *Holy Place* (Leviticus 16:2). We must walk through the door set before us. Here we find a curtain. Why? Because a person who has been born again and is in the initial process of sanctification, *cannot see into the Holy Place* (figuratively speaking). He or she must pass through the curtain by faith in the Word and the Spirit which sanctifies. In the Holy Place, we see "beyond the veil" into the Holy of Holies that pictures the Cherubim, which serves an introduction into the heavenlies or heavenly places. The baptism or filling of the Holy Spirit brings us into contact with heavenly places and the heavenly blessings of Jesus:

Eph 1:3 Blessed *be* the God and Father of our Lord Jesus Christ, who has blessed us with every spiritual blessing in the *heavenly places* in Christ.

Eph 2:6 And raised *us* up together, and made *us* sit together in the *heavenly places* in Christ Jesus.

Along with heavenly blessings, we engage in war with the enemy who dwells in the *heavenlies*, but the Holy Spirit gives us the tools for warfare. (1 Corinthians 12).[†]

Eph 6:12 For we do not wrestle against flesh and blood, but against principalities, against powers, against the rulers of the darkness of this age, against *spiritual hosts of wickedness in the heavenly places.*

Rev 12:7-8 And war broke out in heaven: Michael and his angels fought with the dragon; and the dragon and his angels fought, [8]but

---

[†] [Heavenlies, επουρανιοις - 1) existing in heaven; 1a) things that take place in heaven; 1b) the heavenly regions; 1b.1) heaven itself; the abode of God and angels; 1b.2) the lower heavens, of the stars 1b.3) the heavens, of the clouds; 1c) the heavenly temple or sanctuary; 2) of heavenly origin or nature] (*NetBible Notes*). We will tackle the issue of "the three heavens" later in our study.

they did not prevail, nor was a place found for them in heaven any longer.

The first piece of furniture in the Holy Place was the Candlestick or Lampstand (Exodus 25:31). In actuality, it consisted of an oil lamp with seven branches and seven flames, constructed from 125 pounds of pure gold. Gold represents the divine nature along with oil, the anointing of the Holy Spirit. Gold and light represent *giving the light to men*. We are not that light, but we bear witness to the light:

1 John 1:1-9 [1]That which was from the beginning, which we have heard, which we have seen with our eyes, which we have looked upon, and our hands have handled, concerning the Word of life – [2]the life was manifested, and we have seen, and bear witness, and declare to you that eternal life which was with the Father and was manifested to us – [3]that which we have seen and heard we declare to you, that you also may have fellowship with us; and truly our fellowship *is* with the Father and with His Son Jesus Christ. [4]And these things we write to you that your joy may be full. [5]This is the message which we have heard from Him and declare to you, *that God is light and in Him is no darkness at all.* [6]If we say that we have fellowship with Him, *and walk in darkness, we lie and do not practice the truth.* [7]But if we walk in the light as He is in the light, we have fellowship with one another, and the blood of Jesus Christ His Son cleanses us from all sin. [8]If we say that we have no sin, we deceive ourselves, and the truth is not in us. [9]If we confess our sins; He is faithful and just to forgive us *our* sins and to cleanse us from all unrighteousness.

If we say we are Christians, we must shine light into the darkness. We cannot live in darkness. If we do the deeds of darkness, then we lie and the truth is not in us. If we confess our sins when we fall down, God is faithful. He has forgiven our sins. He continues to pick us back up.

In Rev 1:12-13 and verse 20, we find that the Lampstand is the Church with oil or the anointing. Recall that seven is the Bible's number for completion or perfection. It is the providential design of the LORD which is perfect. It is never accidental. It is as He wills it to be:

Rev 1:12-13, 20 Then I turned to see the voice that spoke with me. And having turned I saw seven golden lampstands, [13]and in the midst of the seven lampstands *One* like the Son of Man, clothed with a garment down to the feet and girded about the chest with a golden band... The mystery of the seven stars which you saw in My right hand, and the seven golden lampstands: The seven stars are the angels of the seven Churches, and the seven lampstands which you saw are the seven Churches.

Jesus said we are the light of the world. We find that if we walk in the Light, bear witness to the Light of God, and have the Light living in us, then we truly are the light of the world. Light is the symbol for truth:

John 9:5 As long as I am in the world, I am the light of the world."

Mat 5:14 "You are the light of the world. A city that is set on a hill cannot be hidden.

The "lampstands" (representing the "Churches") figuratively supported the corporate witness of the Christians in each church ("you are the light of the world"), as they lived in a dark world, shining a bright flame of testimony for all to see (cf. 1 Tim. 3:15). (*Constable's Notes, Revelation*, p. 26)

The next piece of furniture is the *Table of Shewbread (*Exodus 25:23-30; 26:35). It is the symbol of the Word of God and its inward working. The candlestick is meant to portray *an outward shining towards others.* And we should note that the Table of Shewbread also contained wine which was used as a *symbol for fellowship* in the Communion. We see this illustrated in another famous story in Genesis:

> **Gen 14:17-20** [17]And the king of Sodom went out to meet him at the Valley of *Shaveh* (that *is*, the King's Valley), after his return from the defeat of *Chedorlaomer* and the kings who *were* with him. [18]Then Melchizedek king of Salem brought out bread and wine; he *was* the priest of God Most High. [19]And he blessed him and said: "Blessed be Abram of God Most High, Possessor of heaven and earth; [20]And blessed be God Most High, who has delivered your enemies into your hand." And he gave him a tithe of all.

> **Rev 3:20** Behold, I stand at the door and knock. If anyone hears My voice and opens the door, I will come in to him and dine with him, and he with Me.

Shewbread is literally translated *Presence Bread,* or *Bread of Presence,* which was brought to the table by the singers of the Tabernacle or Temple. We come into God's presence through His Word and singing. Bread represents God's presence. God has always wished to dwell with humanity. And His will begins *by His dwelling in the believer today.*

> **Psa 100:2** Serve the LORD with gladness; Come before His presence with singing.

Next, we come to the golden *Altar of Incense* (Exodus 30:1). Physically, it is the highest piece of furniture, and is the symbol of service to God only. In the Holy Place, we see the service of the sons of God (kings and priests of the *Most High*) symbolized:

1. *The candlestick is service to others* – the Light shining in us and through us.
2. *The Table of Shewbread is food for ourselves* – edification to enable us to serve.

3. *The altar of incense is praise, worship, and prayer-service to God,* which also edifies us, but is done totally for God. If this is done as in 1 Tim 2:8, with hands raised, it is the highest service (physically and spiritually).

    1 Tim 2:8 I desire therefore that the men pray everywhere, lifting up holy hands, without wrath and doubting;

Personal as well as corporate prayer, praise, and worship cannot be overemphasized. Therefore, prayer, praise, and worship is the *highest* service and *it is a sacrifice* – that is why it is from an altar. We must take time out of our busy schedules to worship God:

    Psa 141:2 Let my prayer be set before You *as* incense, the lifting up of my hands *as* the evening sacrifice.

    Heb 13:15 Therefore by Him let us continually offer the sacrifice of praise to God, that is, the fruit of *our* lips, giving thanks to His name.

    1 Pet 2:5 You also, as living stones, are being built up a spiritual house, a holy priesthood, to offer up spiritual sacrifices acceptable to God through Jesus Christ.

    1 Pet 2:9 But you *are* a chosen generation, a royal priesthood, a holy nation, His own special people, that you may proclaim the praises of Him who called you out of darkness into His marvelous light.

    Psa 22:3 But You *are* holy, Enthroned in the praises of Israel. But thou *art* holy, *O thou* that inhabitest the praises of Israel. (KJV)

    Rev 8:3-4 [3]Then another angel, having a golden censer, came and stood at the altar. He was given much incense, that he should offer *it* with the prayers of all the saints upon the golden altar which was before the throne. [4]And the smoke of the incense, with the prayers of the saints, ascended before God from the angel's hand.

The altar of incense was also the closest to the Holy of Holies and therefore, the Glory of God or His manifest presence. We believe the Church stands today figuratively before this piece of furniture. Thus, the brazen altar and the laver were, in my (Huffman's) opinion, restored to the Church in the sixteenth century; the candlestick and the shewbread were restored in the twentieth century (the power of the Holy Spirit in the life of the believer and collectively, within the Church). For many in the Church, the altar of incense is now being restored (the importance of praise and worship in the Holy Spirit, which the Charismatic Movement, so called, emphasized beginning in the 1960s). The next thing that God is bringing forth to the Church is not only a restoration (as was present in the first-century Church) but also *a new thing* not fully fulfilled during those days:

> **Hag 2:7-9** [7]And I will shake all nations, and they shall come to the Desire of All Nations, and I will fill this temple with glory,' says the LORD of hosts. [8]'The silver *is* Mine, and the gold *is* Mine,' says the LORD of hosts. [9]'The glory of this latter temple shall be greater than the former,' says the LORD of hosts. 'And in this place, I will give peace,' says the LORD of hosts."

> **Isa 43:19** Behold, I will do a new thing, now it shall spring forth; Shall you not know it? I will even make a road in the wilderness *and* rivers in the desert.

We believe that new thing is the Church entering into the Holy of Holies where the Ark of the Covenant is and where God's glory dwells. As we mentioned, there are no shortcuts from one part of the tabernacle to the other – implying that there are no shortcuts to the Holy of Holies, or the Glory of God. The Church must walk through each part and on through the veil to the manifest presence of God. *The Church must pray and worship into the glory of God in unity. The Church must bring the altar of incense into the Holy of Holies.* As the Church brings the altar of incense into the Holy of Holies by its prayer, praise, and worship – it will *enter into and experience the presence of the Shekinah glory of God.*

Heb 9:2-4 [2]For a tabernacle was prepared: the first [part], in which [was] the lampstand, the table, and the showbread, which is called the sanctuary; [3] and behind the second veil, the part of the tabernacle which is called the Holiest of All, [4] which had the golden censer and the ark of the covenant overlaid on all sides with gold, in which [were] the golden pot that had the manna, Aaron's rod that budded, and the tablets of the covenant.

Notice here that the altar of incense is not pictured in the Holy Place, but in the *Holy of Holies*. We will talk more about this in the section *The Day of Atonement* and when we examine the Book of Hebrews in chapter 9.

THE HOLY OF HOLIES

In the Holy of Holies, we see the Ark of the Covenant, made of shittim wood (aka acacia wood), typical of human weakness or the earthen vessel. The Ark and many facets of the Tabernacle were made with this.[‡] This illustrates that the Ark speaks of an earthly, spiritual attainment since there is no wood (flesh) in heaven itself. It was then overlaid with pure gold, symbolizing God's nature and presence. We know that the Ark manifested the Glory or presence of God. The cherubim of gold above the Ark give us a feeling of the heavenly. And remember, wherever the Ark went, God's Glory went right along with it too. This leads us to the transition point for the next chapter.

At the entrance of the Holy Place, we saw cherubim sewn to the curtain (a taste of God's heavenly presence). In the Holy of Holies, we see cherubim of pure gold (the full *weight* of God's heavenly presence).

[‡] See http://www.dictionary.com/browse/shittim-wood.

2 Cor 4:17 For our light affliction, which is but for a moment, is working for us a far more exceeding [and] eternal *weight of glory.*

DEEP DIVE: EXCEEDINGLY BEYOND EXCEPTIONAL

A far more exceeding - καθ᾽ ὑπερβολὴν εἰς ὑπερβολὴν kath' huperbolēn eis huperbolēn. There is not to be found anywhere a more energetic expression than this. The word (ὑπερβολη huperbolē), used here (whence our word "hyperbole") means properly a throwing, casting, or throwing beyond. In the New Testament, it means excess, excellence, eminence; see 2 Corinthians 4:7. "The excellency of the power." The phrase καθ᾽ ὑπερβολὴν kath' huperbolēn means exceedingly, super-eminently, Romans 7:13; 1 Corinthians 12:31; 2 Corinthians 1:8; Galatians 1:13. This expression would have been by itself intensive in a high degree. But this was not sufficient to express Paul's sense of the glory which was laid up for Christians. It was not enough for him to use the ordinary highest expression for the superlative to denote the value of the object in his eye. He therefore coins an expression, and adds εἰς ὑπερβολὴν eis huperbolēn. It is not merely eminent; but it is eminent unto eminence; excess unto excess; a hyperbole unto hyperbole - one hyperbole heaped upon another; and the expression means that it is "exceeding exceedingly" glorious; glorious in the highest possible degree – Robinson. Mr. Slade renders it, "infinitely exceeding."

The expression is the Hebrew form of denoting the highest superlative; and it means that all hyperboles fail of expressing that eternal glory which remains for the just. It is infinite and boundless. You may pass from one degree to another; from one sublime height to another; but still an infinity remains beyond. Nothing can describe the uppermost height of that glory; nothing can express its infinitude.

Eternal – This stands in contrast with the affliction that is for a moment (παραυτίκα parautika). The one is momentary, transient; so short, even in the longest life, that it may be said to be an instant; the other has no limits to its duration. It is literally everlasting.

Weight – βαρος (baros). This stands opposed to the (ελαφρον elaphron) light affliction. That was so light that it was a trifle. It was easily borne. It was like the most light and airy objects, which constitute no burden. It is not even here called a burden, or said to be heavy in any degree. This is so heavy as to be a burden. Grotins thinks that the image is taken from gold or silver articles, that are solid and heavy, compared with those that are mixed or plated. But why may it not refer to the insignia of glory and honor; a robe heavy with gold, or a diadem or crown, heavy with gold or diamonds: glory so rich, so profuse as to be heavy? The affliction was light; but the crown, the robe, the adornings in the glorious world were not trifles, or baubles, but solid, substantial, weighty. We apply the word weighty now to that which is valuable and important, compared with that which is of no value, probably because the precious metals and jewels are heavy; and it is by them that we usually estimate the value of objects.

Of glory – (δοξης doxēs). The Hebrew word כבוד kabowd denotes weight as well as glory. And perhaps Paul had that use of the word in his eye in this strong expression. It refers here to the splendor, magnificence, honor, and happiness of the eternal world. In this exceedingly interesting passage, which is worthy of the deepest study of Christians, Paul has set in most beautiful and emphatic contrast the trials of this life and the glories of heaven. It may be profitable to contemplate at a single glance the view which he had of them, that they may be brought distinctly before the mind. [Emphasis added]

From *Barnes' Notes on the Bible* (2 Cor 4:17)

To digress, but to employ modern day language as clarification (and inject just a bit of humor): In the 1960s, if something was intense, deep, of great substance, we would say it was "heavy" ("Man, that's really heavy"). Today, if some superlative needs to be emphasized, we use the German "uber" (e.g., "Man, it's uber-cool"). Which suggests that if we wanted to express *exceedingly beyond exceptional* in the parlance of our times, we might express ourselves with a phrase like this: "It's uber-heavy, dude." Christ's glory is *uber-heavy*. However, the authors still prefer *exceedingly beyond exceptional*. We wager the reader agrees.

2 Chr 5:3 And all the men of Israel assembled before the king at the feast that is in the seventh month.

This feast that is in the seventh month refers to the **Feast of Booths** (Lev 23:33-44). Here is a helpful explanation:

The *Feast of Booths*, also known as the *Feast of Tabernacles*, began on the 15th day of the seventh month (in late September or October). It was a seven-day celebration of the autumn harvest. The Israelites lived in temporary shelters (booths) during the feast to remind themselves of the wilderness wanderings (Lev 23:42). All males were required to assemble in the presence of God (Deuteronomy 16:16). (*Logos Faithlife Study Bible* note)]

2 Chr 5:12-14 [12]And the Levites *who were* the singers, all those of Asaph and Heman and Jeduthun, with their sons and their brethren, stood at the east end of the altar, clothed in white linen, having cymbals, stringed instruments and harps, and with them one hundred and twenty priests sounding with trumpets – [13]indeed it came to pass, when the trumpeters and singers *were* as one, to make one sound to be heard in praising and thanking the LORD, and when they lifted up their voice with the trumpets and cymbals and instruments of music, and praised the Lord, *saying: "For He is* good, For His mercy *endures* forever," *that the house, the house of the LORD, was filled with a cloud,* [14]*so that the priests could not continue ministering because of the cloud; for the glory of the LORD filled the house of God.*

God communed with Moses in the Holy of Holies:

Lev 16:2 And the LORD said to Moses: "Tell Aaron your brother not to come at *just* any time into the Holy *Place* inside the veil, before the mercy seat which *is* on the ark, lest he die; *for I will appear in the cloud above the mercy seat.*

Exo 25:21-22 [21]You shall put the mercy seat on top of the ark, and in the ark you shall put the Testimony that I will give you. [22]And there I will meet with you, and I will speak with you from above the mercy seat, from between the two cherubim which *are* on the ark of the Testimony, about everything which I will give you in commandment to the children of Israel.

THREE TYPES OF LIGHT

Note that there are three types of light, symbolizing salvation, revelation (illumination), and God's glory. *These three light the tabernacle:*

1. *The Outer Court* is lit with natural light (sunlight) and at night some light from the burning sacrifice on the brazen altar. God reveals salvation by shedding light on a historical, earthly event – the death of His Son, the Lamb of God. Sunlight (*natural)* was not allowed into the Holy Place or Holy of Holies.

2. *The Holy Place* has the light from the candlestick and some light from the altar of incense (*both symbolism of a spiritual light)*. This is revelation that comes from the Holy Spirit as well as praise and worship to God.

3. *The Holy of Holies* is lit only by the glory of God. We believe the majority of us have not experienced the revelation that comes in the manifest presence of God. We have something incredible to look forward to that exceeds anything the transhumanist movement might have in mind regarding an upgrade to humankind's physical ability, mental capacity, or a high-speed, direct brain-link to the Internet to search Google!

Clearly, the same Divine Pattern resides with the Tabernacle in the Wilderness. God's Plan at the end of the age is to bring the Church into the Holy of Holies, manifest His glory to the Church, and then through His Body that it might present His glory to a dying and desperate world. *God wants His cloud of glory to again fill the house of God, the Church.* For now, we should understand, *This Pattern of the Tabernacle can be summed up as Jesus Christ the Lord – who* **portrays the very pattern for the Church**.

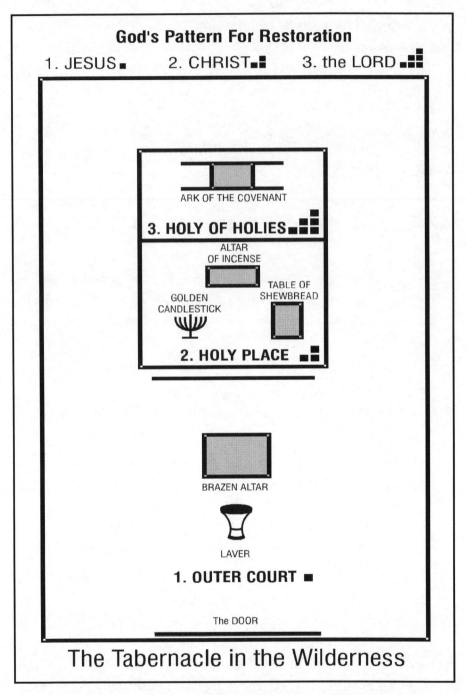

Figure 1 = God's Pattern for Restoration, The Tabernacle
© Gary Huffman 2017

DEEP DIVE: BEING MADE "PERFECT" JUST LIKE JESUS

In the Letter to the Hebrews, Paul lets us in on a secret. Somehow through the incarnation, Jesus Christ was *"made perfect"* through sufferings. This occurred despite the fact that all things were made by God for Him, and He Himself (the *Logos*) made all things. Through the process of the incarnation—*the experience of becoming human and living His life in a body like ours*[§]—He was enabled to be the 'first-born' of many brethren, *"bringing many sons unto glory."* Paul refers to Jesus as *"the captain of our salvation: "For it became him, for whom [are] all things, and by whom [are] all things, in bringing many sons unto glory, to make the captain of their salvation perfect through sufferings."* (Hebrews 2:10)

What does Paul mean by being made *perfect*? Wasn't Jesus already perfect and without sin? Yes. But follow me. Paul uses the term *teleioō (pronounced, tuh-lie-ah-oh)*—and repeats this word over *ten times* in the Book of Hebrews alone (it is used repeatedly in the New Testament as well). Paul is not stating anything regarding the nature of Jesus—no hint exists that Jesus remained less than pure or perfect in regard to sin. Rather, the issue has to do with *accomplishing what He set out to do.* That is, the term conveys 'fully completed' in the sense that the goal was *achieved exactly as planned.* The word *teleioō* is translated 'fulfilled' in Luke 2:43 and 'finished' in John 4:34.[**] Think of its meaning as "mission accomplished." This word confirms God's plan is *predetermined* to be complete in every aspect.

Our tribulations contribute to the process of being made into the glorious image of Jesus Christ. *"By whom also we have access by faith into this grace wherein we stand, and rejoice in hope of the glory of God."* (Romans 5:2)

The Spirit of Christ, given to us as an 'earnest' (i.e., a down payment) commands this inner person (and ultimately outer person) 'makeover.' Visualize if you will, the following quotation from Paul: *"But we all, with open face beholding as in a glass the glory of the Lord, are changed into **the same***

[§] Jesus was "tempted in all ways just as we are yet without sin" (Hebrews 4:15)

[**] It is similar to the word *teleō (tuh-lay-oh)*, used in regard to Jesus accomplishing our salvation on the cross, with the words, "It is *finished (teleō)"* (John 19:30).

image from glory to glory, *[even] as by the Spirit of the Lord."* (2 Corinthians 3:18) We might reflect on the various 'wolf man' movies where the victim of lycanthropy watches his face change from man to beast, viewing his transformation in the mirror. Here Paul visualizes the opposite. We look in the mirror and see ourselves being transformed into the same glory as Jesus Christ! No more hairy face!

Furthermore, Paul indicates the process has already begun. Perhaps the transformation we witness today seems mostly minor; but it begins nonetheless while we live in our mortal bodies. *Our pains are purposeful.* And yet, Paul teaches the aches and pains we go through now are nothing compared to the enjoyment and wonder we will experience later

Paul provides a lengthy dissertation on these matters in 2 Corinthians 4: 16-18, 5:1-8. We should review the entire passage:

*[16] For which cause we faint not; but though our outward man perish, yet the inward man is renewed day by day. [17]For our light affliction, which is but for a moment, worketh for us a far more exceeding and eternal **weight** of glory; [18]While we look not at the things which are seen, but at the things which are not seen: for the things which are seen are temporal; but the things which are not seen are eternal.* (2 Corinthians 4:16-18)

[1] For we know that if our earthly house of this tabernacle were dissolved, we have a building of God, an house not made with hands, eternal in the heavens. [2]For in this we groan, earnestly desiring to be clothed upon with our house which is from heaven: [3]If so be that being clothed we shall not be found naked. [4]For we that are in this tabernacle do groan, being burdened: not for that we would be unclothed, but clothed upon, that mortality might be swallowed up of life. [5]Now he that hath wrought us for the selfsame thing is God, who also hath given unto us the earnest of the Spirit. [6]Therefore we are always confident, knowing that, whilst we are at home in the body, we are absent from the Lord: [7](For we walk by faith, not by sight) [8]We are confident, I say, and willing rather to be absent from the body, and to be present with the Lord. (2 Corinthians 5:1-8)

Paul begins by acknowledging even though our fleshly body undergoes 'entropy'—it runs down and will eventually die and decay—our 'inner being' undergoes renewal day after day (verse 16). Our inner being, our spiritual life, becomes more vital. Paul emphasizes that we are progressing toward our objective, as we behold the glory in the face of Christ. We look into His face when we meet Him in His Word, and often, in the faces of those we serve.

S. Douglas Woodward, *Blood Moon: Biblical Signs of the Coming Apocalypse*, (2014), Faith Happens Books, pp. 276-279 (updated).

Our friend, Derek Gilbert, points out another type or foreshadowing in his recent book, *The Great Inception,* which reiterates what we have shared up to this point about the tabernacle. We will close this chapter concerning the tabernacle with a comparison to what happened on God's Holy Mount at Yahweh's (the Angel of the LORD) meeting with Moses and the Elders of Israel there, for it directly reinforces the same symbolic meaning as does the Tabernacle (and Temple), or should we say, *the tabernacle and Temple reflect Yahweh's Holy mountain.*

The tabernacle and the Temple were representations of Yahweh's holy mountain. As with Eden, the entrances to the tabernacle and temple were on the east side. As with Sinai, the man-made structures were divided into three zones of increasingly restricted access: The base of the mountain was like the outer court with an altar beyond which the Israelites could not pass. Midway up the mountain represented the Holy Place: Moses, Aaron, and his sons (the priests), and the elders of Israel climbed halfway up Sinai to eat a meal with Yahweh; likewise, only the priests could enter the Holy Place in the tabernacle and Temple. And the summit of Sinai was akin to the Holy of Holies, where the visible manifestation of Yahweh descended from heaven. It was open on Sinai only to Moses, and in the tabernacle and Temple only to the high priest.[††]

You see, the pattern that the LORD GOD sets forth, He repeats again and again. Obviously, this stands out as a strategic lesson He wants us to remember. It teaches us that God is Holy, and to dwell with Him, we must

---

[††] Derek P. Gilbert, *The Great Inception*, Crane, MO. Defender Books, 2017, p.97.

be holy too. Thanks be to God, "in Christ" we are through Jesus Christ our LORD.

Rom 7:18-25 [18]For I know that nothing good dwells in me, that is, in my flesh. For I have the desire to do what is right, but not the ability to carry it out.[19] For I do not do the good I want, but the evil I do not want is what I keep on doing.[20] Now if I do what I do not want, it is no longer I who do it, but sin that dwells within me. [21] So I find it to be a law that when I want to do right, evil lies close at hand.[22] *For I delight in the law of God, in my inner being,*[23] *but I see in my members another law waging war against the law of my mind and making me captive to the law of sin that dwells in my members.* [24] Wretched man that I am! Who will deliver me from this body of death? [25] *Thanks be to God through Jesus Christ our Lord!* So then, I myself serve the law of God with my mind, but with my flesh I serve the law of sin. (ESV)

May our experience increasingly reflect the position already established for each of us *in the heavenlies*, until we are filled up to the fullness of God, holy and blameless before Him.

Eph 1:4-6 [3]Blessed be the God and Father of our Lord Jesus Christ, who has blessed us in Christ with every spiritual blessing in the heavenly places, [4]even as he chose us in him before the foundation of the world, *that we should be holy and blameless before him.* In love, [5]he predestined us for adoption to himself as sons through Jesus Christ, according to the purpose of his will, [6]to the praise of his glorious grace, with which he has blessed us in the *Beloved.* (ESV)

3: THE FEASTS OF THE LORD

We mentioned earlier, Luke 24:27, 44-47, when Jesus showed His apostles many (if not all!) of the Old Testament scriptures *that referenced His identity and His mission:*

Luke 24:27, 44-47 [27]And beginning at Moses and all the Prophets, He expounded to them in all the Scriptures the things concerning Himself... [44]Then He said to them, "These *are* the words which I spoke to you while I was still with you, that all things must be fulfilled which *were written in the Law of Moses and the Prophets and the Psalms concerning Me."* [45]And He opened their understanding, that they might comprehend the Scriptures. [46]Then He said to them, *"Thus it is written, and thus it was necessary for the Christ to suffer and to rise from the dead the third day,* [47]and that repentance and remission of sins should be preached in His name to all nations, beginning at Jerusalem.

The apostles used the Old Testament to establish Church doctrine in the New Testament. For instance:

1 Pet 1:10-12 [10]Of this salvation the prophets have inquired and searched carefully, who prophesied of the grace *that would come* to you, [11]searching what, or what manner of time, the Spirit of Christ who was in them was indicating when He testified beforehand the sufferings of Christ and the glories that would follow. [12]*To them it was revealed that, not to themselves, but to us they were ministering the* *things which now have been reported to you* through those who have preached the gospel to you by the Holy Spirit sent from heaven – things which angels desire to look into.

1 Cor 10:1-11 ¹Moreover, brethren, I do not want you to be unaware that all our fathers were under the cloud, all passed through the sea, ²all were baptized into Moses in the cloud and in the sea, ³all ate the same spiritual food, ⁴and all drank the same spiritual drink. For they drank of that spiritual Rock that followed them, and that Rock was Christ. ⁵But with most of them God was not well pleased, for *their bodies were scattered in the wilderness.* ⁶Now these things became our examples, to the intent that we should not lust after evil things as they also lusted. ⁷And do not become idolaters as *were* some of them. *As it is written, "The people sat down to eat and drink, and rose up to play."* ⁸Nor let us commit sexual immorality, as some of them did, and in one day twenty-three thousand fell; ⁹nor let us tempt Christ, as some of them also tempted, and were destroyed by serpents; ¹⁰nor complain, as some of them also complained, and were destroyed by the destroyer. *¹¹Now all these things happened to them as examples, and they were written for our admonition,* upon whom the ends of the ages have come.

Heb 10:1 *For the law, having a shadow of the good things to come, and* not the very image of the things, can never with these same sacrifices, which they offer continually year by year, make those who approach perfect.

Paul, "rightly dividing the Word of Truth", made 80 references to the Old Testament in the Book of Romans, establishing the Gospel of the Grace of God as well as other key doctrines of the Church. Likewise, he made 18 references in the Book of Galatians. The writer of Hebrews (tradition teaches it too was Paul), employed over 100 references. Peter made 30 citations in his first epistle, and John included direct quotes and indirect references to nearly 400 Old Testament scriptures in his gospel, his letters, and in the Book of Revelation.

We can see from this that the Old Testament is vitally important to our understanding of the New Testament and vice versa. We have seen in the previous chapter how the *Tabernacle in the Wilderness is a type and shadow of God's plan for the Church.* For this same reason, we must take a closer look at the Holy Days, aka, the Feasts of the Jews, to discern what important truths we can also discover there. The following provides an outline of these feasts:

I. **Feast of Passover** or *Feast of Unleavened Bread*
    A. Passover (Ex 12:1-23; Lev 23:4,5; Deut 16:1-3)
    B. The Unleavened Bread (Ex 12:18; 23:15; Lev 23:6-8; Deut 16:3-4)
    C. The Sheaf of Firstfruits (Lev 23:10-14)
II. **The Feast of Pentecost,** or the *Feast of Weeks, of Harvest, of Firstfruits* (Ex 23:16; Lev 23:15-21; Deut 16:9-12; Acts 2:1)
III. **The Feast of Tabernacles,** or the *Feast of Booths,* or *Feast of Ingathering*
    A. The Blowing of Trumpets [Rosh Hashanah] (Lev 23:24-32)
    B. The Day of Atonement [Yom Kippur] (Lev 16:23,27-32)
    C. The Feast of Tabernacles [Sukkot] (Lev 23:35, 40; Deu 16:13-15)

I must credit George H. Warnock for many insights shared in this chapter concerning the Feasts of Israel. His book, *The Feast of Tabernacles,* was very influential in the *Latter Rain Movement,* [*]a movement considered a heresy by most Church historians today. Despite that fact, I (Huffman) believe there is a baby in that bathwater that should not be thrown out! Here is what I think Warnock got wrong:

---

[*] Bill Britton, publisher, 1951, (See https://en.wikipedia.org/wiki/Latter_Rain_post%E2%80%93 World_War_II_movement).

he taught that the typology of the Feast of Tabernacles, or the "manifestation of the sons of God" could happen *to only a small group and even only one individual as specific truth was understood.*

As I mentioned in the preface, I hold that the prayer of Jesus in John 17 (which Warnock misinterpreted), will be answered when *there is unity in the Body of Christ.* This feast will therefore be, instead, a **corporate** event. Our assertions in this chapter should correct that error and disclose the true meaning of the feasts of Israel for the Church **at the end of the age.** This is especially so for the feast we know as *Tabernacles.*

THE THREE FEASTS IN SEVEN PARTS

There were three primary feasts divided into seven parts. ***All of Israel's worship centered on these three feasts.*** *There are other worthy celebrations (e.g., Purim and Hanukkah),* but they are not of Moses, not prescribed in the Torah. We see three of these in Deuteronomy 16:16:

> **Deu 16:16** "Three times a year all your males shall appear before the LORD your God in the place which He chooses: at the Feast of Unleavened Bread, at the Feast of Weeks, and at the Feast of Tabernacles; and they shall not appear before the LORD empty-handed."

- ### The Passover

The first feast was *the Passover.* The first Passover, you may recall, was on the eve of Israel's departure from the land of Egypt into the wilderness. God judged Egypt, and their gods, for keeping His people, the Hebrews, in bondage. He sent the angel of death to slay the first-born males of all the land, both animals and humans. The children of the Hebrews were spared if blood was placed over the door of their homes.

Exo 12:12-13 [12]For I will pass through the land of Egypt on that night, and *will strike all the firstborn in the land of Egypt,* both man and beast; and against all the gods of Egypt I will execute judgment: I *am* the LORD. [13]Now *the blood shall be a sign for you on the houses where you are.* And when I see the blood, I will **pass over** you; and the plague shall not be on you to destroy *you* when I strike the land of Egypt.

The Lord made this event the beginning of Israel's calendar or "beginning of months", and thereby established a "new year" on the first of that month. It has come to be known as "New Year's Day" on the Hebrew religious calendar. (Rosh Hashanah is "New Year's Day" on the civil calendar).

Exo 12:1-3 [1]Now the LORD spoke to Moses and Aaron in the land of Egypt, saying, [2]*"This month shall be your beginning of months; it shall be the first month of the year to you.* [3]Speak to all the congregation of Israel, saying: 'On the tenth of this month every man shall take for himself a lamb, according to the house of *his* father, a lamb for a household.

The Passover delivered Israel from the judgment of the firstborn, and prepared them for a new life as a separated, sanctified, and holy nation. In the same way, the cross of Christ is made the beginning for the child of God and delivers that man or woman from judgment.

1. <u>Blood must be used as a covering to avoid judgment.</u>

To appropriate deliverance for each family, the head of the house took responsibility to place blood across the doorpost. Similarly, in our day, the head of the Christian family stands as that family's *High Priest.* It is the head of the family who takes responsibility for his or her family to receive God's blessing.

2. <u>Recall: the lamb must be without blemish.</u>

Exo 12:5 Your *lamb shall be without blemish*, a male of the first year. You may take *it* from the sheep or from the goats.

John 1:29 The next day John saw Jesus coming toward him, and said, "Behold! *The Lamb of God who takes away the sin of the world!*

1 Pet 1:18-19 [18]Knowing that you were not redeemed with corruptible things, *like* silver or gold, from your aimless conduct *received* by tradition from your fathers, [19]but *with the precious blood of Christ, as of a lamb without blemish and without spot.*

To underscore this once more: *Jesus was that Lamb without blemish.*

3.   And make note: the lamb must be killed.

Exo 12:6 Now you shall keep it until *the fourteenth day of the same month*. Then the *whole assembly of the congregation of Israel shall kill it* at twilight.

Jesus, our lamb, was crucified during the time of this feast. He fulfilled the prophecy expressed as a "type" through this feast.

Mat 26:2 (Jesus said) "You know that after *two days is the Passover*, and the Son of Man will be delivered up *to be crucified*."

4.   The blood must be applied to the doorposts of the house.

For us, there must be an individual appropriation, by faith, of the work of the cross.

Rom 10:9-10 That if *you confess with your mouth* the Lord Jesus and believe in your heart that God has raised Him from the dead, you will be saved. [10]For with the heart one believes unto righteousness, and with *the mouth confession is made unto salvation.*

5.   <u>The flesh must be eaten.</u>

Exo 12:8 Then they **shall eat the flesh** on that night; roasted in fire, with unleavened bread *and* with bitter *herbs* they shall eat it.

John 6:53-55 [53]Then Jesus said to them, "Most assuredly, I say to you, *unless you eat the flesh of the Son of Man and drink His blood, you have no life in you.* [54]Whoever *eats My flesh and drinks My blood has eternal life, and I will raise him up at the last day.* [55]For *My flesh is food indeed, and My blood is drink indeed."*

We eat His flesh by *absorbing* the Word, *confessing* our sins, *making supplication* through prayer, and by living *conscious* of our communion with Him (*we practice the presence of God* as taught by the seventeenth century Carmelite monk, Brother Lawrence). As we discern the Lord's Body, all true believers (1 Cor 11:28-29) enter into that communion:

John 1:14 And *the Word became flesh and dwelt among us (literally, "**tabernacled**"),* and we beheld His glory, the glory as of the only begotten of the Father, full of grace and truth.

6.   <u>The people had to depart from where they were.</u>

Exo 12:11 And thus you shall eat it: *with* a belt on your waist, your sandals on your feet, and your staff in your hand. So you shall eat it in haste. It *is* the LORD'S Passover.

Israel was to eat the Passover Lamb with loins girded and shoes on their feet, ready to leave Egypt. Likewise, the moment we receive Christ as our Passover Lamb, we must depart from the world and its corrupting influences and allurements. We must follow our Lord in separation from our old life and consecrate ourselves to a new life.

We will never escape our dependence on the work accomplished through the blood of our Passover Lamb, Jesus. Thus, the feast became an ordinance forever:

> **Exo 12:14** "So this day shall be to you a memorial; and you shall keep it as a feast to the LORD throughout your generations. You shall keep it as a feast by an everlasting ordinance."

- ## Unleavened Bread

The observance of Unleavened Bread was regarded as *the same as the Passover*:

> **Luke 22:1** Now the Feast of Unleavened Bread drew near, which is called Passover.

> **Mat 26:17** Now on the first *day of the* Feast of the Unleavened Bread the disciples came to Jesus, saying to Him, "Where do You want us to prepare for You to eat the **Passover**?"

> **Lev 23:6-8** [6]And on the *fifteenth day of the same month is* the *Feast of Unleavened Bread to the LORD; seven* days you must eat unleavened bread. [7]On the first day you shall have a holy convocation; you shall do no customary work on it. [8]But you shall offer an offering made by fire to the LORD for seven days. The seventh day *shall be* a holy convocation; you shall do no customary work *on it.'"*

The *Passover* was the 14th day of the first month at evening time. *Unleavened Bread* was from the 15th day to the 21st day, a total of seven days altogether.

> **1 Cor 5:6-8** [6]Your glorying *is* not good. Do you not know that a little leaven leavens the whole lump? [7]Therefore purge out the old leaven, that you may be a new lump, since you truly are unleavened. For indeed *Christ, our Passover,* was sacrificed for us. [8]Therefore let us

keep the feast, not with old leaven, nor with the leaven of malice and wickedness, but with the unleavened *bread* of sincerity and truth.

Notice how Paul reinterprets the *elements of Passover*. Unleavened Bread stands as a "type" of their true meaning. Leaven symbolized sin. Leaven possesses characteristics such as "spreading" and "penetrating" – like malice and wickedness that can spread among the believers in the life of an individual Christian or in the body of believers, the Church.

Mat 16:6 Then Jesus said to them, "Take heed and beware of the *leaven of the Pharisees and the Sadducees.*"

Mat 16:12 Then they understood that He did not tell *them* to beware of *the leaven of bread*, but of *the doctrine* of the Pharisees and Sadducees.

To observe the Feast of Unleavened Bread is to live a life free *from the corrupting influences of sin and the flesh.* Jesus used the Feast of Unleavened Bread (at the Lord's Supper) to reveal the significance of the elements of the feast, symbols pointing to the spiritual meaning behind them.

Luke 22:19-20 [19]And *He took bread*, gave thanks and broke *it*, and gave *it* to them, saying, "This is *My body which is given for you;* do this in remembrance of Me." [20]Likewise He also *took* the cup after supper, saying, "This cup *is* the new covenant in *My blood, which is shed for you.*"

• **The Sheaf of Firstfruits**

This particular ordinance was not instituted *until the children of Israel were inside the borders of the promised land*. This distinction is important. Likewise, the New Testament fulfillment came, as we shall see, upon an entrance into the Kingdom of God which was made available by Jesus' death and resurrection:

Lev 23:10-14 [10]"Speak to the children of Israel, and say to them: 'When you *come into the land which I give to you, and reap its harvest, then you shall bring a sheaf of the firstfruits* of your harvest to the priest. [11]He shall wave the sheaf before the LORD, to be accepted on your behalf; *on the day after the Sabbath* the priest shall wave it. [12]And you shall offer on that day, when you wave the sheaf, a male lamb of the first year, without blemish, as a burnt offering to the LORD. [13]Its grain offering *shall be* two-tenths *of an ephah* of fine flour mixed with oil, an offering made by fire to the LORD, for a sweet aroma; and its drink offering *shall be* of wine, one-fourth of a hin. [14]You shall eat neither bread nor parched grain nor fresh grain until the same day that you have brought an offering to your God; it shall be a statute forever throughout your generations in all your dwellings.

The Sheaf of Firstfruits was waved before the Lord "on the morrow after the Sabbath" that was *the same day that Jesus rose from the dead* (Mark 16:9). Before there was a general harvest, one sheaf was taken and waved before the Lord on *the first day of the week during the Feast of Unleavened Bread:*

Mark 16:19 So then, after the Lord had spoken to them, He was received up into heaven, and sat down at the right hand of God.

It was a reminder and a promise of a great harvest from God. In the same way, "Christ, the firstfruits" is a reminder of the great end-time harvest that God will bring.

John 12:24 Most assuredly, I say to you, unless a grain of wheat falls into the ground and dies, it remains alone; *but if it dies, it produces much grain.*

1 Cor 15:20 But now Christ is risen from the dead, *and* has become the firstfruits of those who have fallen asleep.

1 Cor 15:23 But each one in his own order: *Christ the firstfruits,* afterward those *who are* Christ's at His coming.

The *one ripe sheaf* testified that there would be a great harvest from God. We affirm, along with many other teachers, that the saints who arose at His resurrection were also part of this first "sheaf":

Mat 27:52-53 [52]And the graves were opened; and *many bodies of the saints who had fallen asleep were raised;* [53]and coming out of the graves after His resurrection, they went into the holy city and appeared to many.

Paul teaches this truth, citing a prophecy in Psalm 68:18, in regard to the gifts of the Spirit being given to the Church. First, we cite the verse from the Psalms and then its fulfillment according to Paul:

Ps 68:18 Therefore it says, "When He ascended on high, He led captive a host of captives, and He gave gifts to men

Eph 4:8 Therefore it says, "WHEN HE ASCENDED ON HIGH, HE LED CAPTIVE A HOST OF CAPTIVES, AND HE GAVE GIFTS TO MEN."

The book of Acts is the story of the first portion of that harvest (Jesus was the seed – as John 12:24 above states). We will come back to the end-times fulfillment of the Sheaf of Firstfruits later in this book.

- **Feast of Pentecost**

The Feast of Pentecost – also called the *Feast of Harvest, Feast of Firstfruits,* or *Feast of Weeks.* Pentecost is the New Testament name meaning fiftieth (50th). The feast began on the 50th day after the Passover:

Lev 23:15-16 "And you shall count for yourselves from the day after the Sabbath, from the day that you brought the sheaf of the wave offering: *seven Sabbaths* shall be complete. [16] Even unto the morrow after the seventh sabbath *shall you number fifty days; then ye shall offer a new meat offering unto* to the LORD."

On "the morrow after the seventh Sabbath..." After Jesus rose from the dead, He was with the disciples for 40 days, then ascended into heaven. After 10 days, He sent the Holy Spirit on the disciples. *Pentecost was a new feast* (see Lev. 23:16 above); that is, it was not celebrating an event in the past, *but a blessing of the present.* Passover justifies the sinner and he is pardoned. At Pentecost, he is empowered for service:

Acts 1:4-5 And being assembled together with *them,* He commanded them not to depart from Jerusalem, but to wait for the Promise of the Father, "which," *He said,* "you have heard from Me; [5]for John truly baptized with water, but you shall be *baptized with the Holy Spirit* not many days from now."

Acts 2:1-4 When the Day of Pentecost had fully come, they were all with one accord in one place. [2]And suddenly there came a sound from heaven, as of a rushing mighty wind, and it filled the whole house where they were sitting. [3]Then there appeared to them divided tongues, as of fire, and *one* sat upon each of them. [4]And they were all *filled with the Holy Spirit and began to speak with other tongues,* as the Spirit gave them utterance.

Pentecost was called the "Feast of Harvest" because the people had just finished harvesting the firstfruits of their grain:

Exo 23:16 And the Feast of Harvest, the *firstfruits of your labors* which you have sown in the field; and the Feast of Ingathering at the end of the year, when you have gathered *in the fruit of your labors* from the field.

Surely there was a great harvest after Peter's sermon and three thousand persons (not counting women and children) were added that day. This continued indefinitely, of course, at a rapid rate after the Day of Pentecost. The Scripture says the harvest continued:

Acts 4:4 However, many of those who heard the word believed; and the number of the men came to be about five thousand.

Acts 5:14 And believers were increasingly added to the Lord, multitudes of both men and women.

Therefore, Pentecost signified the founding (formation) of the body of Christ. The symbolism of the Old Testament, of bread, sheaves, and loaves, lays the groundwork for *understanding the fellowship of believers and the indwelling of God, through the Holy Spirit, in that body*:

Lev 23:17 You shall bring from your dwellings two wave *loaves* of two-tenths *of an ephah*. They shall be of fine flour; they shall be baked with leaven. *They are* the firstfruits to the LORD.

The *two loaves* of bread speak of **Christ** in union with His **people**:

1 Cor 10:17 For we, *though* many, are one bread *and* one body; for we all partake of that one bread.

Two is the *number of witness* (2 Corinthians 13:1), which is what the early Church was – the two loaves could also speak to the fact that the Jews and gentiles *in the Body of Christ* would be made from the same dough, Jesus, the Bread of Life (John 6:35). Two loaves in that body, kneaded together, comprising one dough:

Eph 2:15 Having abolished in His flesh the enmity, *that is,* the law of commandments *contained* in ordinances, so as to create in Himself *one new man from the two*, *thus* making peace,

Gal 3:28 There is neither Jew nor Greek, there is neither slave nor free man, there is neither male nor female; for *you are all one in Christ Jesus.*

It is not incidental that these two loaves included leaven. We know that the Church still possesses much leaven (a symbol for sin). We know that the glory of the early Church departed because of the leaven that remained. Pentecost was a *feast of firstfruits* (Ex 23:16; Lev 23:17). It was the initial task in the overall process of sanctification of the saints. Thus, the harvest of Pentecost is *both firstfruits but also a promise* of the final perfection of the harvest at the *Feast of Tabernacles*, when God dwells on the earth with men and women.

Ez 48:35 The city [Jerusalem] shall be 18,000 cubits round about; and the name of *the city from that day shall be, 'The Lord is [dwells] there.'"*

Rev 22:1-5 [1]Then he showed me a river of the water of life, clear as crystal, coming from the throne of God and of the Lamb, [2]in the middle of its street. On either side of the river was the tree of life, bearing twelve kinds of fruit, yielding its fruit every month; and the leaves of the tree were for the healing of the nations. [3]There will no longer be any curse; and the throne of God and of the Lamb will be in it, and His bond-servants will serve Him; [4]they will see His face, and His name will be on their foreheads. [5] And there will no longer be any night; and they will not have need of the light of a lamp nor the light of the sun, because the Lord God will illumine them; and they will reign forever and ever.

Note that there is an interval of four months between the last fulfilled feast (Pentecost) for the Body of Christ, and *the Feast of Tabernacles*, the feast yet to be fulfilled in the Church. Perhaps, if the Lord returns before 2,000 years have elapsed from His crucifixion – 32 or 33 AD, that is, until His glorious return – these four months testify to four, 500-year periods, or 2,000 years from His death to His glorification in His saints, *which Tabernacles foreshadows.* Or perhaps it references 40, 50-year Jubilees. There are many that wish to pin it down to a *particular* year. We can only venture a guess that it is very soon.

- ## **The Blowing of Trumpets**

The *Blowing of Trumpets* was an introduction to the **Feast of Tabernacles** or of Ingathering. Like Passover, Tabernacles was a three-fold feast. Mentioned earlier, there was a civil or agricultural calendar in Israel also, which began in the seventh month of the Sacred year (Ex 23:16; 34:22).

> **Exo 34:22** "And you shall observe the *Feast of Weeks,* of the *firstfruits* of wheat harvest, and the Feast of Ingathering at the year's end.

Joel's prophecy is better understood in this light:

> **Joel 2:23** Be glad then, you children of Zion, And rejoice in the LORD your God; For He has given you the former rain faithfully, And He will cause the rain to come down for you – *the former rain, and the latter rain* **in the first month**.

The first month here is the *beginning of the civil year.* Therefore, Joel writes of the same period that the Feast of Tabernacles is to take place (Joel's first month of the civil year equals the seventh month of the sacred year – during the Feast of Tabernacles). We know by the Holy Spirit, speaking through Peter, that Joel references the days *since Pentecost.*

> **Acts 2:16-21** But this is what was spoken by the prophet Joel:[17']And it shall come to pass in the last days, says God, That I will pour out of My Spirit on all flesh; Your sons and your daughters shall prophesy, your young men shall see visions, your old men shall dream dreams. [18]And on My menservants and on My maidservants, I will pour

out My Spirit in those days; and they shall prophesy. [19]I will show wonders in heaven above and signs in the earth beneath: Blood and fire and vapor of smoke. [20]The sun shall be turned into darkness, And the moon into blood, Before the coming of the great and awesome day of the LORD. [21]And it shall come to pass that whoever calls on the name of the LORD Shall be saved.'

And in Joel, chapter 2, we read of the former rain and the latter rain (Joel 2:23). It begins with the *blowing of trumpets:*

Joel 2:1, 11-16, 19-24, 27-32 [1]***Blow the trumpet in Zion, and sound an alarm in My holy mountain!*** ... [12]"Now, therefore," says the LORD, "Turn to Me with all your heart, with fasting, with weeping, and with mourning." [13]So rend your heart, and not your garments; Return to the LORD your God, For He *is* gracious and merciful, slow to anger, and of great kindness; and He relents from doing harm. [14]Who knows *if* He will turn and relent, and leave a blessing behind Him – A grain offering and a drink offering For the LORD your God? [15]*Blow the trumpet in Zion,* consecrate a fast, call a sacred assembly; [16]Gather the people, sanctify the congregation, Assemble the elders, gather the children and nursing babes; Let the bridegroom go out from his chamber, And the bride from her dressing room... [19]The LORD will answer and say to His people, "Behold, I will send you grain and new wine and oil, and you will be satisfied by them; I will no longer make you a reproach among the nations. [23]Be glad then, you children of Zion, and rejoice in the LORD your God; *For He has given you the former rain faithfully, And He will cause the rain to come down for you – the former rain, and the latter rain in the first month.* [24]*The threshing floors shall be full of wheat,* And the vats shall overflow with new wine and oil... [27]Then you shall know that I *am* in the midst of Israel: I *am* the LORD your God and there is no other. My people shall never be put to shame. [28]"And it shall come to pass afterward, *that I will pour out My Spirit on all flesh;* Your sons and your daughters shall prophesy, your old men shall dream dreams, your young men shall see visions. [29]And also on *My* menservants and on *My* maidservants, *I will pour out My Spirit in those days.* [30] "And I will show wonders in the heavens and in the earth: blood and fire and pillars of smoke. [31]The sun shall be turned into darkness, and the moon into blood, *before the coming of the great and awesome day of the LORD.* [32]And it shall come to pass *that* whoever calls on the name of the LORD Shall be saved. **For in Mount Zion and in Jerusalem there shall be deliverance,** *As the LORD has said, among the remnant whom the LORD calls.*

Verses 23, 28-32 refer to the latter rain, which corresponds to the outpouring of the Holy Spirit at Pentecost. The entire passage speaks of the time directly before the day of the Lord (Joel 2:1), which is also *the time of the latter rain.*

According to Joel 2:23, as sure as the former rain came (the fulfillment of Jesus Christ at Passover and the coming of the Holy Spirit at Pentecost), the latter rain shall come down faithfully and finally in the first month of the civil calendar. This latter rain references the "High Holy Days" of Rosh Hashanah, Yom Kippur, and ultimately the Feast of Tabernacles. Thus, at the beginning of Tabernacles, we have the greatest harvest because of the overabundant "rain" of the Holy Spirit that produces the harvest of souls for which the harvest of grain is but a symbol. This is the ingathering from God's harvest field:

Exo 23:16 And the *Feast of Harvest, the firstfruits* of your labors which you have sown in the field; and the *Feast of Ingathering at the end of the year,* when you have gathered in *the fruit of* your labors from the field.

This passage refers to the sacred calendar. Therefore, the phrase "end of the year" here signifies the *Feast of Tabernacles.* It is then that Joel says to *blow the trumpet in Zion* (Joel 2:1,15). The *blowing of the trumpets* occurred in several cases. Specifically, the trumpet was blown for four distinct situations, as the following passage will demonstrate:

> 1. *Calling the assembly (vs 2)*
> 2. *Journeying of the camps (vs 3-6)*
> 3. *Preparation for war (vs 9)*
> 4. *Celebration of the feasts (vs 10)*

Num 10:2-10 ²"Make two silver trumpets for yourself; you shall make them of hammered work; you shall use them for *calling the congregation and for directing the movement of the camps.* ³**When they blow both of them**, all the congregation shall gather before you at the door of the tabernacle of meeting. ⁴But if they **blow *only* one**, then the leaders, the heads of the divisions of Israel, *shall gather to you.* ⁵When you **sound the advance**, the camps that lie on the east side shall then begin their journey. ⁶When you **sound the advance the second time**, then the camps that lie on the south side shall begin their journey; they shall **sound the call for them** to begin their journeys. ⁷And *when the assembly is to be gathered together*, **you shall blow,** but not sound the advance. ⁸The sons of Aaron, the priests, *shall **blow the trumpets***; and these shall be to you as an ordinance forever throughout your generations. ⁹*"When you go to war* in your land against the enemy who oppresses you, then **you shall sound an alarm with the trumpets,** and you will be remembered before the LORD your God, and you will be saved from your enemies. ¹⁰*Also in the **day of your gladness**, in **your appointed feasts**, and at the **beginning of your months**, **you shall blow the trumpets** over your burnt offerings and over the sacrifices of your peace offerings; and they shall be a memorial for you before your God: I *am* the LORD your God."

The two trumpets were made from one whole piece of silver. Recall that *two* is the number of witness. Silver symbolizes *redemption* and *salvation*.

1.   Therefore, God will call His assembly together in the last days:

> **Rev 1:10** I was in the Spirit on the Lord's Day, and I heard behind me a loud voice, as of a **trumpet**...

2.   God calls His people to go forward and possess the land, the inheritance:

> **Eph 1:13-14** [13]In Him you also *trusted,* after you heard the word of truth, the gospel of your salvation; in whom also, having believed, you were sealed with the Holy Spirit of promise, [14]who is the guarantee of our inheritance until the redemption of the purchased possession, to the praise of His glory.

3.   God calls His people to war to possess the land:

> **2 Cor 10:3-6** [3]For though we walk in the flesh, we do not war according to the flesh. [4]For the weapons of our warfare *are* not carnal but mighty in God for pulling down strongholds, [5]casting down arguments and every high thing that exalts itself against the knowledge of God, bringing every thought into captivity to the obedience of Christ, [6]and being ready to punish all disobedience when your obedience is fulfilled.

5.   God calls His people to celebrate the feasts:

> **1 Cor 5:8** Therefore, *let us keep the feast*, not with old leaven, nor with the leaven of malice and wickedness, but with the *unleavened bread* of sincerity and truth.

Paul isn't *indicating that Christians are "under the law" and therefore must keep the feasts as the Jews do.* For Paul, keeping the feast meant the spiritual transformation of salvation and redemption. His teaching is clear in Colossians 2: *the feast, sabbaths, circumcision, are all "shadows of things to come."* Those that twist the scripture to put Christians under the law to observe the same practices as Judaism clearly misunderstand the whole gist of Paul's message:

> **Col.2:16-17** [16] Therefore let no one pass judgment on you in questions of food and drink, or with regard to a *festival* or a *new moon* or a *Sabbath*. [17] These are a shadow of the things to come, but the substance belongs to Christ.

THE DAY OF ATONEMENT

We know that Christ made atonement for everyone through His death on the cross. This event, which Passover foreshadows, justifies us before God and delivers us from His judgment in this life and the next. However, *justification is not the aspect of salvation that delivers us from the power of sin in this mortal, temporal, fleshly life*. Both individually and corporately, we have yet to fully appropriate or "absorb" and then manifest the completed work of atonement. Theologians label this an *"already but not yet"* truth. It is legally established, but not fully consummated. The matter has been settled. We have been cleared of all charges, while the *convicted remain out on bail* for a while longer. We are fully entitled to possess what Christ has supplied, but we have not done so. The convicted claim that we can't. But we can.

On the Day of Atonement, the High Priest made atonement for himself as well as for the people. Two goats were chosen for the atonement of the people. Lots were cast upon the goats. One was destined for sacrifice on the altar, the other was declared the scapegoat. The scapegoat went into the wilderness with the sins imputed (ascribed or credited) to it by the Priest – the sins were carried away. This symbolized a declaration that sin was no longer imputed to the People. They were freed from the sentence of sin and death. They were acquitted. As the scapegoat fled into the wilderness, there became a visible symbol that sin was disconnected and removed.

Lev 16:7-10 [7]"He shall take the two goats and present them before the LORD [at] the door of the tabernacle of meeting. [8]Then Aaron shall cast lots for the two goats: one lot for the LORD and the other lot for the scapegoat. [9]And Aaron shall bring the goat on which the LORD's lot fell, and offer it [as] a sin offering. [10]But the goat on which the lot fell to be the scapegoat shall be presented alive before the LORD, to make atonement upon it, [and] to *let it go as the scapegoat into the wilderness.*"

Michael Heiser sheds light on the second goat (the scapegoat), so designated on the Day of Atonement. He explains that the Hebrew word, "Azazel" can be translated "the goat that goes away." This translation says that the sins of the people are symbolically carried away from the camp and into the wilderness. Heiser goes on to say it isn't that simple:

> However, "Azazel" is really a proper name. In Lev 16:8 one goat is "for Yahweh," while the other goat is "for Azazel." Since Yahweh is a proper name and the goats are described in the same way, Hebrew parallelism informs us that Azazel is also a proper name. What needs resolution is what it means. Azazel is regarded as the name of a demon in the Dead Sea Scrolls and other ancient Jewish books. In fact, in one scroll (4Q 180, 1:8) Azazel is the leader of the angels that sinned in Genesis 6:1–4. The same description appears in the book of 1 Enoch (8:1; 9:6; 10:4–8; 13:1; 54:5–6; 55:4; 69:2). [†]

Heiser points out that in the book of 1 Enoch and others, the rebellious sons of God from Genesis 6 were thrown into the pit or abyss as a prison. Azazel's home was now in the desert or wilderness, away from holy ground – the realm of supernatural evil. He mentions Leviticus 17:7 in this regard: "So they shall no more sacrifice their sacrifices to goat

---

[†] Michael S. Heiser, *The Unseen Realm*, (pp. 176-178) Bellingham, WA: Lexham Press, 2015

demons, after whom they whore" (ESV), and points out the conceptual connection. Heiser tells us that in the ritual of the Day of Atonement, Yahweh's goat was the goat sacrificed. The death of His goat "purges the impurities caused by the people of Israel and purifies the sanctuary. The goat for Azazel was sent away after the sins of the Israelites were symbolically placed on it." He goes on to assert, rightly we might add:

> The point of the goat for Azazel was not that something was owed to the demonic realm, as though a ransom was being paid. The goat for Azazel banished the sins of the Israelites to the realm outside Israel. Why? Because the ground on which Yahweh had his dwelling was holy. Sin had to be "transported" to where evil belonged – the territory outside Israel, under the control of gods set over the pagan nations. The high priest was not sacrificing to Azazel. Rather, Azazel got what belonged to him: *sin.*[‡]

Just as the other feasts were fulfilled, the Day of Atonement must be fulfilled in the Church. Purity was emphasized on the Day of Atonement. The High Priest wore linen clothes – a symbol of purity and righteousness. It was a day of fasting, a most solemn day. The high priest's clothing was changed several times, he bathed five times, and washed his hands and feet ten times. He went three times into the Holiest Place: to offer incense, the blood of a bull, and the blood of a goat. Here, the *Feast of Tabernacles* and the *Holy of Holies of the Tabernacle and Temple* are linked. This Day of Atonement comprises God's solution to humanity's universal problem of sin:

Rom 3:23 For all have sinned and fall short of the glory of God.

Therefore, through the Day of Atonement, as it is being fulfilled in the Church, will see itself forsake or "put off" sin completely as it "puts on Christ." It is the right sort of "put on." We enter the Holy of Holies "sprinkled" with the blood of Jesus and the high praises of God. Here

---

[‡] Ibid.

the Church is filled with the manifest presence of God, His glory that is, because the Church no longer comes up short or misses the mark. Sin is eliminated and no longer stands in the way of dwelling with God, that we might inherit the glory of God! (It is at this point that the "not yet" aspect of Atonement becomes the "already", i.e., a reality) But make note: we will return for another look at the Day of Atonement later.

Gal 3:27 For as many of you as have been baptized into Christ *have put on Christ.*

Rom 13:14 But *put ye on the Lord Jesus Christ,* and make not provision for the flesh, to fulfil the lusts thereof.

Gal 4:19 My little children, of whom I travail in birth again *until Christ be formed in you.*

THE FEAST OF TABERNACLES

The implied perfection of *Atonement* is the completion of corporate maturity of the Body of Christ. The Blowing of Trumpets and the Day of Atonement are both the necessary *preparation for* and *part of* the Feast of Tabernacles. Tabernacles consists, in part, of all that Trumpets and Atonement symbolize. Therefore, we see it paralleled in Ephesians 4:13:

- *Tabernacles is a **feast of victory in war** (Trumpets), and a*
- ***Feast of holiness** (Atonement), and*
- *The Feast of Tabernacles is **a feast of unity**.*

Eph 4:13 Till we all come in **the unity of the faith**, and of the knowledge of the Son of God, **unto a perfect man**, unto the measure of the stature of **the fullness of Christ**.

Lev 23:35 On the first day *there shall be* a holy convocation. You shall do no customary work *on it.*

Convocation means "assembly." The entire Jewish camp came together for one purpose. It was "full and unified." It pictures the completeness of the believer and the Body of Christ – whole and unified.

1. Tabernacles is a feast of joy:

> **Lev 23:40** "And you shall take for yourselves on the first day the fruit of beautiful trees, branches of palm trees, the boughs of leafy trees, and willows of the brook; and you shall rejoice before the LORD your God for seven days."

> **Deu 16:13-15** [13]"You shall observe the Feast of Tabernacles seven days, when you have gathered from your threshing floor and from your winepress. [14]And you shall rejoice in your feast, you and your son and your daughter, your male servant and your female servant and the Levite, the stranger and the fatherless and the widow, who *are* within your gates. [15]Seven days you shall keep a sacred feast to the LORD your God in the place which the LORD chooses, because the LORD your God will bless you in all your produce and in all the work of your hands, so that you surely rejoice.

During the Feast of Tabernacles, *the adult males circled the brazen altar seven times* – a rare, joyous occasion. This was a time of the harvest of the remaining summer grain, grapes, and olives. These plentiful and prized fruits served as a symbol of great joy and provision.

Jeremiah 33 (following) speaks of the time of the end when *Tabernacles has been fulfilled.* Verses 14-17 speak of the time when Jesus (the Branch) will reign and Jerusalem shall dwell safely. Verses 9 and 11 speak of the joy and prosperity that will be known as the Bridegroom and bride and others (mortal humans living in the Millennium) offer up sacrifices of praise to the Lord:

> **Jer 33:9,11** "Then it shall be to Me a name of joy, a praise, and an honor before all nations of the earth, who shall hear all the good

that I do to them; they shall fear and tremble for all the goodness and all the prosperity that I provide for it." [11]The voice of joy and the voice of gladness, the voice of the bridegroom and the voice of the bride, the voice of those who will say: "Praise the LORD of hosts, For the LORD *is* good, For His mercy *endures* forever" – *and* of those *who will* bring the sacrifice of praise into the house of the LORD. For I will cause the captives of the land to return as at the first," says the LORD.

2. Tabernacles is a feast of Ingathering:

   Exo 23:16 "And the Feast of Harvest, the firstfruits of your labors which you have sown in the field; and the *Feast of Ingathering at the end of the year,* when you have gathered in *the fruit of* your labors from the field."

3. Tabernacles is a feast of rain – the Living Water of God (which brings increase and ingathering).

   Deu 11:14 "Then I will give [you] *the rain for your land in its season,* the early rain *and the latter rain,* that you may gather in your grain, your new wine, and your oil."

   Hosea 6:3 Let us know, let us pursue the knowledge of the LORD. His going forth is established as the morning; He will come to us like the rain, like the latter *and* former rain to the earth.

   Joel 2:23-24 [23]Be glad then, you children of Zion, and rejoice in the LORD your God; For He has given you the former rain faithfully, And He will cause the rain to come down for you – the former rain, and the latter rain in the first *month.* [24]The threshing floors shall be full of wheat, And the vats shall overflow with new wine and oil.

Hosea 6:3 teaches that He shall come as the rain unto us. In Joel, the former rain refers to the seed rain (in the Spring) and the latter rain refers to the harvest rain (in the Fall). In Joel 2:23-24, God promises to *give the former—and latter rain in the first month (of the civil year) which is in autumn's harvest time (the time of the Feast of Tabernacles and Ingathering) — the normal time for the latter rain.* This implies a unique event that happens once. It constitutes an *eschatological* event.

> **Hag 2:7-9** [7] "And I will shake all nations, and they shall come to the Desire of All Nations, and I will fill this temple with glory,' says the LORD of hosts. [8] 'The silver *is* Mine, and the gold *is* Mine,' says the LORD of hosts. [9] 'The glory of this latter temple shall be greater than the former,' says the LORD of hosts. 'And in this place, I will give peace,' says the LORD of hosts."

The glory of the last days "temple" (the latter-day Church) through the new covenant, will be greater than the "former temple" – the people of God under the old covenant. The "latter rain" of *the Holy Spirit who grants us the Living Water of God (should it happen immediately after the rapture as we propose in this book),* shall bring about the greatest harvest of souls and of fruit of the Spirit through the translated Body of Christ which will continue to serve in a ministry of evangelism and do marvelous works.

The LORD speaks through the prophet Daniel indicating that in the latter days, God's people shall do great exploits. During these last days, who are the people of God? Energized Jewish evangelists or those sanctified and glorified? But we are getting ahead of our story. Still ponder this passage which we just referenced above:

> **Dan 11:32** And such as do wickedly against the covenant shall he corrupt by flatteries: **but the people that do know their God shall be strong, and do exploits.**

Now let's consider "living water" in more depth, this source of all life from God in heaven:

96

Jer 2:13 "For My people have committed two evils: They have forsaken Me, **the fountain of living waters**, *and* hewn themselves cisterns – broken cisterns that can hold no water."

Ezek 47:1 Then he brought me back to the door of the temple; and there was water, flowing from under the threshold of the temple toward the east, for the front of the temple faced east; the water was flowing from under the right side of the temple, south of the altar.

Ezek 47:9 And it shall be *that* every living thing that moves, wherever the rivers go, will live. There will be a very great multitude of fish, because these waters go there; for they will be healed, and everything will live wherever the river goes.

Ezek 47:12 Along *the bank of the river*, on this side and that, will grow all *kinds of* trees used for food; their leaves will not wither, and their fruit will not fail. They will bear fruit every month, *because their water flows from the sanctuary*. Their fruit will be for food, and their *leaves for medicine."*

In those days, God's *living water* comes from the sanctuary (the Holy of Holies) from under the altar of incense (the altar dedicated to praise and worship). It causes *healing, life, and growth to everything in its path.* Is this verse, which predicts the Temple of the Millennium, a symbol of glorified believers, just as the New Jerusalem is identified with the complete body of believers?

Whether or not there is a rebuilt Jewish Temple established in Jerusalem, the Bible gives us strong indication that the Body of Christ comprises the Temple in the very last of the last days. We believe the Church is the true temple of God, implying that the *living water* from the sanctuary flows from God's presence through the body of Christ to the parched world! Just as Christ used the analogy of the Temple to represent His body ("Tear this Temple down and in three days I will raise it up" –

John 2:19, paraphrased), after the rapture / resurrection of the church, the Head and the Body will be together, in glory, and through both the Head and the Body, the river of life will flow with Jesus being its source:

1 Cor 6:19 Know ye not that your bodies are members of Christ? (KJV)

John 4:10 Jesus answered and said to her, "If you knew the gift of God, and who it is who says to you, 'Give Me a drink,' you would have asked Him, and He would have given you *living water."*

Jesus possesses that *living water;* for He is its source, and He remains eager to give it to all His people who ask for it.

John 7:2, 37-39 [2]Now the Jews' Feast of Tabernacles was at hand... [37]On the last day, that great *day* of the feast, Jesus stood and cried out, saying, "If anyone thirsts, let him come to Me and drink. [38]He who believes in Me, as the Scripture has said, out of his heart will flow *rivers of living water."* [39]But this *He spoke concerning the Spirit, whom those believing in Him would receive; for the Holy Spirit was not yet given,* because *Jesus was not yet glorified.*

Jesus promises rivers of living water to flow from the innermost being of those who believe in Him and receive the Holy Spirit. *It is significant that Jesus chose the last day of the Feast of Tabernacles to disclose this eternal truth.* Nor is it incidental that the eternal life the saints enjoy, forever and ever, begins *with the river of the water of life.*

Rev 22:1 And he showed me a pure river of water of life, clear as crystal, proceeding from the throne of God and of the Lamb.

Rev 22:17 And the Spirit and the bride say, "Come!" And let him who hears say, "Come!" And let him who thirsts come. Whoever desires, *let him take the water of life freely.*

Images of water, latter rain, the Holy Spirit, Christ giving living water, the river of life, the culmination of Tabernacles – all of these reflect the magnificence of the life that the source of Life, Y'shua supplies to us.

4.   Tabernacles is also a *feast of rest*:

> **Lev 23:39** Also on the fifteenth day of the seventh month, when you have gathered in the fruit of the land, you shall keep the feast of the LORD *for* seven days; on the first day, *there shall be a* sabbath-rest, and on the eighth day a *sabbath-rest.*

Again, the number seven signifies divine completion, perfection, and rest. Tabernacles is a feast of sevens**.** All the feasts were on Sabbaths (days of rest for Israel as the Christian Sabbath, Sunday, should be for the Church).

But Tabernacles is, if you will, "especially special" because it is in *the seventh month*. The last day of the feast was on the 21st day (the triple of seven). Thus, it implies *complete rest* (indeed, *sabbath means seventh*). Then the next day (eighth day), comprises another day of rest or a Sabbath, which hints that after the fulfillment of the Feast of Tabernacles, there will be *continual* rest. Tabernacles is the Seventh event in Israel's series of feasts. The feast lasted seven days. God rested from His work of creation on the 7th day:

> **Gen 2:2** And on the seventh day God ended His work which He had done, and He rested on the seventh day from all His work which He had done.

The Feast of Tabernacles is a feast of rest for the Church:

> **Heb 4:4-5, 9** [4]For He has spoken in a certain place of the seventh *day* in this way: *"And God rested on the seventh day from all His works"*; [5]and again in this *place: "They shall not enter My rest."* [9]There remains therefore ***a rest for the people of God.***

5. Tabernacles is also a *feast of Glory*:

Although not stated specifically in Scripture, *Tabernacles constitutes a feast of glory.* According to the Pattern we have disclosed, *the glory of God, or His manifest presence, is a major theme for the third part of the Pattern.* So, by implication, *the fulfillment of Tabernacles would be the period when God's glory is manifested.* We have seen the link between the Holy of Holies, where God's glory dwelt, and Tabernacles on the Day of Atonement. Also, Tabernacles is when God dealt personally with each Jew in separated booths. This implies a special presence of God *with each believer.* Also, the rain, former rain, and the latter rain coming down in one month at the Feast of Tabernacles, signifies the greatest outpouring of the Holy Spirit upon the earth and within the people of God. *It is the manifested presence of God coming into them.* **At their indwelling, it should be expected the LORD will work through His Glorified Body – the Church.**

The Book of Zechariah, which concludes with every nation going forth to Jerusalem to keep the Feast of Tabernacles, speaks repeatedly of *God dwelling with His people, and of His glory being manifest.* Notice also the references in Zechariah to *latter rain, living water, inheritance,* and the *Lordship* (Kingship) of Jesus. Most scholars interpret these passages as occurring *after* the visible return of Christ. But could they happen before?

Zec 2:5, 8 [5]"For I,' says the LORD, 'will be a *wall of fire* all around her, and I will be the *glory in her midst.*'" [8]For thus says the LORD of hosts: "He sent Me after *glory*, to the nations which plunder you"; for he who touches you touches the apple of His eye.

Zec 2:10-13 [10]"Sing and rejoice, O daughter of Zion! For behold, *I am coming and I will dwell in your midst,*" says the LORD. [11]"Many nations shall be joined to the LORD in that day [All Israel?], and they shall become My people [the Church?]. And **I will dwell in your midst**. Then you will know that the LORD of hosts has sent Me

[Y'shua] to you. ¹²And the LORD will take possession of Judah as **His inheritance** in the Holy Land, and will again choose Jerusalem. ¹³Be silent, all flesh, before the LORD, for He is aroused from His holy habitation!"

Zec 6:12-13 ¹²Then speak to him, saying, 'Thus says the LORD of hosts, saying: "Behold, the Man whose name *is* the BRANCH! From His place He shall branch out [becoming many branches!] *And He shall build the temple of the LORD*; ¹³**Yes, He shall build the temple of the LORD**. [Repeating something said by a prophet, is his way of providing dramatic emphasis] *He shall bear the glory, and shall sit and rule on His throne; so He shall be a priest on His throne* [His Church shall reign with Him], *And the counsel of peace shall be between them both.*"'

Zec 8:22-23 Yes, many peoples and strong nations shall come to seek the LORD of hosts in Jerusalem, and to pray before the LORD.²³"Thus says the LORD of hosts: 'In those days ten men from every language of the nations shall grasp the sleeve of a Jewish man, saying, "Let us go with you, for we have heard *that God is with you.*"'"

When the Lord gives *the latter rain*, He will also **"make flashing clouds"** – *the glory of God will be manifested:*

Zec 10:1 Ask the LORD for *rain in the time of the latter rain*. The LORD will make *flashing clouds;* He will give them *showers of rain, grass in the field for everyone.*

Zec 12:8 In that day *the LORD will defend the inhabitants of Jerusalem;* the one who is feeble among them in that day shall be like David, and the *house of David shall be like God, like the Angel of the LORD* before them.

Zec 14:8-9 And in that day, it shall be *that living waters shall flow from Jerusalem,* Half of them toward the eastern sea and half of them toward the western sea; In both summer and winter it shall occur. [9]And *the LORD shall be King over all the earth*. In that day it shall be – "the LORD *is* one," and His name one.

Zec 14:16 And it shall come to pass *that* everyone who is left of all the nations [those who were not already raptured before the day of the Lord, or killed during the time of Great Tribulation] which came against Jerusalem [even members of attacking armies or the peoples represented by them] shall go up from year to year *to worship the King, the LORD of hosts, and to keep **the Feast of Tabernacles.***

Zec 14:18-19 If the family of Egypt will not come up and enter in, they *shall have* no *rain;* they shall receive the plague with which the LORD strikes the nations who do not come up to keep the Feast of Tabernacles. [19]This shall be the punishment of Egypt and the punishment of all the nations that do not come up to keep the Feast of Tabernacles.

Peter understood the *connection between God's manifest presence and the Feast of Tabernacles.* He was eager to celebrate Tabernacles with Jesus, Moses and Elijah, right then and there, in the midst of God's *shekinah glory* enveloping Jesus at the Transfiguration:

Mat 17:1-5 Now after six days Jesus took Peter, James, and John his brother, led them up on a high mountain by themselves; [2]and He was transfigured before them. His face shone like the sun, and His clothes became as white as the light. [3]And behold, Moses and Elijah appeared to them, talking with Him. [4]Then Peter answered and said to Jesus, "Lord, it is good for us to be here; if You wish, let us make here three tabernacles: one for You, one for Moses, and one for Elijah." [5]While he was still speaking, behold, a bright cloud overshadowed them; and suddenly a voice came out of the cloud, saying, "This is My Beloved Son, in whom I am well pleased. Hear Him!"

DEEP DIVE: THE SHEKINAH [KABOD] GLORY OF GOD

The word shekinah does not appear in the Bible, but the concept clearly does. [*Kabod* is the Hebrew word, Shekinah actually comes from the Kaballah.] The Jewish rabbis coined this extra-biblical expression, a form of a Hebrew word that literally means "he caused to dwell," signifying that it was a divine visitation of the presence or dwelling of the Lord God on this earth. The Shekinah was first evident when the Israelites set out from Succoth in their escape from Egypt. There the Lord appeared in a cloudy pillar in the day and a fiery pillar by night: "After leaving Succoth they camped at Etham on the edge of the desert. By day the LORD went ahead of them in a pillar of cloud to guide them on their way and by night in a pillar of fire to give them light, so that they could travel by day or night. Neither the pillar of cloud by day nor the pillar of fire by night left its place in front of the people" (Exodus 13:20–22). God spoke to Moses out of the pillar of cloud in Exodus 33, assuring him that His Presence would be with the Israelites (v. 9).

Verse 11 says God spoke to Moses "face to face" out of the cloud, but when Moses asked to see God's glory, God told Him, "You cannot see My face; for no man shall see Me, and live" (v. 20). So, apparently, the visible manifestation of God's glory was somewhat muted. When Moses asked to see God's glory, God hid Moses in the cleft of a rock, covered him with His hand, and passed by. Then He removed His hand, and Moses saw only His back. This would seem to indicate that God's glory is too awesome and powerful to be seen ...

The visible manifestation of God's presence was seen not only by the Israelites but also by the Egyptians: "During the last watch of the night the LORD looked down from the pillar of fire and cloud at the Egyptian army and threw it into confusion. He made the wheels of their chariots come off so that they had difficulty driving. And the Egyptians said, 'Let's get away from the Israelites! The LORD is fighting for them against Egypt'" (Exodus 14:24-25). Just the presence of God's Shekinah glory was enough to convince His enemies that He was not someone to be resisted.

In the New Testament, Jesus Christ is the dwelling place of God's glory. Colossians 2:9 tells us that "in Christ all the fullness of the Deity lives in bodily form," causing Jesus to exclaim to Philip, "Anyone who has seen me has seen the Father" (John 14:9). In Christ, we see the visible manifestation of God Himself in the second person of the Trinity. Although His glory was also veiled, Jesus is nonetheless the presence of God on earth. Just as the divine Presence dwelled in a relatively plain tent called the "tabernacle" before the Temple in Jerusalem was built, so did the Presence dwell in the relatively plain man who was Jesus. "He had no beauty or majesty to attract us to him, nothing in his appearance that we should desire him" (Isaiah 53:2). But when we get to heaven, we will see both the Son and the Father in all their glory, and the Shekinah will no longer be veiled (1 John 3:2).

Retrieved from https://www.gotquestions.org/shekinah-glory.html

King Solomon discovered the connection between God's manifest presence and Tabernacles:

2 Chr 5:1 So all the work that Solomon had done for the house of the LORD was finished; and Solomon brought in the things which his father David had dedicated: the silver and the gold and all the furnishings. And he put *them* in the treasuries of the house of God.

2 Chr 5:3 Therefore all the men of Israel assembled with the king at the feast, *which was in the seventh month.*

2 Chr 5:12-14 [12]And the Levites *who were* the singers, all those of Asaph and Heman and Jeduthun, with their sons and their brethren, stood at the east end of the altar, clothed in white linen, having cymbals, stringed instruments and harps, and with them *one hundred and twenty priests sounding with trumpets –* [13]indeed it came to pass, *when the trumpeters and singers were as one,* to make one sound to be heard in praising and thanking the LORD, and when they lifted up their voice with the trumpets and cymbals and instruments of music, and praised the LORD, *saying: "For He is* good, For His mercy *endures* forever," that the house, *the house of the LORD, was **filled with a cloud**,* [14]*so that the priests could not* *continue ministering **because of the cloud**; for the **glory of the LORD filled the house of God**.*

We live today under the impression that God's glory cannot manifest. But is this true? It was manifested before Israel as the Temple was completed and anointed with worship and praise. Could something like this happen when the Rapture occurs and the *then living* believers (along with the *then resurrected* but who currently sleep now) are made complete and anointed with the Glory of God?

In 2 Chronicles, we learn that Solomon's temple (a symbol of the worship of God during the time of rest from war) was dedicated with worship and singing. This was done during the "feast which was in the seventh month" – that is, *Tabernacles* – and God shows His approval by filling His house with His glory. God filled His Temple with His glorious presence in the appearance of a cloud that was so heavy the priests could not perform their duties. This is God's supreme intent for the Body of Christ, the Temple of God in the last days. *God will again fill His house with His Glory! His presence will be obvious to everyone.*

TABERNACLES IS THE FEAST OF FEASTS

Therefore, to recap, the Feast of Tabernacles is perhaps the most comprehensive statement of the salvation for which we are destined. Its meaning includes all the following:

1. **Victory in War**
2. **Holiness**
3. **Unity**
4. **Joy**
5. **Ingathering**
6. **Living Water**
7. **Rest**
8. **Glory**

While the ultimate glorification of the Church awaits when we return with Christ at His visible return, let us allow the Holy Spirit of God to manifest the truth of Tabernacles in our lives even now. Let us appropriate these truths today, as God guides, inspires, and indwells us ever more fully.

We are not to defer or delay the realization of sanctification which will yield, through the power of the Holy Spirit, the glory of God in our lives. This would be an act of unbelief and disobedience. Our lives are to witness to His glory, even today, as the "leaven" is "thrown out" and as we "put on" Christ. We should manifest – now – the victory that Jesus won for us over the world, the flesh, and the devil (1 John 2:16), as we allow the holiness of Jesus, the Bread of Life, to be "kneaded into our lives". For without holiness, the Scripture tells us plainly, we cannot see Him, "Follow... holiness, *without which no man shall see the Lord.*" (Hebrews 12:14)

- Let us lay aside our differences and dwell together in unity.
- Let the joy of the Lord be our strength, rather than that which the world gives.
- Let us go forth and gather in the harvest that is waiting for us.
- Let the Living Water flow from God's throne to the thirsty world.
- Let us enter God's rest, and allow Him to do even greater works than Jesus did (John 14:12) through His Body the Church, with Jesus as Head.
- Let us do "great exploits" as the LORD told Daniel His people would do.
- Let us realize that as we grow into a mature, unified body, God's glory will manifest itself, in His Church, from "glory to glory", advancing toward the fullness that will be realized *in the revealing of the Children of God.*

    Hosea 12:9 (KJV) And I that am the LORD thy God from the land of Egypt will yet make thee to *dwell in tabernacles*, as in the days of the solemn feast.

4: THE GLORY OF GOD

THE KINGDOM OF GOD AND THE KINGDOM OF HEAVEN (GOD'S GLORY REVEALED)

The Triune God has revealed His Plan to us *in triad* ways. For the remainder of this study we will study and keep in mind the three truths that comprise this pattern. In Numbers 14:21, God swears:

Num 14:21 But truly, as I live, all the earth shall be filled with the glory of the LORD...

David prays this in Ps 72:19.

Psa 72:19 And blessed *be* His glorious name forever! And let the whole earth be filled *with* His glory. Amen and Amen.

When God swears it and David (the man after God's own heart) prays it – there should be no doubt that it will happen. The whole earth will be filled with God's glory. Romans 8:13-25, among many others, gives some insight about the glory to be revealed in this world through us.

Rom 8:13-25 ¹³For if you live according to the flesh you will die; but if by the Spirit you put to death the deeds of the body, you will live. ¹⁴For as many as are led by the Spirit of God, these are sons of God. ¹⁵For you did not receive the spirit of bondage again to fear, but you received the Spirit of adoption by whom we cry out, "Abba, Father." [16]The Spirit Himself bears witness with our spirit that we are children of God, [17]and if children, then heirs – heirs of God and joint heirs with Christ, if indeed we suffer with *Him*, that we may also be glorified together. [18]*For I consider that the sufferings of this present time are not worthy to be compared* **with the glory which shall be revealed in us.** [19]*For the earnest expectation of the creation eagerly waits for* **the revealing of the sons of God.** [20]*For the creation was subjected to futility,* ‧ *not willingly, but because of Him who subjected it in hope;* [21]*because the creation itself also will be delivered from the bondage of corruption* **into the glorious liberty of the children of God.** [22]For we know that the whole creation groans and labors with birth pangs together until now. [23]Not only *that,* but we also who have the firstfruits of the Spirit, *even we ourselves groan within ourselves, eagerly waiting for the adoption, the redemption of our body.* [24]For we were saved in this hope, but hope that is seen is not hope; for why does one still hope for what he sees? [25]But if we hope for what we do not see, we eagerly wait for *it* with perseverance.

These verses speak of the manifestation of the sons of God, which occurs when the Body of Christ receives its inheritance in Christ. Verse 18 says that God's glory shall be revealed in us *at this time.* Notice from verses 18-23 that the glory revealed in us – the adoption of sons, the deliverance of the creation, the redemption of our body, and the blessed hope – are all closely related. We will talk more about this in a later chapter.

The Kingdom of God and *the Kingdom of Heaven*...Most of us think of these two concepts as identical. I (Huffman) will highlight why I believe the Bible reveals a difference between the two.

‧ *Futility* is substituted for *vanity* in the KJV. This references Genesis 3:17. What is the curse? It is a technical theological matter on God's act after Adam's sin. See the Deep Dive, "The Creation Was Subjected to Corruption for Our Glory." (p. 154-155)

Luke 17:20-21 [20]Now when He was asked by the Pharisees when the kingdom of God would come, He answered them and said, "The kingdom of God does not come with observation; [21]nor will they say, 'See here!' or 'See there!' For indeed, the kingdom of God is within you."

Rom 14:17 For the kingdom of God is not eating and drinking, but righteousness and peace and joy in the Holy Spirit.

The Kingdom of God is where God is King. The Kingdom of God is the reign of God in the universe over all His creatures and includes time, eternity, heaven, and earth.

Mark 9:1 And He said to them, "Assuredly, I say to you that there are some standing here who will not taste death till they see the kingdom of God present with power."

Luke 9:27-29 [27]But I tell you truly, there are some standing here who shall not taste death till they see the kingdom of God." [28]Now it came to pass, about eight days after these sayings, that He took Peter, John, and James and went up on the mountain to pray. [29]As He prayed, the appearance of His face was altered, and His robe *became* white *and* glistening.

Mat 16:28 Assuredly, I say to you, there are some standing here who shall not taste death till they see the Son of Man coming in His kingdom."

In Mark 9:1 above, "Power" – Greek word *"dunamis"* – means an exhibition of power (from which our WORD "dynamite" comes). This power of God through signs and wonders was exhibited by Jesus Christ and *these signs and wonders authenticated His divine mission:*

Act 2:22 "Men of Israel, hear these words: Jesus of Nazareth, a Man attested by God to you by miracles, wonders, and signs which God did through Him in your midst, as you yourselves also know--"

Mark 9:2-8 tells the story of the "Kingdom of God come with power."

Mark 9:2-8 [2]Now after six days Jesus took Peter, James, and John, and led them up on a high mountain apart by themselves; and He was transfigured before them. [3]His clothes became shining, exceedingly white, like snow, such as no launderer on earth can whiten them. [4]And Elijah appeared to them with Moses, and they were talking with Jesus. [5]Then Peter answered and said to Jesus, "Rabbi, it is good for us to be here; and let us make three tabernacles: one for You, one for Moses, and one for Elijah" – [6]because he did not know what to say, for they were greatly afraid. [7]And a cloud came and overshadowed them; and a voice came out of the cloud, saying, "This is My Beloved Son. Hear Him!" [8]Suddenly, when they had looked around, they saw no one anymore, but only Jesus with themselves.

In Matt 16:28, Jesus calls this event "the Son of Man coming in His Kingdom" – and in Luke 9:27, "seeing the Kingdom of God."

2 Pet 1:16-18 [16]For we did not follow cunningly devised fables when we made known to you the power and coming of our Lord Jesus Christ, but were eyewitnesses of His majesty. [17]For He received from God the Father honor and glory when such a voice came to Him from the *Excellent Glory*: "This is My Beloved Son, in whom I am well pleased." [18]And we heard this voice which came from heaven when we were with Him on the holy mountain.

What did they see? The cloud of glory! Moreover, the cloud of "Excellent Glory." So, the sign *"authenticating the divine mission of the doer"* was the cloud of glory – the same sign that God gave the Israelites in the wilderness. The Kingdom of God was within Jesus and God chose to manifest that Kingdom to three men in the form of the cloud of Glory. By implication: *The Kingdom of God **within** can be manifest **without** in the form of the Glory of God.*

Jesus describes the Kingdom of Heaven in Matthew 20 and in seven parables in Matthew 13. These describe different aspects of the Church during the "Church age". This is the Kingdom of God manifest through the Church to the world. Indeed, the *Kingdom of Heaven is the outward manifestation of the Kingdom of God in space and time.* God must first be King within for His Kingdom to be manifest without. *The full manifestation of the Kingdom of God features the Glory of God.*

There was more to this episode than merely revealing HIS GLORY to those disciples on the mount. Michael Heiser makes clear that the most logical candidate for the "high mountain" is Mount Hermon, because of its height, proximity to Caesarea Philippi and its symbolic religious associations. He places this vital point in the context of the descent of the sons of God in Genesis 6:1-4. In other words, tradition is wrong. *The Transfiguration was not on Mount Tabor, but on Mount Hermon.* The evil brought to humanity through the 200 watchers discussed in the Book of Enoch was to be reversed there and then. Heiser writes:

> Jesus picks Mount Hermon to reveal to Peter, James, and John exactly who He is – the embodied glory – the essence of God, the divine Name made visible by incarnation. The meaning is just as transparent: I'm putting the hostile powers of the unseen world on notice. I've come to earth to take back what is mine. The Kingdom of God is at hand.[†]

Heiser asserts that this is the transition point of Jesus' ministry. After the Transfiguration, Jesus moves toward His death at Jerusalem. While the enemy knows who Jesus is, the enemy is not aware of His plan. Thus, Jesus baits the forces of darkness to act against Him, those evil powers not knowing that Jesus is using them and their hatred toward Him to accomplish His goal. We know now, but they did not know then, that death is how Jesus launched the Kingdom of God.

[†] Heiser, op. cit., pp. 285-287.

Therefore, we must underscore the fact that the Kingdom of God is revealed *for* us, but is also now revealed *against the forces of darkness.*

Acts 2:1-4 [1]When the Day of Pentecost had fully come; they were all with one accord in one place. [2]And suddenly there came a sound from heaven, as of a rushing mighty wind, and it filled the whole house where they were sitting. [3]Then there appeared to them divided tongues, as of fire, and *one* sat upon each of them. [4]And they were all filled with the Holy Spirit and began to speak with other tongues, as the Spirit gave them utterance.

The Kingdom of God in unity and prayer brought forth (in answered prayer) the Church (the Kingdom of Heaven). This included the sign of the tongues of fire or a small pillar of fire (Glory of God) over every head. Now that was very significant to every devout Jew in town! This same

KINGDOM OF GOD	THE KINGDOM OF HEAVEN
Everywhere – Infinite	A Certain Place – Finite
Eternal – Infinite	A Certain Time – Finite
Within Us and Without Us	We Are in This Kingdom

Figure 2 - The Kingdom of God, the Kingdom of Heaven
© Gary L. Huffman, 2017

pillar of fire had led their ancestors through the wilderness. In other words, while the symbolism could suggest a baptism of fire by which their sins were purged (somewhat like the hot coal placed on the mouth of Isaiah – Isaiah 6:6-7); more importantly, it symbolized that each new believer had become a "pillar of fire" albeit on a small scale. And this small body of little fires would surely grow hotter and spread.

Following is a small chart to contrast the two kingdoms: (The Kingdom of Heaven comprises a subset or *part* of the Kingdom of God):

Figure 3 - *Conceiving of the Kingdom of God*
© Gary Huffman, 2017

God is working in us to be King in every part of our lives so that He can work through us to manifest His Kingdom throughout the whole earth.

Mat 6:10 Your kingdom come. Your will be done on earth as *it is* in heaven.

The King James Version translates Matthew 6:10, "on earth" but it might possibly imply "in earthen vessels" not just a worldly domain. The thousand-year reign of Christ on the earth will be the fulfillment of the Kingdom of Heaven – or the Kingdom of God manifest on the earth (in this place and time). *That Kingdom includes God's glory dwelling with us and through us.*

THE KINGDOM AND THE GLORY OF GOD

Glory – as defined in *The New Compact Bible Dictionary*:

Concerning God, it is the display of His divine attributes and perfections... In both Testaments, there are references to the Shekinah glory of God, although not by name, for the word occurs in the Targums[‡] not in the Bible. To avoid anthropomorphisms (ascription of physical characteristics to God) which might lead to erroneous doctrine, the Targum writers spoke of *the glory of the Shekinah. This was the actual, physical manifestation of the presence of God, as seen in the pillars of cloud and fire.* New Testament references to the Shekinah glory are seen in John 1:14 and Romans 9:4. *Glory culminates in the changing of the bodies of the saints to the likeness of their glorified Lord* (Philippians 3:20-21, emphasis added).

John 1:14 And the Word became flesh and dwelt among us, and we beheld **His glory**, the glory as of the only begotten of the Father, full of grace and truth.

[‡] The Targums were commentaries of the Jewish scriptures for the benefit of Jews after the captivities who ceased to understand the sacred tongue. – *Dake's Bible.*

Rom 9:4 who are Israelites, to whom *pertain* the adoption**, the glory**, the covenants, the giving of the law, the service *of God,* and the promises;

Phil 3:20-21 For our citizenship is in heaven, from which we also eagerly wait for the Savior, the Lord Jesus Christ, [21]who will transform our lowly body that *it may be conformed to His glorious body*, according to the working by which He is able even to subdue all things to Himself.

The New Compact Bible Dictionary defines Shekinah as the "dwelling of God. The visible presence of Jehovah. It is alluded to in such places as Isaiah 60:2 by the phrase 'His Glory' and in Romans 9:4 by the phrase *'the glory.'* Moses calls this phenomenon, the 'cloud'..." We read in the scripture:

Exo 13:21 And the LORD went before them by day *in a pillar of cloud* to lead the way, and *by night in a pillar of fire* to give them light, so as to go by day and night.

Exo 14:19-20 [19]And the Angel of God, who went before the camp of Israel, moved and went behind them; and the pillar of cloud went from before them and stood behind them. [20]So it came between the camp of the Egyptians and the camp of Israel. Thus, it was a cloud and darkness *to the one,* and it gave light by night *to the other,* so that the one did not come near the other all that night.

Dake's Bible cites Luke 2:9 as an example of *God's Shekinah glory:*

Luke 2:9: And, lo, the angel of the Lord came upon them, and the glory of the Lord shone round about them: and they were sore afraid. Dr. Smith's *Smaller Scripture History* says: "To give the Israelites a visible manifestation of God's continual presence with them, on the very night in which they began their march, *the visible symbol of that presence went before them, in the Shekinah, or pillar* *of fire by night and of a cloud by day,* giving by its advance or halt the signal for their march or rest." (p. 92, emphasis added)

Num 14:10-21 [10]And all the congregation said to stone them with stones. Now the *glory of the LORD* appeared in the tabernacle of meeting before all the children of Israel. [11]Then the LORD said to Moses: "How long will these people reject Me? And how long will they not believe Me, with all the signs which I have performed among them? [12]I will strike them with the pestilence and disinherit them, and I will make of you a nation greater and mightier than they." [13]And Moses said to the LORD: "Then the Egyptians will hear *it,* for by Your might You brought these people up from among them, [14]and they will tell *it* to the inhabitants of this land. They have heard that You, LORD, *are* among these people; that You, LORD, are seen face to face and *Your cloud stands above them, and You go before them in a pillar of cloud by day and in a pillar of fire by night.* [15]Now *if* You kill these people as one man, then the nations which have heard of Your fame will speak, saying, [16]'Because the LORD was not able to bring this people to the land which He swore to give them, therefore He killed them in the wilderness.' [17]And now, I pray, let the power of my Lord be great, just as You have spoken, saying, [18]'The LORD is longsuffering and abundant in mercy, forgiving iniquity and transgression; but He by no means clears *the guilty,* visiting the iniquity of the fathers on the children to the third and fourth *generation.'* [19]Pardon the iniquity of this people, I pray, according to the greatness of Your mercy, just as You have forgiven this people, from Egypt even until now." [20]Then the LORD said: "I have pardoned, according to your word; [21]but truly, as I live, *all the earth shall be filled with the glory of the LORD.*

The sin of the people was a setback, but God will not settle for a people that keep on sinning. One day, His glory would be global. And His people will show forth that glory everywhere.

Psa 85:9 Surely His salvation *is* near to those who fear Him, that *glory* may dwell in our land.

Psa 72:19 And blessed *be* His glorious name forever! And let *the whole earth be filled with His glory*. Amen and Amen.

Psa 63:1-2 [1]O God, You *are* my God; Early will I seek You; My soul thirsts for You; My flesh longs for You In a dry and thirsty land Where there is no water. [2]So I have looked for You in the sanctuary, *to see Your power and Your glory*.

Psa 90:16 Let Your work appear to Your servants, And Your *glory* to their children.

Psa 97:1-6 [1]The LORD reigneth; let the earth rejoice; let the multitude of isles be glad *thereof*. [2]Clouds and darkness *are* round about him: righteousness and judgment *are* the habitation of his throne. [3]A fire goeth before him, and burneth up his enemies round about. [4]His lightnings enlightened the world: the earth saw, and trembled. [5]The hills melted like wax at the presence of the LORD, at the presence of the Lord of the whole earth. [6]The heavens declare His righteousness, and <u>all</u> *the people see His glory.*

Psalm 97 relates the judgments of God and then Christ's reign during the millennium. Read verse 1 and verse 6 which conveys to us that "All the people (shall) *see His glory*."

Exo 16:7 And in the morning *you shall see the glory of the LORD;* for He hears your complaints against the LORD. But what *are* we, that you complain against us?"

Exo 16:10 Now it came to pass, as Aaron spoke to the whole congregation of the children of Israel, that they looked toward the wilderness, and behold, *the glory of the LORD appeared in the cloud.*

Exo 33:18-23 [18]And he said, "Please, show me Your glory." [19]Then He said, "*I will make all My goodness pass before you*, and I will proclaim the name of the LORD before you. I will be gracious to whom I will be gracious, and I will have compassion on whom I will have compassion." [20]But He said, "You cannot see My face; for no man shall see Me, and live." [21]And the LORD said, "Here is a place by Me, and you shall stand on the rock. [22]So it shall be, *while My glory passes by*, that I will put you in the cleft of the rock, and will cover you with My hand while I pass by. [23]Then I will take away My hand, and you shall see My back; but My face shall not be seen."

Exo 34:28-30 So he was there with the LORD forty days and forty nights; he neither ate bread nor drank water. And He wrote on the tablets the words of the covenant, the Ten Commandments. [29]Now it was so, when Moses came down from Mount Sinai (and the two tablets of the Testimony *were* in Moses' hand when he came down from the mountain), that Moses did not know *that the skin of his face shone while he talked with Him.* [30]*So when Aaron and all the children of Israel saw Moses, behold, the skin of his face shone, and they were afraid to come near him.*

Exo 34:33 And when Moses had finished speaking with them, he put a veil on his face.

Isa 35:2 It shall blossom abundantly and rejoice, even with joy and singing. The glory of Lebanon shall be given to it, the excellence of Carmel and Sharon. They shall see the glory of the LORD, The excellency of our God.

Isa 40:5 *The glory of the LORD shall be revealed, And all flesh shall see it togethe*r; For the mouth of the LORD has spoken."

Isa 60:2 For behold, the darkness shall cover the earth, And deep darkness the people; But the LORD will arise over you, *And His glory will be seen upon you.*

Isa 66:18 "For I *know* their works and their thoughts. It shall be that I will gather all nations and tongues; and they *shall come and see My glory.*

Compare Moses to Jesus' disciples' Transfiguration experience:

Mat 17:2 And He was transfigured before them. *His face shone like the sun,* and His clothes became as white as the light.

Mat 17:5 While he was still speaking, behold, *a bright cloud overshadowed them;* and suddenly a voice came out of the cloud, saying, "This is My Beloved Son, in whom I am well pleased. Hear Him!"

Mark 9:3 *His clothes became shining,* exceedingly white, like snow, such as no launderer on earth can whiten them.

Luke 9:29-35 [29]As He prayed, the appearance of His face was altered, and His robe *became* white *and* glistening. [30]And behold, two men talked with Him, who were Moses and Elijah, [31]*who appeared in glory* and spoke of His decease which He was about to accomplish at Jerusalem. [32]But Peter and those with him were heavy with sleep; and when they were fully awake, *they saw His glory* and the two men who stood with Him. [33]Then it happened, as they were parting from Him, *that* Peter said to Jesus, "Master, it is good for us to be here; and let us make three tabernacles: one for You, one for Moses, and one for Elijah" – not knowing what he said. [34]While he was saying this, *a cloud came and overshadowed them;* and they were fearful as they entered the cloud. [35]And a voice came out of the cloud, saying, "This is My Beloved Son. Hear Him!"

Many times, *the cloud of glory is referred to simply as "cloud"* as in Luke 9 above. Now, let's consider the *ministry of Jesus in glory* and to His disciples after His death:

Luke 24:4 And it happened, as they were greatly perplexed about this, that behold, two men stood by them *in shining garments*.

Mat 28:2-4 ²And behold, there was a great earthquake; for an angel of the Lord descended from heaven, and came and rolled back the stone from the door, and sat on it. *³His countenance was like lightning, and his clothing as white as snow.* ⁴And the guards shook for fear of him, and became like dead *men*.

2 Pet 1:16-18 ¹⁶For we did not follow cunningly devised fables when we made known to you the power and coming of our Lord Jesus Christ, but *were eyewitnesses of His majesty*. ¹⁷For He received from God the Father *honor and glory* when such a voice came to Him from *the Excellent Glory*: "This is My Beloved Son, in whom I am well pleased." ¹⁸And we heard this voice which came from heaven when we were with Him on the holy mountain.

This was the *cloud of glory* as recorded in Luke 9. Being a Jew, Peter understood the importance of that cloud of glory. It supplied strength to Peter, not just to Jesus. Likewise, *seeing the glory of God*, Stephen was emboldened in Acts 7:55.

Acts 7:55 But he, being full of the Holy Spirit, gazed into heaven *and saw the glory of God*, and Jesus standing at the right hand of God.

Jesus saw the progenitors of the Old Covenant. Moses and Elijah represented the law and the prophets at the display of Jesus' glory before His death. Stephen saw the New Covenant. Jesus was imbued with glory at the right hand of God before Stephen was murdered. Did the Jews, who were stoning Stephen to death, see the glory of God? The Scripture doesn't indicate this. But we shouldn't rule out that possibility. Note that the forebears of the New Covenant witnessed God's glory within and around Jesus. Stephen saw it at his death. James, Peter and

John saw it at the Transfiguration. John the Baptist saw the Holy Spirit descend upon Jesus in the shape of a dove. Paul was blinded (temporarily) *by the glory of Jesus* at his conversion on the road to Damascus (in Paul's experience, Luke tells us that Jesus' voice spoke *"from the glory of God"*). Importantly, this same thing, this occurrence, took place on the Mount of Transfiguration, when the Father's voice spoke "from the cloud".

> **Acts 22:6-11** [6]Now it happened, as I journeyed and came near Damascus at about noon, suddenly a great light from heaven shone around me. [7]And I fell to the ground and heard a voice saying to me, 'Saul, Saul, why are you persecuting Me?' [8]So I answered, 'Who are You, Lord?' And He said to me, 'I am Jesus of Nazareth, whom you are persecuting.' [9]*"And those who were with me indeed saw the light and were afraid, but they did not hear the voice of Him who spoke to me.* [10]So I said, 'What shall I do, Lord?' And the Lord said to me, 'Arise and go into Damascus, and there you will be told all things which are appointed for you to do.' [11]And since I could not see *for the glory of that light*, being led by the hand of those who were with me, I came into Damascus.

In the Old Testament, *the glory of God was the sign that God's presence and blessing was with Israel*. Likewise, to these "New Covenant" Jews, the glory of God showing forth from Jesus showed them that He was the Messiah, the Anointed One, the Son of God. *This experience of glory demonstrated that God's presence and blessing were upon Jesus*. In Luke 2:9, *God's glory* was also a sign to the Jewish shepherds that this birth was confirmation that God was its author – the God of Abraham, Isaac, Jacob, and Moses. This event was like other moments of the display of God's glory as had been told to them by their ancestors. "The cloud" led the children of Israel through the wilderness. "The cloud" filled Solomon's temple. In the same way, there was no mistaking the meaning of what was happening. *The glory of God authenticated the event of Messiah's birth.*

Luke 2:9 And behold, an angel of the Lord stood before them, and *the glory of the Lord shone around them*, and they were greatly afraid.

A physical, visible manifestation of God's presence in glory is emphasized throughout scripture as something tremendous, something so extraordinary its meaning lies beyond our comprehension! We may echo Ezekiel 3:12, *"Blessed be the Glory of the Lord from His place."*

It often goes missed that the deep conviction of the Apostles was mightily influenced by witnessing the glory of God and the glory of Jesus. The glory of God – sensing it, seeing it – no doubt was a major factor influencing the spiritual wherewithal of those foundational leaders of our faith. As we noted above, Peter, James, John, Stephen, and Paul directly experienced it. At the resurrection of Jesus when a great earthquake occurred, on the road to Damascus, and possibly at the death of Stephen, *non-believers saw the glory of God* – however, it was seen in a faith-enhancing way. When Jesus ascended, the glory of God appeared again in "the cloud." This is an important point to keep in mind as we continue. *God's glory appears during key events in the life of the Church. At selected moments, in situations of greatest import, many witness God's glory.* Therefore, we are led to ask, "When the Church has been raptured, should we expect God's glory to be *re*-presented then?" If we say, "No," do we doubt because we have grown to be "naturalists?" Why would the rapture not show forth the glory of God? Is there a more important event for the Church other than Christ's own resurrection?

THE RESURRECTION OF THE DEAD

The resurrection of the dead is a foundational truth that we must understand before going on to maturity.

Heb 6:1-3 [1]Therefore, leaving the discussion of the elementary *principles* of Christ, let us go on to perfection, not laying again the foundation of repentance from dead works and of faith toward God,

[2]of the doctrine of baptisms, of laying on of hands, of *resurrection of the dead*, and of eternal judgment. [3]And this we will do if God permits.

In other words, as God permits, *we will go on to maturity – even unto perfection.*

So, we pose a question: Does the writer of Hebrews mention heaven as a foundational truth? Our answer is, "No" *because "going to heaven" is just one aspect of the magnitude of the resurrection.* At the resurrection, those who have previously gone to heaven will return to earth and dwell here, at least for a thousand years. Heaven as it is traditionally understood considers the "afterlife" the "mansion in the sky" (John 14:1-3) But for the mature in our faith, it would be far more accurate to think of "heaven" as a temporary holding place for those who have died in Christ. There is even conjecture about whether the New Jerusalem should be considered "heaven" before it descends from the third heaven and becomes the dwelling place of God, Christ, and believers from all time.[§]

We have body, soul, spirit. Before rebirth (born again experience) our spirit is dead. At rebirth our spirit is made alive by God's Holy Spirit:

- The first birth – body and soul born (natural birth).
- The second birth – spirit born (spiritual birth) – "born again".

[§] Randall Price, in his essay on the New Jerusalem, points out this issue (along with many others we intend to touch on later). "We must also look to another context to explain the "the bride, the wife of the Lamb" as already in the New Jerusalem before the eternal state, if it is contended the New Jerusalem begins with the eternal state rather than is preexistent. Regardless of when the New Jerusalem descends from heaven, it is the prophetic promise of it as the eternal home of God's people which at the conclusion of John's Revelation, compels the prayer of the saints, "Amen. Come, Lord Jesus" (Revelation 22:20). Randall Price, *The New Jerusalem*, p. 7. Retrieved June 4, 2017 from http://www.worldofthebible.com/Bible%20Studies/The%20New%20Jerusalem.pdf

John 3:3 Jesus answered and said to him, "Most assuredly, I say to you, unless one is born again, he cannot see the kingdom of God."

At death, the body goes to earth, while spirit and soul go to the third heaven to dwell with God (and Hebrew's "great cloud of witnesses"), the saints who have died and gone before us. At the resurrection/rapture, the complete body, soul, and spirit are reunited so that we might have fellowship with God as a whole person.

Psa 139:13-16 [13]For You formed my inward parts; You covered me in my mother's womb. [14]I will praise You, for I am fearfully *and* wonderfully made; Marvelous are Your works, and *that* my soul knows very well. [15]My frame was not hidden from You, When I was made in secret, *and* skillfully wrought in the lowest parts of the earth. [16]Your eyes saw my substance, being yet unformed. And in Your book, they all were written, the days fashioned for me, when *as yet there were* none of them.

Every physical, earthly element of David's body was prepared by God before David's birth and recorded. God knew every molecule and wrote it down in 'His Book.' This is the same truth for each of us.

Mat 10:30 But the very hairs of your head are all numbered.

Jesus' statement, of course, implies every aspect of our body is precious to God — not just our hair! [I (Huffman) don't know about you, but God would not be challenged by counting the few hairs left on my head!]

So, now we see how God can resurrect the body – dimensions, elements – down to the atoms if He so intends. Cremation, nuclear annihilation – no problem for God. We will be resurrected with a new body.

Luke 24:39-40 Behold My hands and My feet, that it is I Myself. Handle Me and see, *for a spirit does not have flesh and bones as you see I have."* [40]When He had said this, He showed them His hands and His feet.

Jesus' same body was resurrected minus His shed blood. His blood had to stay before the Father on the altar in the heavenly tabernacle for you and me. But the scars on His hands, His feet, and pierced side will always be visible – to remind us of the price He paid for our salvation.

1 Cor 15:4 And that He was buried, and that He rose again the third day *according to the Scriptures,*

Of course, the "Scriptures" here means the Old Testament.

Psa 71:20-21 *You,* who have shown me great and severe troubles, shall revive me again, And bring me up again from the depths of the earth. [21]You shall increase my greatness, And comfort me on every side.

Psa 16:10 For You will not leave my soul in Sheol, nor will You allow Your Holy One to see corruption.

These passages reveal David's confidence in the resurrection. But remember, David has yet to see that resurrection as we write these words in *The Revealing, on May 31, 2017.*

Acts 2:29 "Men *and* brethren, let *me* speak freely to you of the patriarch David, that he is both dead and buried, and his tomb is with us to this day."

And God's promise to Abraham cannot be fulfilled until the resurrection.

Gen 17:8 Also I give to you and your descendants after you the land in which you are a stranger, all the land of Canaan, as an everlasting possession; and I will be their God."

Isa 26:19 Your dead shall live; *Together with* my dead body they shall arise. Awake and sing, you who dwell in dust; For your *dew is like the dew of herbs, And the earth shall cast out the dead.*

The *dew* is the Holy Spirit which brings forth the fruit of resurrection. The Spirit is the Living Water. Those that have become dust will be reconstituted (rehydrated!) with the water of Life.

Dan 12:1-3 [1]"At that time Michael shall stand up, the great prince who stands *watch over the sons of your people*; And there shall be a time of trouble, such as never was since there was a nation, *even* to that time. And at that time your people shall be delivered, everyone who is found written in the book. [2]And many of those *who sleep in the dust of the earth shall awake, some to everlasting life, Some to shame and everlasting contempt.* [3]Those who are wise *shall **shine** like the brightness of the firmament,* and those who **turn many to righteousness** like the stars forever and ever.

WHAT HAPPENS IMMEDIATELY AFTER THE RAPTURE?

During this "time of trouble", also known as the Great Tribulation, is this shining – of which Daniel speaks – to be understood as a symbol or does it in fact signify the glory of God? With the significant testimony of Scripture we have already reviewed, the conclusion should be that *such a signing will take place.* That is why we conclude *the manifest presence of God in His people will be made known at some point during the last days.* The issue of course, is whether this shining for those resurrected – and raptured (before the visible return of Christ) – becomes evident to the "earth dwellers" during the Tribulation. Will they see our glory with Christ's?

Hos 6:2-3 After two days He will revive us; On the third day, He will raise us up, that we may live in His sight. [3]Let us know, let us pursue the knowledge of the LORD. His going forth is established as the morning; *He will come to us like the rain, Like the latter and former rain to the earth.*

Just as He rose on the third day, so will He raise us all through His power (1 Corinthians 6:14, Ephesians 1:19). This resurrection is for all those who "follow on (make progress) to know the Lord". The "latter rain" of the Holy Spirit came at Pentecost until now. The "rain, the former rain and the latter rain" will come at one time in the last days to flood the earth in the Spirit of God to bring in the most abundant harvest of all time! From Hosea, we can infer that the Former and Latter Rain, whose fulfillment comprises the Feast of Tabernacles, *closely coincides with the resurrection of believers up to that moment in time.*

Let's take another look at *the Sheaf of Firstfruits* (recall this was the third portion of the Passover feast):

Lev 23:11 He shall wave the sheaf before the LORD, to be accepted on your behalf; on the day after the Sabbath the priest shall wave it.

Mat 27:52-53 [52]And the graves were opened; and many bodies of the saints who had fallen asleep were raised; [53]and coming out of the graves after His resurrection, *they went into the holy city and appeared to many.*

This was a partial fulfillment of John 12:24 and of the Old Testament *Feast of Firstfruits.* Those who were resurrected appeared as a witness to those in Jerusalem.

Will those who are resurrected at the time of the resurrection/rapture disappear to "heaven" – not to appear again until Jesus returns with them (i.e., "the clouds of heaven") at his visible return to judge the "earth dwellers?" Or will those resurrected/raptured appear on the earth in some fashion as a witness to what is happening in the last days? There were saints that did this at the first resurrection. Will there be resurrected witnesses appearing to unbelievers after the Rapture?

John 12:24 Most assuredly, I say to you, unless a grain of wheat falls into the ground and dies, it remains alone; but if it dies, it produces much grain.

Jesus was the seed of wheat that died to bring forth much fruit. The Old Testament saints *rose as a testimony to this truth and a fulfillment of the Feast of Firstfruits.* Jesus and these saints together were the sheaf of firstfruits waved before the Lord at this resurrection time. This was celebrated in the Old Testament times before the general harvest. That fulfillment in the New Testament happened before the vast resurrection harvest to come when the Feast of Tabernacles is fulfilled on the earth in the last days.

Allow me to underscore that this also served as an assurance that all others – dead and buried in Jesus – would be resurrected. Matthew 27:53 indicates that these saints had been resurrected once and for all. And the word "appears" *indicates glorified bodies like their Lord who could "appear" and "disappear" at will.* It is only quite reasonable to assume that these saints who had resurrected with Jesus, also ascended into heaven with Him. Consider that Acts 1:9-11 teaches Jesus' ascent into and return from heaven will closely parallel each other.

Acts 1:9-11 [9]Now when He had spoken these things, while they watched, He was taken up, and a cloud received Him out of their sight. [10]And while they looked steadfastly toward heaven as He went up, behold, two men stood by them in white apparel, [11]who also said, "Men of Galilee, why do you stand gazing up into heaven? This *same*

Jesus, who was taken up from you into heaven, *will so come in like manner as you saw Him go into heaven."*

Mark 13:26 Then they will see *the Son of Man coming in the clouds with great power and glory.*

Zec 14:5 Then you shall flee *through* My mountain valley, For the mountain valley shall reach to Azal. Yes, you shall flee as you fled from the earthquake in the days of Uzziah king of Judah. Thus, **the LORD my God will come, and all the saints with You**.

Jude 1:14 Now Enoch, the seventh from Adam, prophesied about these men also, saying, *"Behold, the Lord comes with ten thousands of His saints...*

Mark 13:26 says "in the clouds" while Zechariah 14:5 and Jude 14 say "with His saints." Jesus was taken up into heaven in a cloud. We are only following precedent by pointing out the implied parallel (in Acts 1:11) by suggesting that Christ ascended into heaven together with those of His saints who were resurrected at that time. *The use of* **cloud** *is key.*

Heb 12:1 Therefore we also, *since we are surrounded by so great a* **cloud** *of witnesses,* let us lay aside every weight, and the sin which so easily ensnares *us,* and let us run with endurance the race that is set before us,

Hebrews 12:1 links Old Testament saints with a "cloud". Was this choice of words coincidental? What might it imply about glory? It does not say, "A *crowd* of witnesses, but a *cloud* of witnesses: who are clearly saints from the context just read in Chapter 11. The word for cloud is νέφος néphos, (nef'-os), whose Latin form, according to Strong's, aligns with nubes or *nebula,* and thus, identical to the English word, *nebula,* which means "an interstellar cloud." But there is more. *Says Wikipedia (definition):* "A nebula is an interstellar cloud of dust, hydrogen, helium and other ionized gases. Originally, nebula was a name for any diffuse astronomical object, including galaxies beyond the Milky Way. The Andromeda Galaxy, for instance, was once referred to as the Andromeda Nebula before the true nature of galaxies was confirmed in the early 20th century by Vesto Slipher, Edwin Hubble and others." We may say that a nebula is a cloud formed from millions of stars. And that fits into the concept of the glory of angels and of saints compared to that of stars. [See the later *Deep Dive* in this chapter on "Being as the Stars in Heaven."]

This usage of cloud would fulfill the typology of the Firstfruits in the Old Testament and exactly parallel Jesus' return from Heaven mentioned in Zechariah 14:5 and Jude 1:14. It only stands to reason by citing the scriptural precedent. These were *firstfruits*, as is Christ, and as will be those who are "at Christ's *coming*":

1 Cor 15:22-23 [22]For as in Adam all die, even so in Christ all shall be made alive. [23]But each one in his own order: Christ the firstfruits, afterward those *who are Christ's at His coming.*

The word translated *coming* is the Greek word **parousia**, mainly used in the New Testament to *denote Christ's second coming for the Church* as the Bridegroom to take His Bride – what most Christians call the "Rapture." "They that are Christ's" indicates possession or ownership. Ephesians 1:14 states: "redemption of the purchased possession" – *possession* indicates full surrender and obedience; but also, that Christ "paid the price" to redeem us – which employs an Old Testament term that means "to buy back" *one that has been already sold into slavery.*

For every single promise concerning Christ's First Advent there are five promises concerning His Second Advent. How much more will the Lord exhibit those glorified during this process. God's emphasis is a witness to the value He places on this event! Allow us to propose there are (at least) five purposes in Christ's second coming:

1. Christ, the Bridegroom, comes for the Church, His bride. (Rev 21:2,9-11)
2. To save *nationally* (in some sense) the people of Israel. (Rom 11:26-27)
3. To overthrow the antichrist and Satan. (Rev 12:5,9-11;19:11-20)
4. To judge the Gentile nations and their gods. (Matt 25:31-32)
5. To establish His thousand-year kingdom on earth. (Isa 24:23; Rev 20:4)

The truth introduced to us recently by the scholarship of Dr. Heiser, a sixth purpose should be included also: *To judge the deposed Divine Council members and install the newly adopted Sons of God – the glorified members of the Body of Christ. (Psalm 82)*

1 Th 4:15-17 [15]For this we say to you by the word of the Lord, that we who are alive *and* remain until the coming of the Lord will by no means precede those who are asleep. [16]For the Lord Himself will descend from heaven with a shout, with the voice of an archangel, and with the trumpet of God. And the dead in Christ will rise first. [17]Then we who are alive *and* remain shall be caught up together with them *in the clouds* to meet the Lord in the air. *And thus, we shall always be with the Lord.*

"We shall be caught up" (gr. *harpazo*) which means a "sudden, swift violent grab." "To snatch out of". Revelation 16:15 and Matthew 24:42-43 use the term in this way, but Jesus will snatch up only what is His (the jewels from the earth).

Rev 16:15 "Behold, I am coming as a thief. Blessed *is* he who watches, and keeps his garments, lest he walk naked and they see his shame."

Mat 24:43 But know this, that if the master of the house had known what hour the thief would come, he would have watched and not allowed his house to be broken into.

In 1 Thessalonians 4:17, the word "air" is the Greek *aer*. *It should be distinguished from aether – aether referring to a higher air more distant from the earth.* **Aer** denotes a "lower air" in immediate contact with the earth's surface. Paul indicates *that the meeting of the Lord and His saints will take place in the **lower air** – closer to the surface of the earth.* Would this event be visible? Would the glory of Christ and His Bride be seen?

There appear to be different phases to the first resurrection, but we will not examine these in our study. We will remain with the rapture doctrine as traditionally set forth by Pre-Tribulational and Mid-Tribulational believers, (and those who ascribe to the Pre-Wrath view) – namely, that the Rapture occurs sometime before the visible Second Coming of Christ in Matthew 24:29-31, which is also when "every eye shall see Him." (Revelation 1:7) Of course, the classic passage from Paul in 1 Corinthians, reveals to us "the mystery" of the catching up of the saints – both living and asleep:

> **1 Cor 15:35-44** [35]But someone will say, "How are the dead raised up? And with what body do they come?" [36]Foolish one, what you sow is not made alive unless it dies. [37]And what you sow, you do not sow that body that shall be, but mere grain – perhaps wheat or some other *grain.* [38]But *God gives it a body as He pleases*, and to each seed its own body. [39]All flesh *is* not the same flesh, but *there is* one *kind of* flesh of men, another flesh of animals, another of fish, *and* another of birds. [40]*There are* also celestial bodies and terrestrial bodies; but the glory of the celestial *is* one, and the *glory* of the terrestrial *is* another. [41]*There is* one glory of the sun, another glory of the moon, and another glory of the stars; for *one* star differs from *another* star in glory. [42]So also *is* the resurrection of the dead. The body is sown in corruption, it is raised in incorruption. [43]It is sown in dishonor, *it is raised in glory*. It is sown in weakness, it is raised in power. [44]It is sown a natural body, it is raised a spiritual body. *There is a natural body, and there is a spiritual body.*

DEEP DIVE: A NEW BODY IS LIKE MOVING INTO A BRAND-NEW HOUSE

Paul teaches in 2 Corinthians 4:17-18, that our afflictions amount to very little and are only temporary; nonetheless, they work on our behalf to create in us that which far exceeds in value the 'price we are paying' now. It comprises a property which will last for all eternity—a "weight of glory" (the meaning of which we will discuss more later). We are paying but a small monthly rent now—but we will soon own a mansion (in ourselves), the deed included, without any further payments due. "For our light affliction, which is but for a moment, is working for us a far more exceeding *and* eternal weight of glory, while we do not look at the things which are seen, but at the things which are not seen. For the things which are seen *are* temporary, but the things which *are* not seen are eternal."

This new life amounts to a creation. Paul is building toward that conclusion later in 2 Corinthians 5:17. ("We are a new creation"). That is why he states here, *"For it is the God who commanded light to shine out of darkness, who has shone in our hearts to give the light of the knowledge of the glory of God in the face of Jesus Christ."* (2 Corinthians 4:6) *Already (but not yet),* we have the seed within us that will blossom into a fully glorified body. He teaches, *"But we have this treasure in earthen vessels, that the excellence of the power may be of God and not of us."* (verse 7) Our mortality allows *God to shine through us.* We read, *"always carrying about in the body the dying of the Lord Jesus, that the life of Jesus also may be manifested in our body... For we who live are always delivered to death for Jesus' sake, that the life of Jesus also may be manifested in our mortal flesh."* (verse 8-9, 11) And finally, "Even though our outward *man* is perishing, yet the inward man is being renewed day by day." (verse 16)

In verse 18, Paul reminds us that we must set our 'eyes' (today we would say 'our focus'), on eternal things not seen. For Paul, *'seeing is **disbelieving**!'* We must focus on what is eternal, what we see only "with the eyes of faith."

In Chapter 5, verse 1, Paul justifies directing our focus in this manner because our bodies on earth are growing older and running down minute-by-minute. But in heaven our eternal bodies are like houses that cannot depreciate even one penny. *"For we know that if the tent that is our earthly home is destroyed, we have a building from God, a house not made with hands, eternal in the heavens."*

In verses 2-4, Paul continues this analogy. We live in a dilapidated house now; we sigh and groan and hope for the day when we will obtain our 'new house.' Not that we want to have *no* house at all—for we do not want to be found living without one. After all, he tells us, *being naked* indicates we do not possess a new house 'to come home to'—perhaps because we did not deserve one! Perish the thought!

In verse 5, Paul advises us not to worry. God's promise to us regarding owning a new house in heaven has been guaranteed by an earnest payment: He has given us *the Holy Spirit as a constant companion.* His Spirit in us confirms the house will be waiting for us to move in immediately when we arrive! *"He who has prepared us for this very thing is God, who has given us the Spirit as a guarantee."*

In verse 6, he switches subjects slightly, even lamenting a bit. While we live in the 'old house' we are not residing in God's neighborhood! However, just as soon as we move out of the old house, we instantly move into the new one next door to where God is! (As a quick sidebar, Paul states, *"Remember now... we live by the truth of what we know, our faith, not by what we see"* (verse 7 paraphrased). "For we walk by faith not by sight." He finally concludes this discussion by saying, "You know I am so confident about this, I had rather be absent from my body right now and be in my new house, in the new neighborhood, present with the LORD." Paul is brimming with confidence. "We would rather be away from the body and with the Lord."

Perhaps we should ask ourselves whether we readily concur with Paul's wish. *Do we believe our prospects to be so bright we would rather change houses right away?* Or do we just want to cling to the old real estate? Are we ready to move into the new neighborhood? Or do we want to stay put?

S. Douglas Woodward, based on a passage from *Blood Moon: Biblical Signs of the Coming Apocalypse*, (2014), Oklahoma City: Faith Happens Books, pp. 279-280.

Human beings need a different type of body to reside in the heavens (the sky, "outer space," and the heavenlies). God will provide such a body. And remember that heaven is not the reward that we anticipate. However, in receiving our glorified bodies, we are enabled to operate in the heavens (the sky as well as "outer space") as well as upon the earth. Where the LORD calls us to work, we will be empowered to serve Him. He has a job for us (at least one!) in the ages to come. Indeed, all of creation is eagerly waiting for **the revealing**... the "manifestation of the sons of God". (Romans 8:19)

That venerable scholar writing at the end of the Nineteenth Century, G.H. Pember, broke ground on the so-called Gap Theory of creation, the relationship of Orthodox Christianity to the heretical Theosophy of Madame Helena Petrovna Blavatsky, and fascinating speculation regarding the nature of Satan's domain as "prince and power of the air". Presented here is Pember's fascinating teaching on these subjects which complements what we have presented in this book.

DEEP DIVE: REPLACING THE PRINCE OF THE AIR AND HIS POWERS AND PRINCIPALITIES WITH THE GLORIFIED CHILDREN OF GOD

G. H. Pember

But (Satan) is also called "the Prince of the Power of the Air." [Ephesians 2:2] This principality would seem to be the same as "the heavenly places" – our version incorrectly translates "high places" – which, as Paul tells us, swarm with the spiritual hosts of wickedness. It is by no means necessary to restrict it to the eighty or a hundred miles of atmosphere supposed to surround the earth: for if Satan's power extends to the sun, as we suggested above, and so to the whole of our solar system, the kingdom of the air would include the immense space in which the planets of our center revolve; and in such a case it seems not unlikely that the throne of its prince may be situated in the photosphere of the sun... [Note: Pember was a man of the nineteenth century!]

What, then, is the nature of the power indicated by these titles of Satan? To understand it we must glance at the general hints of Scripture concerning spiritual agencies. For, though unseen and little suspected by the rulers of earth, there are also spiritual powers, all originally appointed by God, whether they be loyal to Him now or not. Rank above rank these watchers stand, each passing on his account to a superior until it reaches the Most High at the apex of the pyramid. So in Zachariah's first vision, those whom the Lord had sent to walk to and fro upon the earth are represented as delivering their report to the Angel of the Lord, who then appeals to the Almighty Himself. And hence we read of thrones, dominions, principalities, powers, archangels, and angels. Nor can we know much of Scripture without discovering that vast numbers of these invisible beings, who supervise the affairs of men and their world, are in open rebellion against the Almighty; that there are principalities, powers, and world-rulers of darkness, with whom, as Paul tells us, we have to wage a fearful warfare. These all render account to Satan, their prince, who, in his reports to the Most High, makes use of their intelligence to accuse ourselves and our brethren before God day and night.

It is then plainly revealed that *spiritual as well as human powers are concerned in the administration of our earth.* And these diverse agencies are mentioned as making up the totality of its government in a verse of Isaiah, where we are told *that the Lord at His coming will depose and punish two distinct governing bodies, "the **High Ones that are on high**, and the **Kings of the Earth** upon the earth."* Of these, the former are manifestly identical with Satan and his angels [Heiser might say, "the corrupted members of the divine counsel"]; the latter with the antichristian world-powers. Nor will Christ alter the form of government, though He change the rulers. *For Himself and His Church will then take the place of the High Ones that are on high,* while the first rank among the Kings of the Earth upon the earth will be given to the seed of Abraham according to the flesh... *it is probable that they are the appointed successors of Satan's ministers,* who will hereafter take possession of the elements to use them in the execution of the wrath to come. For until the Devil be deposed from the throne of the air, it is likely that he will exercise control, to a great extent at least, *over atmospheric phenomena* [UFOs maybe?]. In the

Book of Job, we find him even wielding the lightning: for at his bidding the fire of God fell from heaven, and consumed both the flocks and servants of the patriarch. And when, many centuries afterwards, our Lord arose from His sleep and "rebuked" the winds and the sea, it cannot be supposed that He was chiding the mere rush of the blast, or the senseless waves; but rather, *those malignant spirits of air and water which had combined to excite the storm…*

Seeing, then, that *the government which Christ will shortly take upon His shoulders appears to be exactly identical with that which was once committed to Satan,* and that God's first arrangements were of necessity perfection, does it not seem likely that, when the times of restitution arrive, the original order of things, will begin to be restored in Christ's Millennial kingdom?

If so, we can easily discover the outline of Satan's pre-Adamite world [an assertion of the Gap Theory, that before Adam (Pember, Dake, and many others contend) there was another race of humanoids upon the earth].

For in the Millennium, Christ and His Church, the members of which will then have been made like unto Himself, are to reign in the heavenly places over earth and its inhabitants. So, probably in remote ages, before the first whisper of rebellion against God, *Satan, as the great governing head and the viceroy of the Almighty, assisted by glorious beings of his own nature, ruled over the sinless dwellers upon earth.* At the same time, he directed the worship of his subjects, and expounded to them the oracles of the all-wise Creator. (emphasis added)

(Pember M. A., G. H. (2012-06-20). *Earth's Earliest Ages and Their Connection with Modern Spiritualism and Theosophy* (Kindle Locations 776-784, (Kindle Locations 800-816, 889-897, 968-976, 1211-1218). Kindle Edition.)

A STARRY-EYED GROOM AND GLORIOUS BRIDE MEET ABBA

<u>**2 Cor 4:14**</u> Knowing that He who raised up the *Lord Jesus will also raise us up with Jesus, and will **present us with you**.*

The scripture suggests that we will be presented to the Father by Jesus, in the same way a bridegroom would present his bride to his father and mother, and "glory" in her! This presenting of His Bride possibly happens immediately after the moment we are translated.

2 Cor 4:17-18 For our *light affliction, which is but for a moment, is working for us a far more exceeding and **eternal weight of glory,*** [18]while we do not look at the things which are seen, but at the things which are not seen. For the things which are seen *are* temporary, but the things which are not seen *are* eternal.

Please make note: we will not be naked when clothed with the glory of God, just as Adam and Eve before the fall.** In addition to a white robe, the glory of God will gleam bright. *This is the special clothing God has always intended for His children.* Nevertheless, there will be different orders of glory for not all children did great works after their salvation (by faith alone):

2 Cor 5:1-5 For we know that if our earthly house, *this* tent, is destroyed, we have a building from God, a house not made with hands, eternal in the heavens. [2]For in this we groan, *earnestly desiring to be clothed with our habitation which is from heaven,* [3]if indeed, having been clothed, we shall not be found naked. [4]For we who are in *this* tent groan, being burdened, not because we want to be unclothed, but further clothed, that mortality may be swallowed up by life. [5]Now He who has prepared us for this very thing *is* God, *who also has given us the Spirit as a guarantee.*

Gen 15:5 Then He brought him outside and said, "Look now toward heaven, and *count the stars* [a double meaning] if you are able to number them." And He said to him, "*So shall your descendants be.*"

** Some scholars assert that Adam and Eve were "innocent" but not glorified. Michael Heiser argues that they were living in a state of glorification. Huffman sides with Heiser on this matter. Woodward believes the glorification in Eden was real, but not anywhere near the level after we are glorified and share in Christ's glory imputed to us.

Gen 22:17 Blessing I will bless you, and multiplying I will multiply your descendants *as the stars of the heaven* [implying multiple meanings as we will see below] and as the sand which *is* on the seashore; and your *descendants shall possess the gate of their enemies.*

GOD'S PROMISE TO ABRAHAM HAS MULTIPLE MEANINGS

In a paper presented at the *2016 Society for Biblical Literature* meeting entitled, '"So Shall Your Seed Be", **David A. Burnett** presented a detailed study, a portion of which we reference here. His title: "Paul's application of Genesis 15:5 used in Romans 4:18 in Light of Early Jewish Deification Traditions." He also published this material in the *Journal for the Study of Paul and his Letters, Vol. 5, No. 2 – Fall, 2015.* His primary thesis is this: he argues for the "qualitative" as well as the "quantitative" interpretation of God's words, in Gen 15:5 and 22:17 cited above. His paper is an outstanding one and we recommend you read it. However, Because of copyright issues and the expressed wishes of the author Burnett, we provide only a brief recap of his worthy scholarship here.

DEEP DIVE: BECOMING AS THE STARS OF HEAVEN

Scholar David Burnett provides an important insight into Paul's understanding of the Genesis account regarding God's promises to Abraham as presented by Paul in Romans 4:18, "In hope he believed against hope, that he should become the father of many nations, as he had been told, 'So shall your offspring be.'" Burnett indicates the traditional quantitative interpretation is not the only way scholars have explained Paul's teaching concerning Genesis 15:5 and 22:17. While it is certainly true that Abraham's descendants could be described as *"countless, innumerable, or vast"* Paul conveys Abraham's seed will also possess powerful capabilities, equaling, or exceeding the angels in heaven.

This view stands in contrast to most contemporary scholars who emphasize the meaning of Yahweh's promises strictly refers to "the

139

multitude" of offspring. However, there are several "ancient" Jewish sources who challenge that point of view, suggesting there is more to it than that.

Burnett points to Philo, Sirach, and the author(s) of the Apocalypse of Abraham, who interpreted the promises to mean that Abraham's descendants would possess a likeness to stars and powers exceeding those of humankind.

Assuming Burnett is correct, we can easily see that the "seed of Abraham" exposition Paul provides in Romans, chapter 4, supports a much more extensive promise than scholars typically admit. "For the promise to Abraham and his offspring that he would be heir of the world did not come through the law but through the righteousness of faith" (Romans 4:13, ESV) Furthermore, we feel safe to see in this interpretation, one which reinforces Dr. Michael Heiser's insights into (1) the divine council of the Old Testament that we have covered previously as well as, (2) the future role of the saints in the Millennial Kingdom.

Burnett indicates there is a tradition in early Judaism that asserted Abraham's offspring would one day replace the sons of God (i.e., the stars of heaven) taking on similar power and authority to the angels; thus, "inheriting" the nations as their possession. In this respect, Paul can be seen to agree with other contemporary Jewish interpreters. Therefore, it would appear to be biblically accurate to understand the promise of "becoming as the stars of heaven" as a simile, but one far greater than modern scholars have allowed. Based upon the demonstration of Abraham's faith at the "binding of Isaac" (known in Judaism as the Aqedah – Genesis 22), God's promise to Abraham involves far more than fertility or progeny. It asserts his offspring will rule the nations. Burnett suggests that Paul connects the promises of God to comprise more than the number of descendants, but to the creation (the cosmos) and the resurrection of the dead. "And many of those who sleep in the dust of the earth shall awake, some to everlasting life, some to shame *and* everlasting contempt. Those who are wise *shall shine like the brightness of the firmament,* and those who turn many to righteousness *like the stars forever and ever." (Daniel 12:2-3).*

Burnett references Origen, the early Church father (Origen's Commentary on Romans 4:6-7) who stated (citing Origen): *"Your seed and your works can ascend to heaven and become works of light and be compared to the splendor and brilliance of the stars, so that when the day of resurrection arrives, you will stand out in brightness as one star differs from another star"* (4.6.9). Therefore, it appears it was not just the Jewish contemporaries of Paul who taught that Abraham's seed would become as *the stars of heaven*, but one of the early Church Fathers as well, understanding in Paul's exposition of Romans 4 to be *both qualitative as well as quantitative.*

In short, those that are true sons and daughters of Abraham will become like the angels in power after their resurrection and, apparently, rule not just the earth, but the cosmos. They will be given this authority instead of the corrupted "principalities and powers", i.e., the divine council established by God at the division of nations after the Tower of Babel incident.

The physical bodies of men and women are adapted to express and satisfy the soul – but their new resurrected body will be adapted to express and fulfill God's highest spiritual aspirations for humanity.

Prov 3:35 The *wise shall inherit glory*, but shame shall be the legacy of fools.

1 Cor 15:47-49 [47]The first man *was* of the earth, *made* of dust; the second Man *is* the Lord from heaven. [48]As *was* the *man* of dust, so also *are* those *who are made* of dust; and as *is* the heavenly Man, so also *are* those *who are* heavenly. [49]And as we have borne the image of the *man* of dust, *we shall also bear the image of the heavenly Man.*

1 Cor 15:51-53 [51]Behold, I tell you a mystery: We shall not all sleep, but we shall all be changed – [52]in a moment, in the twinkling of an eye, at the last trumpet. For the trumpet will sound, and the dead will be raised incorruptible, and we shall be changed. [53]For this corruptible must put on incorruption, and this mortal *must* put on immortality.

Phil 3:20-21 [20]For our citizenship is in heaven, from which we also eagerly wait for the Savior, the Lord Jesus Christ, [21]*who will transform our lowly body that it may be conformed to* **His glorious body**, according to the working by which He is able even to subdue all things to Himself.

The transformation of our bodies is the last chapter in God's total redemption of humanity. When our individual bodies are changed at the resurrection, the full and complete Body of Christ is ready to serve God in all dimensions of creation – physical and spiritual – with Jesus as the Head over His Body, the Church. The secret of resurrection power, however non-intuitive it is, remains the secret of spirituality: *one must die to oneself before we can receive this life from God.*   To die to oneself means to put the priorities of serving Christ and doing His will before your own will. It means trusting in Him that He will save you from the wrath to come. It means believing His Spirit has come to dwell in you, enabling you to live a new life, as a new creation. It means to join with the lives of others in the Body of Christ so that all may be glorified together.

2 Corinthians 5:17 Therefore, if anyone is in Christ, he is a new creation. The old has passed away; behold, the new has come. (ESV)

Whether we are physically alive or are "asleep" when Jesus returns, during our earthly existence, we must have died to self, that is – acknowledging our sins and inviting Christ into our spirits to save us from sin, *if we are to receive His resurrection power*. And this while *dying to self* is a metaphor... *it remains more than a metaphor*.   Our "old life" must be crucified before our "new life" can be appropriated. For demonstrating resurrection power in our everyday lives are proportionate to our dying to self and allowing the life of Christ to live and work through us.

Galatians 2:20 I am crucified with Christ: nevertheless, I live; yet not I, but Christ liveth in me: and the life which I now live in the flesh I live by the faith of the Son of God, who loved me, and gave himself for me.

5: THE INHERITANCE

WHAT AWAITS THE MANIFESTED CHILDREN OF GOD

The Scripture plainly teaches that we have an inheritance awaiting us, an inheritance that includes joining with Jesus Christ to rule and reign throughout the Cosmos.

Eph 1:10-11 [10]That in the dispensation of the fullness of the times He might gather together in one all things in Christ, both which are in heaven and which are on earth – in Him. [11]*In Him also we have obtained an inheritance,* being predestined according to the purpose of Him who works all things according to the counsel of His will,

Eph 1:13-14 [13]In Him you also *trusted,* after you heard the word of truth, the gospel of your salvation; in whom also, having believed, *you were sealed with the Holy Spirit of promise,* [14]*who is the guarantee of our inheritance* until the redemption of the purchased possession, to the praise of His glory.

Rom 8:16-17 [16]The Spirit Himself bears witness with our spirit that we are children of God, [17]and if children, then heirs – *heirs of God and joint heirs with Christ,* if indeed we suffer with *Him,* that we may also be glorified together.

Rom 8:22-23 [22]For we know that the whole creation groans and labors with birth pangs together until now. [23]Not only *that,* but we also who have the *firstfruits of the Spirit,* even we ourselves groan within ourselves, eagerly *waiting for the adoption,* the redemption of our body.

Definition of earnest: *A token of what is to come, pledge. Inheritance, real estate, etc. Usually a small amount of what is to come.*

The baptism of the Holy Spirit is spoken of in Ephesians and Romans as the earnest of the inheritance and the firstfruits – also a pledge of what is to come. Firstfruits is the first, early part of the harvest indicating what the harvest might be like. When the Israelites spied out the promised land, they were not aware that their heroics would one day signify the resurrection of the People of God. But their inspection of the land of Canaan, was the first incident of bringing forth "first fruits:"

Num 13:1-2 [1]And the LORD spoke to Moses, saying, [2]"Send men to spy out the land of Canaan, which I am giving to the children of Israel; from each tribe of their fathers you shall send a man, everyone a leader among them."

Num 13:17-20 [17]Then Moses sent them to spy out the land of Canaan, and said to them, "Go up this *way* into the South, and go up to the mountains, [18]and see what the land is like: whether the people who dwell in it *are* strong or weak, few or many; [19]whether the land they dwell in *is* good or bad; whether the cities they inhabit *are* like camps or strongholds; [20]whether the land *is* rich or poor; and whether there are forests there or not. Be of good courage. And bring some of the fruit of the land." Now the time *was* the season of the first ripe grapes.

The season of the first ripe grapes signifies the firstfruits of harvest – the giant grapes were literally a huge sign to the Israelites of the great harvest that could be theirs if they would go forth into the promised land and take what God had given them. These grapes were the earnest of their inheritance from God. Let's review the full story:

Num 13:23-33 [23]Then they came to the Valley of Eshcol, and there cut down a branch with one cluster of grapes; they carried it between two of them on a pole. *They* also *brought* some of the pomegranates and figs. [24]The place was called the Valley of Eshcol, because of the cluster which the men of Israel cut down there. [25]And they returned from spying out the land after forty days. [26]Now they departed and came back to Moses and Aaron and all the congregation of the children of Israel in the Wilderness of Paran, at Kadesh; they brought back word to them and to all the congregation, and showed them the fruit of the land. [27]Then they told him, and said: "We went to the land where you sent us. It truly flows with milk and honey, and this *is* its fruit. [28]Nevertheless the people who dwell in the land *are* strong; the cities *are* fortified *and* very large; moreover, we saw the descendants of Anak there. [29]The Amalekites dwell in the land of the South; the Hittites, the Jebusites, and the Amorites dwell in the mountains; and the Canaanites dwell by the sea and along the banks of the Jordan." [30]Then Caleb quieted the people before Moses, and said, "Let us go up at once and take possession, for we are well able to overcome it." [31]But the men who had gone up with him said, "We are not able to go up against the people, for they *are* stronger than we." [32]And they gave the children of Israel a bad report of the land which they had spied out, saying, "The land through which we have gone as spies *is* a land that devours its inhabitants, and all the people whom we saw in it *are* men of *great* stature. [33]There we saw the giants (the descendants of Anak came from the giants); and we were like grasshoppers in our own sight, and so we were in their sight."

Num 14:7-9 [7]And they spoke to all the congregation of the children of Israel, saying: "The land we passed through to spy out *is* an exceedingly good land. [8]If the LORD delights in us, then He will bring us into this land and give it to us, 'a land which flows with milk and honey.' [9]Only do not rebel against the LORD, nor fear the people of the land, for they *are* our bread; their protection has departed from them, and the LORD *is* with us. Do not fear them."

This account is a prefiguring or illustration of the firstfruits or earnest of our inheritance. If the infilling of the Holy Spirit is a token of what will be given to believers (as the huge grapes were to the Israelites), then our inheritance must be something beyond imagination. Notice that receiving the inheritance includes overcoming the enemy, even when the enemy is of giant proportions. But no problem, *they are bread for us.* After we take responsibility and wage war against the giants inhabiting the land (the enemies we face today), comes our full inheritance.

Deu 10:9 Therefore Levi has no portion nor inheritance with his brethren; the LORD *is* his inheritance, just as the LORD your God promised him.)

Deu 9:29 Yet they *are* Your people and Your inheritance, whom You brought out by Your mighty power and by Your outstretched arm.'

Deu 32:9 For the LORD'S portion *is* His people; Jacob *is* the place of His inheritance.

These three verses from Deuteronomy indicate that the inheritance of the priests (we are such priests) is God and that God's inheritance is His people. We read in 1 Peter 2:9, *"But ye are a chosen generation, a **royal priesthood,** an holy nation, a peculiar people; that ye should shew forth the praises of him who hath called you out of darkness into his marvelous light."* "For ye are...a royal priesthood." Paul's teaching in the Book of Ephesians demonstrates the same truth:

Eph 1:13-14 [13]In him you also, when you heard the word of truth, the gospel of your salvation, and believed in him, were sealed with the promised Holy Spirit, [14]who is the guarantee of our inheritance until the redemption of the purchased possession, to the praise of His glory. who is the guarantee of our inheritance until we acquire possession of it, to the praise of his glory. (ESV)

Eph 1:18 The eyes of your understanding being enlightened; that you may know what is the hope of His calling, what are the *riches of the glory of His inheritance in the saints.*

THE ADOPTION OF SONS

There are three closely related Greek words which signify the stages of a child's growth to maturity: *teknion, teknon,* and *vios.*

- *Teknion* (gr, τεκνίον) – baby, or small child (Strong's 5040)
- *Teknon* (gr, τεκνον) – a child, or descendant (Strong's 5043)
- *Vios* (gr, υιοις pronounced hwee-os) – a son (Strong's 5207)

Here, the original text quotes Mary calling Jesus, "**Teknon**", or child:

Luke 2:48 So when they saw Him, they were amazed; and His mother said to Him, "*Son*, why have You done this to us? Look, Your father and I have sought You anxiously."

Here, the Father, in the original text, calls Jesus His beloved *vios*:

Luke 3:22 And the Holy Spirit descended in bodily form like a dove upon Him, and a voice came from heaven which said, "You are My Beloved Son; in You I am well pleased."

From this time on, Jesus, *the mature Son*, is called *vios*.

Gal 3:24-29 [24]Therefore the law was our tutor *to bring us* to Christ, that we might be justified by faith. [25]But after faith has come, we are no longer under a tutor. [26]For you are all sons of God through faith in Christ Jesus. [27]For as many of you as were baptized into Christ have *put on Christ.* [28]There is neither Jew nor Greek, there is neither slave nor free, there is neither male nor female; for you are all one in

Christ Jesus. [29]And if you *are* Christ's, then you *are Abraham's seed, and heirs according to the promise.*

Gal 4:1-5 [1]Now I say *that* the heir, as long as he is a child, does not differ at all from a slave, though he is master of all, [2]but is under guardians and stewards until the time appointed by the father. [3]Even so we, when we were children, were in bondage under the elements of the world. [4]But when the fullness of the time had come, God sent forth His Son, born of a woman, born under the law, [5]to redeem those who were under the law, that we might receive the adoption as sons.

Galatians 4:5 states, "*vios*-adoption" (a transliteration) or "son-adoption." All Galatians' references to "son" are translated from *vios*. Every believer possesses this "son-adoption" legally in Christ, but not yet in our experience. That's why Romans 8:15 also says we have the Spirit of "son-adoption", that is, *the Holy Spirit working in us towards adoption yet to come.* This is another "already but not yet," vis-à-vis *the adoption of sons.* We see the word *adoption used once* more in the translation from the phrase, "son-adoption.' Referring to Galatians 3:6–9, 26–29, Michael Heiser writes:

> In Christ, believers are "the sons of God." The language of inheritance is crystal clear. It derives from and advances the Old Testament idea that humans were meant to be in the family of God all along. It's no coincidence that the New Testament writers repeatedly describe salvation into Yahweh's family with words like "adoption," "heir," and "inheritance" to describe what the Church really is – the reconstituted divine-human family of God. The believer's destiny is to become what Adam and Eve originally were: immortal, glorified imagers of God, living in God's presence as his children.[*]

Rom 8:15 For you did not receive the spirit of bondage again to fear, but you received *the Spirit of adoption* by whom we cry out, "Abba, Father."

---

[*] Heiser, op. cit., p. 308.)

1 Pet 2:2 As newborn babes, desire the pure milk of the word, that you may grow thereby, [3]if indeed you have tasted that the Lord *is* gracious.

- Starting as babes:

1 John 2:28 And now, little children, abide in Him, that when He appears, we may have confidence and not be ashamed before Him at His coming.

- Growing up to children, and then "adoption" as God terms it:

Luke 2:51 Then He went down with them and came to Nazareth, and was subject to them, but His mother kept all these things in her heart.

Gal 4:1 Now I say *that* the heir, as long as he is a *child*, does not differ at all from a slave, though he is master of all.

Eph 1:5 Having predestined us to adoption as *sons* by Jesus Christ to Himself, according to the good pleasure of His will.

Rom 8:23 Not only *that,* but we also who have the firstfruits of the Spirit, even we ourselves groan within ourselves, eagerly waiting *for the adoption,* the redemption of our body.

- Jesus, though He was "Lord of all," was subject to His parents until God's appointed time. At His baptism by John, He received the fullness of the Spirit:

John 3:34-35 For He whom God has sent speaks the words of God, for God does not give the Spirit by measure. [35]The Father loves the Son, and has given all things into His hand.

We have received a measure, but not that fullness:

2 Cor 1:22 who also has sealed us and given us the Spirit in our hearts as a guarantee.

- The *earnest* (the guarantee) is a small part of the inheritance to come.

Luke 4:1 Then Jesus, being filled with the Holy Spirit, returned from the Jordan and was led by the Spirit into the wilderness.

Luke 4:14 Then Jesus returned in the power of the Spirit to Galilee, and news of Him went out through all the surrounding region.

Luke 4:18-21 [18]*"The Spirit of the Lord is upon Me, because He has anointed Me to preach the gospel to the poor; He has sent Me to heal the brokenhearted, to proclaim liberty to the captives and recovery of sight to the blind, to set at liberty those who are oppressed;* [19]*to proclaim the acceptable year of the Lord."* [20]Then He closed the book, and gave it back to the attendant and sat down. And the eyes of all who were in the synagogue were fixed on Him. [21]And He began to say to them, "Today, this Scripture is fulfilled in your hearing."

Luke 4:36 Then they were all amazed and spoke among themselves, saying, "What a word this *is!* For with authority and power He commands the unclean spirits, and they come out."

Luke 4:41 And demons also came out of many, crying out and saying, "You are the Christ, the Son of God!" And He, rebuking *them,* did not allow them to speak, for they knew that He was the Christ.

John 1:32-33 [32]And John bore witness, saying, "I saw the Spirit descending from heaven like a dove, and He remained upon Him. [33]I did not know Him, but He who sent me to baptize with water said to me, 'Upon whom you see the Spirit descending, and remaining on Him, this is He who baptizes with the Holy Spirit.'

- <u>This was the promise of the Father:</u>

   Gal 3:14 that the blessing of Abraham might come upon the Gentiles in Christ Jesus, that we might receive the promise of the Spirit through faith.

   Gal 3:16-18 [16]Now to Abraham and his Seed were the promises made. He does not say, "And to seeds," as of many, but as of one, *"And to your Seed,"* who is Christ. [17]And this I say, *that* the law, which was four hundred and thirty years later, cannot annul the covenant that was confirmed before by God in Christ, that it should make the promise of no effect. [18]For if the inheritance *is* of the law, *it is* no longer of promise; but God gave *it* to Abraham by promise.

   Gal 3:29 And if you *are* Christ's, then you are Abraham's seed, and heirs according to the promise.

   Gal 4:7 Therefore you are no longer a slave but a son, and if a son, then an heir of God through Christ.

Therefore, through the "Anointed One," we participate in His inheritance, the earnest of the Spirit now, and the fullness to come (the "already, but not yet!"). In the King James Version, John 1:12 says we have the power to become sons (*vios*) of God. This is not necessarily doctrinally incorrect, because we are *becoming* the mature sons of God, and in Jesus Christ *we are already the sons of God*. However, most modern translations have the idea correct: we have *the right to become children (technon) of* God. Either way, we are now children, growing into sonship.

   John 1:12 But as many as received Him, to them He gave the *right to become children of God,* to those *who believe* in His name:

   1 John 3:1-2 [1]Behold what manner of love the Father has bestowed on us, that we should be called children of God! Therefore, the world does not know us, because it did not know Him. [2]Beloved, now we are children of God; and it has not yet been revealed what we shall be, but we know *that when He is revealed, we shall be like Him,* for we shall see Him as He is.

I John 3, verse 1 and 2, we are not called a baby, but "children of God". The NKJV and Amplified Bible have correctly translated what could be thought of as an adolescent; but regardless of physical age, the concept constitutes a "direct descendant."

Rom 8:14-25 [14]For as many *as are led by the Spirit of God, these* are sons of God. [15]For you did not receive the spirit of bondage again to fear, but you received the Spirit of adoption by whom we cry out, "Abba, Father." [16]The Spirit Himself bears witness with our spirit that we are children of God, [17]and if children, then heirs – heirs of God and joint heirs with Christ, if indeed we suffer with *Him,* that we may also be glorified together. [18]*For I consider that the sufferings of this present time are not worthy to be compared with the glory which shall be revealed in us.* [19]For the earnest expectation of the creation eagerly waits for *the revealing of the sons of God.* [20]For the creation was subjected to futility, not willingly, but because of Him who subjected *it* in hope; [21]because the creation itself also will be delivered from the bondage of corruption into the glorious liberty of the children of God. [22]For we know that the whole creation groans and labors with birth pangs together until now. [23]Not only *that,* but we also who have the firstfruits of the Spirit, even we ourselves groan within ourselves, eagerly waiting for the adoption, the redemption of our body. [24]For we were saved in this hope, but hope that is seen is not hope; for why does one still hope for what he sees? [25]But if we hope for what we do not see, we eagerly wait for *it* with perseverance.

Romans 8 shows this distinction well – the sons of God will be led by the Spirit – 100% – like Jesus (verse 14). Whenever we operate 100% in the Spirit, we are acting as a mature son or daughter of God at that moment.

We cannot be adopted and receive our inheritance until we "lock in" to our *corporate maturity. This is not accomplished by an individual without the corporate body of Christ participating.* Being in fellowship with other like-minded believers is one of the activities necessary to grow more like Christ. Note: the NKJV correctly translates "children" (*teknon*) and "sons" (*vios*).

Heb 2:10 For it was fitting for Him, for whom *are* all things and by whom *are* all things, *in bringing many sons to glory*, to make the captain of their salvation *perfect through sufferings.*

God wants to bring many sons and daughters unto glory. And rest assured: He will! God will use *an imperfect creation* to make this happen.

DEEP DIVE: THE CREATION WAS SUBJECTED TO EVIL FOR OUR GLORY

Christians reject the notion *the creation is evil.* Instead, we believe an originally good creation was cursed because our sin (originating from humans and not God) altered what was initially made good.† Ultimately, both 'the sinner' and the creation are slated for full redemption by the Creator. In other words, the death of Jesus did more than pay the penalty for humankind's sin; it legally set the creation free to be made right again once Christ returns in glory. That comprises Paul's argument in Romans 8:

"For the creature [creation]‡ was made subject to vanity, not willingly, but by reason of him who hath subjected the same in hope, because the creature

---

† Remember after every day (save one) those statements by God in Genesis— "And God saw what He had made and said, 'It is Good.'" This language was an emphatic rebuttal to virtually all other religions blaming evil on the creation. God's commentary constitutes an unmistakable exclamation point for just how good it is! God takes personally those that "dis" the creation. He reigns as the proud Creator.

‡ The word for creation and creature is one and the same: *ktisis*, (pronounced, key-teh-sees). Thus, it can be translated either way depending upon the context. The KJV seems to mistranslate it in the Romans 8 passage Woodward references here.

[creation] itself also shall be delivered from the bondage of corruption into the glorious liberty of the children of God."

In other words, God has a reclamation plan for our world and we are right at the very center of it! For our sakes, the creation in its entirety was subjected to futility. This plan incorporates the essential gospel mystery. As Paul says, "*...we speak the wisdom of God in a mystery, [even] the hidden [wisdom], which God ordained before the world **unto our glory**"* (I Corinthians 2:7). While evil sought to wreck the creation due to our sin, God intervened in our world—in history—to redeem us and His creation. God planned from the beginning *to bring good from what was corrupted.* It was done this way "unto our glory"—for the purpose of *our being glorified one day.* Paul goes on to say: *For we know that the whole creation groaneth and travaileth in pain together until now. And not only they, but ourselves also, which have the first fruits of the Spirit, even we ourselves groan within ourselves, waiting for the adoption, to wit, the redemption of our body.*

Once fully redeemed, we will overcome *"the bondage of corruption and obtain the glorious liberty of the children of God"* as quoted earlier. We are instructed this struggle was necessary to transform us into *glorified children of God.* For from the beginning, we were predestined to become like Jesus Christ: *For whom He did foreknow, He also did predestinate [to be] conformed to the image of His Son, that He might be the firstborn among many brethren. Moreover, whom He did predestinate, them He also called: and whom He called, them He also justified: and whom He justified, them He also glorified* (Romans 8:29)

Salvation consists of a many-step process. In God's eyes, however, all the steps have been accomplished already. There is no suspense. Everything has already been settled. Though our experience today does not include the perfection we call *glorification*, nevertheless, we are told this next step is as good as finished (or as they say in my home Oklahoma, 'it is a done deal'). According to Paul's gospel, God 'called us' for this express purpose: *"Whereunto He called you by our gospel, to **the obtaining of the glory of our Lord Jesus Christ**."* (2 Thessalonians 2:14)

The Lord God planned from the beginning to have many millions (at least) of sons and daughters glorified with *the same glory present in Jesus Christ*. [For a technical discussion of the language used "in the curse" see the following paper, http://www.icr.org/article/creation-curse/.]

S. Douglas Woodward, *Blood Moon: Biblical Signs of the Coming Apocalypse*, (2014), Oklahoma City: Faith Happens Books, pp. 276-279.

From a great saint (recently gone to be with the LORD, DeVern Fromke, who we will hear from again later), we read these helpful words:

We are now waiting! As His own begotten ones we are waiting for the return of our Lord in the air when we shall be caught away to be presented before Him "without spot or wrinkle or any such thing." Such is the hope that should purify us!

Yet not only do we hope and wait, but the rest of creation is also waiting as in a sort of universal travail. Waiting— *not to be caught away, but to be delivered; it is a groaning, waiting for the manifestation of the sons of God, a waiting for the day of adoption or unveiling which will signal its deliverance from the curse.* Yes, it is in that glorious day of unveiling that the Father will display to a wondering universe His Son and sons.

In that day, we will be ready with the Lord Jesus to share in the government which shall be upon His shoulder (Rom. 8: 19-25; Eph. 3: 10-11; 5: 27.) J. B. Phillips has so well portrayed this in Romans 8: 18:

"In my opinion, whatever we may have to go through now is less than nothing compared with the magnificent future God has planned for us. The whole creation is on tip-toe to see the wonderful sight of the sons of God coming into their own."[§]

[§] Fromke, DeVern F. *The Ultimate Intention* (Kindle Locations 2601-2611). Hauraki Publishing. Kindle Edition.

1 Cor 15:40-44 [40]*There are* also celestial bodies and terrestrial bodies; but the glory of the celestial *is* one, and the *glory* of the terrestrial *is* another. [41]*There is* one glory of the sun, another glory of the moon, and another glory of the stars; for *one* star differs from *another* star in glory. [42]So also *is* the resurrection of the dead. *The body* is sown in corruption, it is raised in incorruption. [43]It is sown in dishonor, it is raised in glory. It is sown in weakness, it is raised in power. [44]It is sown a natural body, it is raised a spiritual body. There is a natural body, and there is a spiritual body.

Heb 3:1-6 [1]Therefore, holy brethren, partakers of the heavenly calling, consider the Apostle and High Priest of our confession, Christ Jesus, [2]who was faithful to Him who appointed Him, as Moses also *was faithful* in all His house. [3]For this One has been counted worthy of more glory than Moses, inasmuch as He who built the house has more honor than the house. [4]For every house is built by someone, but He who built all things *is* God. [5]And Moses indeed *was* faithful in all His house as a servant, for a testimony of those things which would be spoken *afterward,* [6]but Christ as a Son over His own house, whose house we are if we hold fast the confidence and the rejoicing of the hope firm to the end.

Christ is the faithful son over His House.

Eph 4:11-15 [11]And He Himself gave some *to be* apostles, some prophets, some evangelists, and some pastors and teachers, [12]for the equipping of the saints for the work of ministry, for the edifying of the body of Christ, [13]till *we all come to the unity of the faith and of the knowledge of the Son of God, to a perfect man, to the measure of the stature of the fullness of Christ;* [14]that we should *no longer be children,* tossed to and fro and carried about with every wind of doctrine, by the trickery of men, in the cunning craftiness of deceitful plotting, ¹⁵but, speaking the truth in love, *may grow up in all things into Him who is the head – Christ,*

Eph 1:5 Having *predestined us to adoption as sons* by Jesus Christ to Himself, according to the good pleasure of His will.

Mat 23:15 Well done, good and faithful servant; thou hast been faithful over a few things, I will make thee ruler over many things.

Luke 16:10 He who is faithful in a very little thing is faithful also in much.

God is working in us by the Holy Spirit through circumstances and the five ministries mentioned in Ephesians 4 above to bring the body of Christ to maturity. If we submit to these ministries and the discipline of the Holy Spirit, God will surely bring us to son-adoption and our full inheritance in Christ! "To be faithful in little things, is a big thing." – Saint Augustine.

WHAT IS AVAILABLE TO US TO WALK IN THE SPIRIT?

Teaching these truths usually raises the question of what is available to us and what is not, *or what is imputed and what is imparted.* Once again, this is the "already, but not yet" concept in theology. We believe that God has made Himself available to us but much remains in a legal sense because of our own sin and failings (immaturity). "By His stripes we were healed" – yet look at our experience in sickness and healing. "He is our peace"..."He is our righteousness" – He has made available everything that we need in Jesus. Look at these verses for imputed vs. imparted:

Heb 2:8 *You have put all things in subjection under his feet."* For in that He put all in subjection under him, He left nothing *that is* not put under him. But now we do not yet see all things put under him.

Legally, all things are in subjection to Jesus, but we have yet to see the manifestation of it.

Heb 4:3 For we who have believed do enter that rest, as He has said: *"So I swore in My wrath, 'They shall not enter My rest,'"* although the works were finished from the foundation of the world.

Heb 4:6-11 ⁶Since therefore it remains that some *must* enter it, and those to whom it was first preached did not enter because of disobedience, ⁷again He designates a certain day, saying in David, *"Today,"* after such a long time, as it has been said: *"Today, if you will hear His voice, do not harden your hearts."* ⁸For if Joshua had given them rest, then He would not afterward have spoken of another day. ⁹There remains therefore a rest for the people of God. ¹⁰For he who has entered His rest has himself also ceased from his works as God *did* from His. ¹¹Let us therefore be diligent to enter that rest, lest anyone fall according to the same example of disobedience.

Hebrews 4:3 teaches we who believe *enter into rest*, and verse 11 says we need to seek earnestly to enter into that rest. Legally (aka "positionally"), we already have rest in Jesus, but we must seek it intensely to experience it. The inheritance worked like this – it was not something you would have obtained when the father died. It was the family business – you would have it *when you were mature enough to handle the authority and responsibility that follows*. Yet before that time, you lived and worked there and partook of the benefits of that inheritance even as a servant would. When the father was ready (because you were ready) you received his authority. Then you could run the family business.

GOD'S FAMILY BUSINESS

Michael Heiser provides further explanation of God's family business by showing that believers are "the sons of God" – meaning that they are members of God's governing council, a divinely appointed administration. Adam and Eve were to start the spread of Eden – God's kingdom rule – and that purpose hasn't changed. He reminds us that God's family is also His Council, and that New Testament writers use family terms for the Church right along with divine council terminology. He quotes Ephesians 1:5, 11–19 for starters:

> [5] *Having predestined us to adoption through Jesus Christ to himself according to the good pleasure of his will ... [11] in whom also we were chosen, having been predestined according to the purpose of the One who works all things according to the counsel of his will, [12] that we who hoped beforehand in Christ should be for the praise of his glory, [13] in whom also you, when you heard the word of truth, the gospel of your salvation, in whom also when you believed you were sealed with the promised Holy Spirit, [14] who is the down payment of our **inheritance**, until the redemption of the possession, to the praise of his glory... [15] Because of this I also, hearing of your faith in the Lord Jesus and your love for all the saints, [16] do not cease giving thanks for you, making mention in my prayers, [17] that the God of our Lord Jesus Christ, the glorious Father, may give you a spirit of wisdom and revelation in the knowledge of him [18] (the eyes of your hearts having been enlightened), so that you may know what is the hope of his calling, what are the riches of the glory of his **inheritance** among the **saints**, [19] and what is the surpassing greatness of his power toward us who believe.*

Heiser explains: "The English translation obscures an important Old Testament connection back to the divine council. The word for "saints" in verse 18 (and elsewhere in the New Testament) is *hagioi*, which means "holy ones." Paul tells the Ephesians that believers have a *glorious inheritance **among the holy ones.***"[**] [emphasis added] Heiser goes on to say that "holy ones" in the Old Testament is a term used for divine beings in the divine council of Yahweh (e.g., Job 5:1; 15:15; Psalm 89:5–7; Zechariah

---

[**] Michael S. Heiser, *The Unseen Realm*, op. cit., pp. 310-312.

14:5). The term is also used for believing and loyal people (Psalm 16:3; 34:8; cp. Leviticus 26:14–33). Citing Heiser in his own words:

> We saw earlier, in chapter 30, that both uses come together in a crucial chapter—Daniel 7. That chapter had the second Yahweh figure in human form, the son of man, receiving an everlasting kingdom from the enthroned Ancient of Days. The kingdom was also given to the holy ones—both divine and human (Dan 7:22, 27). The passage conveyed the idea of joint rulership in God's kingdom.[††]

Heiser cites Paul speaking of the same inheritance among the holy ones in his letter to the Ephesians. Not only are we heirs and children in God's family, but our inheritance is also to rule and reign with Jesus (Col 1:11–13). Heiser contends that when the nations restored to Yahweh, the present corrupted divine council (see Psalm 82) will lose their domination of the nations and be replaced by believers. As Paul wrote, believers will "judge angels" (1 Corinthians 6:3). He also mentions that the Apostle John states as much in Revelation, chapter two.

> **Rev 2:25–28** [25] Nevertheless, hold fast to what you have until I come. [26] And the one who conquers and who keeps my works until the end, I will give him *authority over the nations,* [27] and "he will shepherd them with an iron rod; he will break them in pieces like jars made of clay," [28] as I also have received from my Father, and I will give him *the morning star.*

Heiser points out that the power of this passage is to be found in John's citation (in verse 27) of Psalm 2, which depicts the messiah's reign. Before telling the Messiah, "You will break them with an iron rod," Yahweh proclaims to Him, *"You are my son; today I have begotten you. Ask from me and I will make the nations your heritage, and your possession the end of the*

[††] Ibid.

earth" (Psalm 2:7–8). Jesus, who is the Messiah, will inherit the kingdom. He then shares it with His brothers and sisters who are "those who overcome" until Jesus' return. John tells us (Revelation 3:21) that those who overcome *rule and reign with Jesus*:

> **Rev 3:20-21**[20] *Behold, I stand at the door and knock! If anyone hears my voice and opens the door, indeed I will come in to him and dine with him, and he with me.* [21] *The one who conquers, I will grant to him to **sit down with me on my throne**, as I also have conquered and have sat down with my Father on his throne.*

Heiser continues to relate that the destiny of the believer is not only a place in God's home, but dominion with Jesus "among the holy ones" (Ephesians 1:18). Paul prays for his readers that our kingdom inheritance will be...

> **Col 1:11–13** [11] Enabled with all power, according to his glorious might, for all steadfastness and patience with joy, [12] giving thanks to the Father who has qualified you for a share of the inheritance of the saints [holy ones] in light, [13] who has rescued us from the domain of darkness and transferred us to the *kingdom* of the Son he loves.[‡]

Heiser contends further that when the nations are restored to Yahweh, the *divine council will lose their domination of the nations and be replaced by believers*. As Paul wrote, believers will "judge angels" (1 Cor 6:3). He also mentions that the apostle John says the same in Revelation 2:25-28: "Nevertheless, hold fast to what you have until I come. *And the one who conquers and who keeps my works until the end, I will give him **authority over the nations**, and "he will shepherd them with an iron rod*; he (Jesus but also resurrected believers of all ages will break them in pieces like jars made of clay," as I also have received from my Father, and I will give him the morning star.

[‡] Ibid.

Our inheritance in Christ works much the same way. We are now partaking of much of the benefits of inheritance *in a limited way* as servants. When we are mature, we receive His full inheritance and authority. This teaching is not intended to let you sit back and wait until the full inheritance comes. Instead, it is intended to motivate you to "labor" to enter in to everything that is available to us as believers now. We are yet to see the fullness the **earnest** of our inheritance guarantees!

PARALLEL TRUTHS

Below are several *parallel truths* with accompanying references:

- Adoption of sons (Rom 8:5)
- Redemption of the body (Rom 8:23)
- Resurrection of the dead (I Cor 15:23; 51-53)
- Rapture or taking up (I Th 4:13-18)
- When He shall appear or Parousia (I Jn 2:28;1 Th 4:13-18; 2:19)
- Receiving our inheritance (Eph 1; Heb 6:5,10-12; Rom 8:17)
- God's redemption of the purchased possession (Eph 1; 1:18-20; 1 Cor 6:20; 1 Pet 1:18-19)
- Manifestation of the Sons of God (Rom 8:14,19)
- Purifying and blessed hope (I Jn 3:3; Tit 2:13)
- When we receive a crown (I Pet 5:4)
- Glorification of believer's bodies (Rom 8:18; Col 3:4)
- When we shall all be changed (I Cor 15:52-54)
- Receiving our incorruptible bodies (I Cor 15:52-54)
- The Parousia (Matt 24:27; 2 Th 2:8)
- Jacob's Ladder (Gen 28:11-19)
- When "all Israel shall be saved" (Rom 11:26-27)

We identify these points as "parallel truths" because the events are identical or run parallel to one another at the end of the age. We have already discussed some of these topics. However, we will address all these points in the remainder of this book.

DEEP DIVE: PREACHING "TOTAL" SALVATION TO UNBELIEVERS

Until we receive our inheritance, we have a job to do. As C.S. Lewis wrote, we must recognize the marvelous glory awaiting those *who call upon the name of the LORD* and are saved by His death. During the time that remains, we are challenged to 'grow the family' of God by seeking others – helping them realize the wonderful gift of His love and salvation. God is Love. And as we reach out to others, our own natures grow more like His.

The Apostle John shares this stunning insight: *"Herein is our love made **perfect** [fully realized], that we may have boldness in the Day of Judgment: Because as He is, so are we in this world."* (I John 4:17) As God is Love and His love transforms those who believe in Him, we too are meant to have our love *perfected* during this time. Our love is to transform others even as His love transforms us. God sets forth this duty for us now and until the day we are caught up to be with Christ. By having our love perfected (fully completed), we may be bold when we stand before Christ at the judgment for believers.

Understand, this judgment is not the 'White Throne' judgment of Revelation 20:11 (expressly for unbelievers) but the so-called *bēma* seat of Christ (*bēma* referenced a low platform from which civil judgments were made in the Roman Empire). "For we must all appear before the judgment seat (bēma) of Christ; that everyone may receive the things [done] in [his] body, according to that he hath done, whether [it be] good or bad." (2 Corinthians 5:10) Vines comments on the believer's judgment: "At this *bēma* believers are to be made manifest, that each may "receive the things done in (or through) the body," according to what he has done, "whether it be good or bad." There they will receive rewards for their faithfulness to the Lord. [But] For all that has been contrary in their lives to His will they will suffer loss." However, it is a judgment of works, not of sin for sin has been dealt with – "Therefore there is no condemnation for those who are in Christ Jesus." (Romans 8:2)

Finally, we are to acquire the keen eyes God has for all those who surround us. *We are to see them as prospective fellow heirs to the glory of God.* We must maintain a high level of motivation. We must share the full extent of the salvation that Christ has won for us. Keeping this incredible gift in mind that is available for all who will accept it, we must express love for others and to take to heart the importance, the eternal significance, of their opportunity to share in *this weight of glory!*

Are we motivated to share the gospel **because of the glory that awaits** *those who profess faith in Jesus Christ?* That is the message that the Lord God asks us to carry forth to every man, woman, and child. We should implore each and every one to believe in Jesus Christ, that they may each obtain a weight of glory that exceeds our most sublime imagining. "Keeping watch" as Jesus taught us, requires we be mindful of this glory that awaits. It is crucial to the days ahead when we are persecuted, and perhaps are martyred for our faith. It is for the "joy set before us" that we will, like Jesus, determine that giving our life, our all, is required.

S. Douglas Woodward, drawn from *Blood Moon: Biblical Signs of the Coming Apocalypse,* (2014), Oklahoma City: Faith Happens Books, pp. 285-287 (updated).

6: THE PAROUSIA

THE PAROUSIA AND THE OLIVET DISCOURSE

We begin this chapter with selections from the Olivet Discourse, our Lord's most detailed teaching on biblical prophecy and His return. In Greek, the word for His return is *parousia*. This word is the word most often associated with the second coming of Christ.

Mat 24:3 Now as He sat on the Mount of Olives, the disciples came to Him privately, saying, "Tell us, when will these things be? And what *will be* the sign of Your ***coming***, and of the end of the age?"

Mat 24:20-31 ²⁰And pray that your flight may not be in winter or on the Sabbath. ²¹For then there will be great tribulation, such as has not been since the beginning of the world until this time, no, nor ever shall be. ²²And unless those days were shortened, no flesh would be saved; but for the elect's sake those days will be shortened. ²³"Then if anyone says to you, 'Look, here *is* the Christ!' or 'There!' do not believe *it.* ²⁴For false christs and false prophets will rise and show great signs and wonders to deceive, if possible, even the elect. ²⁵See, I have told you beforehand. ²⁶"Therefore if they say to you, 'Look, He is in the desert!' do not go out; *or* 'Look, *He is* in the inner rooms!' do not believe *it.* ²⁷*For as the lightning comes from the east and flashes to the west, so also will the coming of the Son of Man be.* ²⁸*For wherever the carcass is, there the eagles will be gathered together.* ²⁹"Immediately after the tribulation of those days the sun will be darkened, and the moon will not give its light; the stars will fall from heaven, and the powers of the heavens will be shaken. [30]Then the sign of the Son of Man will appear in heaven, and then all the tribes of the earth will mourn, and they will see the Son of Man **coming** on the *clouds of heaven with power and great glory.* [31]*And* He will send His angels with a great sound of a trumpet, and they will gather together His elect from the four winds, from one end of heaven to the other.

Much of this chapter follows the teaching in Ray Stedman's book, *What on Earth's Going to Happen?* Stedman (1917 – 1992) was one of the country's foremost pastors. But before we consider his words, we need to have some insight into the Greek words relevant to our study.

In Matthew 24, two words are translated as "coming;" one is the Greek word *parousia*, and the other is word *erkoma*. **Parousia** means (1) presence and (2) a coming, an arrival, advent, often of the second coming of Christ. **Erkoma** means "to come, to go, the coming one," i.e., the Messiah. *The word "parousia" is the word used in the New Testament for Christ's coming for His Bride, or what we have come to call* **the "rapture."** The second Greek word denotes the coming of Christ in power and great glory to judge and then to rule the earth.

One of the questions the disciples ask is, "what shall be the sign of thy 'parousia'?" At first Jesus gives us a brief rundown on the last 2000 years of history and then of the last 3½ years, which is also called the Great Tribulation (Matt 24:21). Jesus explains that there will be false prophets talking of His presence in the desert, here, and there at the time of the Great Tribulation. Then He gives them a picture of how His presence will truly be manifested during this time (last 3½ years).

Stedman's comments go far to *corroborate our most unusual thesis in this book.* Please read the following carefully:

> The word the Lord uses for "coming" here is the now familiar "parousia." It is quite a different word than he uses a few verses farther

on when he speaks of "the Son of man coming on the clouds of heaven with power and great glory." It is easy to confuse these two comings because of his reference to lightning in verse 27. Since lightning is a form of power and glory, many feel the Lord is using it as a symbol of his coming in glory. But note carefully what he says. Lightning flashes in the east, but the effect of it is seen all over the sky. Yet the flash itself does not involve the whole inverted dome of the heavens from east to west. When he uses the symbol of lightning, therefore, he is not describing a universally visible manifestation of his glory, but the universal effect of his presence behind the scenes. Like lightning flashes, he will be seen by his own in different places, at all different times, but the effect of those appearances will be felt throughout the earth. Furthermore, lightning is sovereign, unpredictable, uncontrollable. So will be the presence, the parousia, of the Son of man. He will appear and disappear at will. Whenever there is need for him he will be there, just as he was during the post-resurrection period. *

Stedman goes on to say that people will not be able to search for Him, but He will be "wherever he finds a heart ready to know him. In the passage parallel to this in Luke 17, Jesus says, 'For as the lightning flashes and lights up the sky from one side to the other, so will the Son of man be in his day'" ... Then, using a common proverb of the day, Jesus indicates the proper way to find him in that day, "Wherever the body is, there the eagles will be gathered together."

Like lightning flashes, "so shall also the parousia of the Son of man be." Jesus will appear and disappear at will, just as He did after His resurrection. Remember the sheaf of firstfruits. This is the great ingathering. In referring to the eagles, or vultures, Jesus means the same as the phrase "where there's smoke, there's fire." Wherever He manifests His presence during this time, the signs will be evident, just as you know

---

* Ray Stedman, *What on Earth's Going To Happen?* (pp. 106-107) Glendale, CA: Regal Books, 1970.

where a carcass is by the vultures circling above. This parallels the post-resurrection period. We should also make note that *the eagle also symbolizes the spiritually strong.* Ray Stedman explains:

> During that forty-day period the disciples of Jesus were what we might call "Pre-church Christians." They believed in Jesus but they were not yet members of the church, for the church was not formed until the day of Pentecost when the Holy Spirit was poured out. During the close of the age, the disciples (or as Jesus calls them "the elect") will be what we might call "Post-church Christians." The church has been removed from the world, at least from any visible participation in world affairs. Since we know that Christians will be given glorified bodies like their Lord's (and Paul says that, once removed from this life, the church will be forever "with the Lord"), it seems highly likely that church Christians will join the Lord Jesus in this ministry behind the scenes during the tribulation. They will be like Moses and Elijah who appeared with the transfigured Christ on the Mount. The picture then is clear. Jesus will come for his church and take the members into a new relationship with him. Then he, with them, will remain throughout the "end of the age" period, appearing only to those whose hearts are ready to believe in him. Rumors of his presence will continually be spread abroad, so that men will be saying in that day as they said during the forty-day period, "Where is he?" Authorities will search for him and will not be able to find him, but false prophets will claim to know where he is.[†]

Stedman on the culmination or "epiphany" of the *Parousia*:

> But we must be careful to understand it in relation to the parousia, the presence of Jesus, which has been going on since the Church was taken out of the restrictions of time before the end of the age began. This flaming advent is part of the parousia, actually the event that marks *the end of the secret presence*. It is the outshining of his presence *before*

[†] Ibid., pp. 100-101.

the eyes of the whole world. What he has been in secret to his own during the dark days of the tribulation, he now will be openly before the whole world. He will especially manifest himself to the Lawless One. Paul says, "The Lord Jesus will slay him with the breath of his mouth and destroy him by his appearing and his coming" (2 Thessalonians 2:8). That last phrase, "his appearing and his coming," is literally, "the epiphany of his parousia." Epiphany is a word that means unveiling, or outshining. Taken in that sense, Paul is calling this dramatic appearance of Jesus Christ, "the unveiling of his presence." It is the startling climax of the whole period which Jesus calls "the close of the age."[‡]

Then Ray Stedman provides a possible meaning for *the Sign of the Son of Man:*

...This violent upheaval in nature is followed immediately by the sign of the Son of man in heaven and the visible appearing of Jesus Christ to all the earth:

> "Then will appear the sign of the Son of man in heaven, and then all the tribes of earth will mourn, and they will see the Son of man coming on the clouds of heaven with power and great glory."

As we have already noted, this is the outshining of his glory; the sudden unveiling of his presence. It is often called the "second coming," though in truth that term covers the whole period of Christ's secret presence. But it will be the second time the world sees Jesus Christ. The last time it saw him was on a bloody cross, writhing in the agonies of death, apparently a shameful failure with no glory, no power and no success. But when it sees him again it will see him coming triumphant in power and glory.

The event will be preceded by the appearance of "the sign of the Son of man" in the heavens. The disciples had asked him at the beginning of this discourse: "What will be the sign of your coming?"

[‡]Ibid., pp. 111-112.

This question he now answers, though not as completely or clearly as they or we might have liked.

When the disciples asked the question they did not mean, as we frequently take it, "What is the sign that will mark the time of your coming?" Inevitably we associate signs with schedules. But the disciples knew better than that. They meant, "What is the event which will reveal the meaning of your coming?" This is always the purpose of signs in Scripture. That sign, Jesus now says, will appear in the sky just before he is made visible.

Let us not miss the fact that he links this sign with the statement, "then all the tribes of the earth will mourn." We shall examine that more fully a bit later, but from other Scripture it appears *that he means the tribes of Israel*. Since this sign is thus linked with Israel it strongly suggests that the sign will consist of *the reappearance of the cloud of glory which accompanied the nation Israel as they journeyed through the wilderness for forty years*. It was called the Shekinah, and was the sign of God's presence with his people. Much later, when the Temple was built and Solomon dedicated it to God, the Shekinah glory came down and took rest in the holy of holies upon the Ark of the Covenant as the sign that God was dwelling with His people.

This shining cloud may well be what Jesus himself is referring to when he says, "They will see the Son of man coming on the clouds of heaven." There is an obvious reference to this same event in Revelation 1:7. There John says: "Behold, he is coming with the clouds, and every eye will see him, everyone who pierced him; and all tribes of the earth will wail on account of him." Of course, it can simply refer to the atmospheric clouds, but the repeated emphasis seems suggestive of more. When Jesus thus appears it will mark the close of the age, but it will also be the opening event of a new age, and the supreme characteristic of that new age will be that God dwells with His people. In Revelation 21:3, John describes it, "Behold, the dwelling of God is with men. He will dwell with them." Since the Shekinah is the sign of God's presence with man, it is fitting that it should reappear as the sign that explains, clarifies, and reveals the meaning of Christ's coming. He comes that he may be, as the Old Testament prophets whispered, "Immanuel-God with us."§

John 7:2,10 Now the Jews' Feast of Tabernacles was at hand. ³His brothers therefore said to Him, "Depart from here and go into Judea, that Your disciples also may see the works that You are doing. But when His brothers had gone up, then He also went up to the feast, not openly, but as it were in secret.

Just like the *Parousia*, the fulfillment of the Feast of Tabernacles, starts secretly and then eventually manifests God's glory. Jesus came to the Feast secretly (only a few knew of His presence), and then on the last day of Tabernacles (the last trumpet was blown on the Day of Atonement), he openly revealed himself (His voice was *like a trumpet*, for He cried out):

John 7:37-38 On the last day, that great *day* of the feast, Jesus stood and *cried out*, saying, "If anyone thirsts, let him come to Me and drink. ³⁸He who believes in Me, as the Scripture has said, out of his heart will flow rivers of living water."

Indeed, rivers of God's Living Water will flow like never before when Y'shua fulfills the Feast of Tabernacles. (Compare Matthew 24:29-31 with 2 Thessalonians 2:8).

2 Th 2:8 And then the lawless one will be revealed, whom the Lord will consume with the breath of His mouth and destroy with the brightness of His coming.

As we learned from Stedman's words, Paul's "brightness of His coming" is literally, "the epiphany (επιφανεια) of His parousia (παρουσια)." Epiphany means unveiling, or outshining. So, Paul is saying, in effect, "the unveiling of His presence." So, we find that the second phase of Christ's second coming is the out-shining of His secret, hidden presence or *parousia* that has continued

§ Ibid., pp. 116-118.

for the last 3 1/2 years. The disciples were not asking for a sign to alert them to Christ's coming, but rather *what sign would reveal the meaning of Christ's coming*. Jesus said that sign will appear in the sky just before He unveils His presence. Since this sign is over Israel the implication is that this will be the appearance of the Shekinah cloud of glory, the same cloud that led Israel through the wilderness. The cloud was the sign of God's presence with His people. The cloud appeared in the Holy of Holies of Solomon's temple to show God was dwelling with His people. Therefore, to reiterate: the cloud was the sign of God's presence with His people. The cloud appeared in the Holy of Holies of Solomon's temple to show God was dwelling with His people.[**]

If we are correct, this shining (the glory of Christ and His Body, the previously raptured believers), *will be brilliantly displayed over Zion*. That is the significance of the image on the cover of our book. It will be "The Revealing" of Christ with His Church for all the world, the "earth dwellers" as Stedman called them, and the meaning of His secret presence

> **Rev 1:7** Behold, He is *coming with clouds*, and every eye will see Him, even they who pierced Him. And all the tribes of the earth will mourn because of Him. Even so, Amen.

The repeated emphasis of *clouds* suggests much more than mere rain clouds. This signifies the beginning of the God's "new age" – Yahweh dwelling with His people in His manifest presence.

> **Rev 21:3** And I heard a loud voice from heaven saying, "Behold, the *tabernacle of God is with men*, and He will dwell with them, and they shall be His people. God Himself will be with them *and be* their God.

This reappearance of the Shekinah cloud of glory will explain and reveal the meaning of Christ's coming to the earth: "God with us" – God come to dwell with man. Recall another name for God from Isaiah:

[**] Ibid., pp. 111-117.

Isa 7:14 Therefore the Lord himself shall give you a sign; Behold, a virgin shall conceive, and bear a son, and shall call his name *Immanuel.*

Mat 1:23 *"Behold, the virgin shall be with child, and bear a Son, and they shall call His name Immanuel,"* which is translated, "God with us."

As Isaiah 7:14, and Matthew 1:23 states, He is Immanuel – God with us. God's dwelling in and alongside His people will be demonstrated (manifested) at the time of which Jesus spoke in Matthew 24.

Therefore, let's combine *our study of the resurrection* and *parousia* together. We concluded that *Jesus will come with a cloud of saints, and later in a cloud of glory.* Both testify to two parts of the same reality. Philippians 3:20-21 illustrates perfectly this culmination of glory.

Phil 3:20-21 For our citizenship is in heaven, from which we also eagerly wait for the Savior, the Lord Jesus Christ, [21]who will transform our lowly body *that it may be conformed to His glorious body,* according to the working by which He is able even to subdue all things to Himself.

This verse literally asserts we will be "conformed to His body of glory." That is, just as Jesus has a body of glory, so shall we. This is guaranteed by "Christ in you, the hope of glory" (Colossians 1:27). When Jesus reigns in our body, soul, and spirit, He will "subdue all things unto Himself." He can transform every molecule and fiber of our being – from corruption to incorruption, from dishonor to glory, from weakness to power.

At the Transfiguration, Jesus' raiment was white and glistening, and His countenance was altered; the Apostles who were witnesses testified that "His clothing shined *white* like lightning." One account stated his robes were whiter than even the best launderer can make them (think the best cleaning agent used at a "dry cleaners"). We can conjecture, reasonably we might add, that John is likely referencing the Transfiguration at the opening of his gospel:

John 1:14 And the Word became flesh and dwelt among us, and *we beheld His glory*, the glory as of the only begotten of the Father, full of grace and truth.

John says, "We beheld His glory." There are many appearances of the resurrected Jesus, where His glory did not shine, including appearances in John's gospel (see John 20 and 21). Jesus could, as He willed, "dim the lights." Nevertheless, we should have no trouble concluding that Jesus' glorified body was the same post-resurrection as at the Transfiguration; otherwise the New Testament writers would not have identified it as a "glorified body" or a "body of glory." We can rest assured from all our studies so far that our body will be the same as His. We too will glisten with glory, be partakers of the divine nature, and thus *manifest the presence of God*. We are not then and never will be Yahweh. But we will be considered, in the words of Dr. Heiser, *little elohim*; moreover, *those who partake of God's glory.*

2 Pet 1:4 By which have been given to us *exceedingly great and precious promises, that through these you may be partakers of the divine nature*, having escaped the corruption *that is* in the world through lust.

We know that if we gather several thousand lighted candles, the assembly of light would be very bright. Likewise, when the gathered glorified saints are together in one place, with the Head of the Body, Jesus Christ, "the brightness of His Glory" (Hebrews 1:3), the light will blind those who have only ordinary eyes. We will indeed express copious amounts of lightning-bright light. From far away, the cloud of saints with their Lord *would look like a larger version of the cloud of glory* that led Israel through the wilderness.

Exo 14:19: And the Angel of God, who went before the camp of Israel, moved and went behind them; and *the pillar of cloud went from before them and stood behind them.*

THE ANGEL, THE NAME, THE PRESENCE

Michael Heiser supplies a compelling argument as to what the Scriptures say about the Angel of God, His name, and His presence: We begin in Exodus:

Exo 23:20–22 [20] "Look, I *am about to* send an angel before you to guard you on the way and to bring you to the place that I have prepared. [21] Be attentive to him and listen to his voice; do not rebel against him, because he will not forgive your transgression, *for my name is in him.* [22] But if you listen attentively to his voice and do all that I say, I will be an enemy to your enemies and a foe to your foes."

Heiser points out:

There's something strange about God's description to Moses that tells us that this is no ordinary angel. This angel has the authority to pardon sins or not, a status that belongs to God. More specifically, God tells Moses that the reason this angel has this authority is "my name is in him" (verse 21).[††]

Moses immediately knew what that phrase meant. By God saying that His name was in the angel *meant that He, Himself was in the angel – His very presence.* Quoting Heiser, "The I AM of the burning bush would accompany Moses and the Israelites to the promised land and fight for them. Only he could defeat the gods of the nations and the descendants of the Nephilim whom Moses and Joshua would find there."[‡‡]

[††] Heiser, op. cit., pp. 142-144.
[‡‡] Ibid.

Heiser then identifies other passages confirming his perspective (which these authors share) that this angel is none other than Yahweh (and the pre-incarnate Christ):

Lev 11:45 I *am* Yahweh, who brought you up from the land of Egypt to be for you as God.

Josh 24:17–18a [17]Yahweh our God brought us and our ancestors from the land of Egypt, from the house of slavery, and did these great signs before our eyes. He protected us along the entire way that we went, and among all the peoples through whose midst we passed. [18]And Yahweh drove out all the people before us...

Duet 4:35-38 [35]You yourselves were shown this wonder in order for you to acknowledge that Yahweh is the God; there is no other God besides him. [36] From heaven he made you hear his voice to teach you, and on the earth, he showed you his great fire, and you heard his words from the midst of the fire. [37] And because he loved your ancestors he chose their descendants after them. And he brought you forth from Egypt with his own presence, by his great strength, [38] to drive out nations greater and more numerous than you from before you, to bring you and to give to you their land as an inheritance, as it is this day .

Jud 2:1 And the angel of Yahweh went up from Gilgal to Bokim and said, "I brought you up from Egypt, and I brought you to the land that I had promised to your ancestors"

Says Heiser:

These passages interchange Yahweh, the Angel of Yahweh, and the "presence" (*panim*) of God as the identity of the divine deliverer of Israel from Egypt. There weren't three different deliverers. They are all the same. One of them, the angel, takes human form. If Deuteronomy 4:37 is read in light of Exodus 23:20–23, then the presence and the

Angel are co-identified. This makes good sense in view of the meaning of the "Name" which was in the Angel.[§§]

Jesus Christ was that cloud in the wilderness, just as He will be amidst the cloud of glory along with His saints (His holy ones – the Church). He will lead Israel through the spiritual wilderness they are in. Recall that in our resurrection discussion, we learned Jesus ascended into heaven via a cloud. *Our logical conclusion was that this cloud comprised Old Testament saints as firstfruits of the end-time harvest.*

As Ray Stedman explained, at the end of the age Jesus and His saints will appear to "post-church Christians." *The church is visibly removed from the world, yet will appear like Moses and Elijah on the Mount of Transfiguration with Jesus.* They will appear to those whose hearts are ready to believe in Him. Rumors of His presence will be spread, so that men will be saying, "where is He?" Jesus' answer to that question, before it is asked is, "where the body is, there the eagles will gather."

THE GREAT TRIBULATION (THE DAY OF THE LORD)

To grasp the essence of the Great Tribulation and of what it consists, which most scholars regard as synonymous with *The Day of the Lord,* we must compare Daniel 9:24-27 to Matthew 24:15-28:

> **Dan 9:24-27** [24]"Seventy weeks are determined for your people and for your holy city, to finish the transgression, To make an end of sins, To make reconciliation for iniquity, To bring in everlasting righteousness, To seal up vision and prophecy, And to anoint the Most Holy. [25]"Know therefore and understand, *that* from the going forth of the command to restore and build Jerusalem Until Messiah the Prince, *there shall be* seven weeks and sixty-two weeks; The street shall be built again, and the wall, Even in troublesome times. [26]"And after the sixty-two weeks Messiah shall be cut off, but not for

---

[§§] Ibid.

Himself; and the people of the prince who is to come shall destroy the city and the sanctuary. The end of it *shall be* with a flood, and till the end of the war desolations are determined. [27]Then he shall confirm a covenant with many for one week; *but in the middle of the week He shall bring an end to sacrifice and offering.* And on the wing of abominations shall be one who makes desolate, even until the consummation, which is determined, is poured out on the desolate."

Mat 24:15-28 [15]"Therefore when you see the *'abomination of desolation,'* spoken of by Daniel the prophet, standing in the holy place" (whoever reads, let him understand), [16]"then let those who are in Judea flee to the mountains. [17]Let him who is on the housetop not go down to take anything out of his house. [18]And let him who is in the field not go back to get his clothes. [19]But woe to those who are pregnant and to those who are nursing babies in those days! [20]And pray that your flight may not be in winter or on the Sabbath. [21]For then there will be *great tribulation*, such as has not been since the beginning of the world until this time, no, nor ever shall be. [22]And unless those days were shortened, no flesh would be saved; but for the elect's sake those days will be shortened. [23]"Then if anyone says to you, 'Look, here *is* the Christ!' or 'There!' do not believe *it.* [24]For false christs and false prophets will rise and show great signs and wonders to deceive, if possible, even the elect. [25]See, I have told you beforehand. [26]"Therefore if they say to you, 'Look, He is in the desert!' do not go out; *or* 'Look, *He is* in the inner rooms!' do not believe *it.* [27]For as the lightning comes from the east and flashes to the west, so also will the coming of the Son of Man be. [28]For wherever the carcass is, there the eagles will be gathered together.

Jesus speaks of the final 3½ years before the kingdom is established on earth. We know this because the abomination of desolation, vs 15, is the same as in Daniel 9:27 in the 70th week, which is the last week (7) of years. There were 70 weeks (7's) altogether (Dan 9:25). In the midst of the last week is the abomination and therefore at the 3½ year mark. In Matthew

24:21 Jesus says this 3½ year period will consist of great tribulation – and from this descriptive phrase came the name "Great Tribulation" The words "Great Tribulation" appear in Rev 2:22 and (possibly) in 7:14.***

Rev 2:22 Indeed I will cast her into a sickbed, and those who commit adultery with her into *great tribulation*, unless they repent of their deeds.

Rev 7:14 And I said to him, "Sir, you know." So he said to me, "These are the ones who come out of (the) *great tribulation*, and washed their robes and made them white in the blood of the Lamb.

Jesus also marks this as the time of His parousia or secret presence in Matthew 24:27. Then, He proclaims in verses 29-30, that immediately after the tribulation of those days, He will return in power and great glory.

2 Th 2:1-8 [1]Now, brethren, *concerning the coming of our Lord Jesus Christ* and our gathering together to Him, we ask you, [2]not to be soon shaken in mind or troubled, either by spirit or by word or by letter, as if from us, as though the day of Christ had come. [3]Let no one deceive you by any means; for *that Day will not come unless the falling away comes first, and the man of sin is revealed, the son of perdition,* [4]who opposes and exalts himself above all that is called God or that is worshiped, so that he sits as God in the temple of God, showing himself that he is God. [5]Do you not remember that when I was still with you I told you these things? [6]And now you know what is restraining, that he may be revealed in his own time. [7]For the

---

*** Although some have pointed out that this verse could be translated "great sufferings, distress, or difficulties" – the Greek word being *thlipsis*, which is translated differently in various places in the New Testament; thus the word in Revelation 7:14 is not necessarily a reference to the "Great Tribulation." It might not refer specifically to the final 3 and ½ years. See the book *Then His Voice Shook the Earth*, by David W. Lowe, for which Woodward wrote a foreword.

mystery of lawlessness is already at work; only He who now restrains *will do so* until He is taken out of the way. [8]And then the lawless one will be revealed, whom the Lord will consume with the breath of His mouth and destroy with the brightness of His coming.

Here Paul says that the *Day of Christ will not come until there is a falling away, and the man of sin is revealed... but by what? The abomination.* He beseeches them by the coming (lit. *parousia*) of the Lord Jesus Christ. So, here is the same 3½ years called the day of Christ and a reference to the *parousia* in verse 1 and verse 8 (unveiling of His *Parousia*).

1 Th 5:2 For you yourselves know perfectly that the day of the Lord so comes as a thief in the night.

Paul refers to this as the Day of the Lord, which comes as a thief in the night just as Jesus teaches in a parable from Matthew 24:43.

Mat 24:43 But know this, that if the master of the house had known what hour the thief would come, he would have watched and not allowed his house to be broken into.

1 Th 5:23 Now may the God of peace Himself sanctify you completely; and may your whole spirit, soul, and body be preserved blameless at the *coming* of our Lord Jesus Christ.

Paul prays for the whole man to be preserved until the coming (*parousia*) of the Lord. From these verses, we gather the "Great Tribulation" is the 3½ years directly before Jesus returns in power and great glory, and that the "Parousia" occurs before or sometime during this period (but before the coming of Jesus with the clouds of heaven, to judge the nations and establish His Kingdom). Note Old Testament counterparts exist for The Great Tribulation and The Day of Christ (e.g., "the Indignation", "the Day of the Lord," and "Jacob's Trouble."). We see these in the following passages:

Jer 30:3-7 [3]For behold, the days are coming,' says the LORD, 'that I will bring back from captivity My people Israel and Judah,' says the LORD. 'And I will cause them to return to the land that I gave to their fathers, and they shall possess it.'" [4]Now these *are* the words that the LORD spoke concerning Israel and Judah. [5]"For thus says the LORD: 'We have heard a voice of trembling, Of fear, and not of peace. [6]Ask now, and see, whether a man is ever in labor with child? So why do I see every man *with* his hands on his loins like a woman in labor, and all faces turned pale? [7]Alas! *For that day is great,* so that none *is* like it; *And it is* **the time of Jacob's trouble,** *but he shall be saved out of it.*

Isa 10:25 For yet a very little *while and* **the indignation** *will cease,* as will My anger in their destruction."

Isa 13:6 *Wail, for the* **day of the LORD** *is at hand!* It will come as destruction from the Almighty.

Isa 26:20 Come, my people, enter your chambers, and shut your doors behind you; hide yourself, as it were, for a little moment, until **the indignation** is past.

Here, Isaiah speaks of the chambers, or *tabernacles* that the church will enter *during the fulfillment of the Feast of Tabernacles.* This will be God's protecting Glory on behalf of believers, comprising the Body of Christ in the last days, possibly before or at the outset of the Great Tribulation (*The Indignation*) when the wrath of God is poured out upon the "earth dwellers" (as Ray Stedman calls those refusing to accept the gracious offer of salvation through Jesus Christ and "miss the Rapture"). Therefore, this does not mean the church will be inactive during the Great Tribulation. On the contrary, it will be the church's "shining hour."

Isa 34:2 For *the indignation* of the LORD *is* against all nations, And *His* fury against all their armies; He has utterly destroyed them, He has given them over to the slaughter.

Joel 2:1 Blow the trumpet in Zion, and sound an alarm in My holy mountain! Let all the inhabitants of the land tremble; For the day of the LORD is coming, for it is at hand:

Joel 2:15 Blow the trumpet in Zion, consecrate a fast, call a sacred assembly.

Psa 75:2 "When I choose the proper time, I will judge uprightly."

Rev 11:2-3 [2]But leave out the court which is outside the temple, and do not measure it, for it has been given to the Gentiles. And they will tread the holy city underfoot for forty-two months. [3]And I will give *power* to my two witnesses, and they will prophesy one thousand two hundred and sixty days, clothed in sackcloth."

Rev 12:6 Then the woman fled into the wilderness, where she has a place prepared by God, that they should feed her there *one thousand two hundred and sixty days.*

Rev 13:5-7 [5]And he was given a mouth speaking great things and blasphemies, and he was given authority to continue *for forty-two months.* [6]Then he opened his mouth in blasphemy against God, to blaspheme His name, His tabernacle, and those who dwell in heaven. [7]It was granted to him to make war with the saints and to overcome them. And authority was given him over every tribe, tongue, and nation.

These references concern the same 3½ years (whether 42 months or 1260 days). After God receives the congregation (the Church at the beginning of the Parousia), His judgments begin. In Revelation 13, we see the Antichrist blaspheming God, His tabernacle, and those who dwell (literally, "pitch their tents", chambers, or tabernacles) in heaven during the Day of the Lord. *This is the Parousia, the Body of Christ dwelling in the heavens above the earth.* Although we can't be dogmatic, we believe it could either be the "second heaven," (outside the atmosphere where celestial bodies such as the sun and moon reside), or possibly "the first heaven" – the atmosphere – as "the Prince and power of the air" along with his angels lose their position of rulership there (the Divine Council has been displaced and is cast down to the earth). The evil principalities' occupation has ended and the Body of Christ replaces them. We read of this moment in Revelation, chapter 12:

> **Rev 12: 6-8** [6] And the woman fled into the wilderness, where she has a place prepared by God, in which she is to be nourished for 1,260 days. [7] Now war arose in heaven, Michael and his angels fighting against the dragon. And the dragon and his angels fought back, [8] but he was defeated, and there was no longer any place for them in heaven.

The corrupted supernatural beings that have ruled the earth since Adam handed over the deed to Eden when he chose the serpent's (*nachash*) word over Yahweh's, are finally displaced. These powerful beings fall to earth,[†††] to the terrestrial domain solely, and as the Scriptures says, "Woe unto those that dwell on the earth for the Devil has lost his place in heaven and he has totally lost it too! He knows his time is now very short." (Revelation 12:12, paraphrased)

It is now "total war" as the Devil and his Antichrist go about the process of annihilating those that dwell in Israel along with anyone else who believes in Jesus as Messiah. In these last days, he is given power to overcome the saints and extends his power over *every tribe, tongue, and*

[†††] These beings are not demons. Demons already dwell here on earth and roam about looking for a desirable place to reside. Demons are the spirits of the Nephilim from before, and possibly after the flood of Noah which still appeared "post-flood."

nation (not just in the Middle East as the "Islamic Antichrist Theory" professes. See Revelation 13:7, on the preceding page).

For those who believe in the Pre-Tribulation Rapture or the Pre-Wrath Rapture, this group of post-Rapture believers are known as "Tribulation saints." Of course, those students of Bible prophecy who ascribe to a Post-Tribulation Rapture, dispute the existence of this body of believers – since there are no believers raptured at all prior to the resurrection beginning the Kingdom. For "Post-Tribbers," the Church and Israel all remain with upon the face of the earth throughout the Great Tribulation – even during the outpouring of God's wrath. We treat Post-Tribbers as beloved brothers and sisters, but believe 1 Thessalonians 5:9 teaches differently, "For God has **not** destined us for wrath, but for obtaining salvation through our Lord Jesus Christ.: Understanding the "*mystērion*" of the Church suggests the Body of Christ does exit (is snatched up) at some point before the Great Tribulation begins, but certainly before the wrath of God is poured out upon the earth.

Let's return to Isaiah 26:20 once more and consider what it might imply concerning the Great Tribulation period of the last days:

> **Isa 26:20** Come, my people, enter your *chambers*, and shut your doors behind you; hide yourself, as it were, for a little moment, until the indignation is past.

If the woman in Revelation 12:6 is Israel (and not the Church) as many commentators contend, then at the time that her citizens receive her Messiah these will find some protection, perhaps not only by escaping to the wilderness, but in fulfilling the prophetic type of the Shekinah glory of God. God calls upon them to return to their chambers, to their booths, and shut the doors behind them. Recall that during Old Testament times, the Israelites met God in their tents (their booths) during the Feast of Tabernacles. Might this be what is implied in Isaiah 26:20? We think so.

Israel will meet again with God through their true Messiah. However, our thesis, in light of and supported by the previous presentation up to this point, is that believers in Messiah will also be His glorified sons and daughters. However, those glorified at the resurrection, the Body of Christ, is the family destined to take the place of the corrupted Divine Counsel. The Shekinah, the cloud of glory, may appear (as the cover of this book illustrates) over Israel during the Indignation (i.e., the Time of Jacob's Trouble). God's translated family may also aid in Israel's protection and elsewhere as the LORD wills.

Next, let's reconsider the Seven Trumpets of Revelation and the "Last Trump" of 1 Corinthians:

Rev 8:2-6 [2]And I saw the seven angels who stand before God, and to them were given seven trumpets. [3]Then another angel, having a golden censer, came and stood at the altar. He was given much incense, that he should offer *it* with the prayers of all the saints upon the golden altar which was before the throne. [4]And the smoke of the incense, with the prayers of the saints, ascended before God from the angel's hand. [5]Then the angel took the censer, filled it with fire from the altar, and threw *it* to the earth. And there were noises, thunderings, lightnings, and an earthquake. [6]So the seven angels who had the seven trumpets prepared themselves to sound.

Immediately before the seven angels sound their trumpets, there is incense offered from the golden altar before the throne of God. Remember, this is the heavenly Day of Atonement, part of the Feast of Tabernacles and the necessary "ritual that makes holy" God's people. Could this begin the Parousia? This can be bravely conjectured because the Altar of Incense is within the Holy of Holies before God's presence – the golden censor was taken into the Holy of Holies on one day only – the Day of Atonement. This may indicate the Parousia begins at or near the midpoint of the seven years before Jesus visibly returns.

Rev 10:7 But in the days of the sounding of the seventh angel, when he is about to sound, the mystery of God would be finished, as He declared to His servants the prophets.

Rev 11:15 Then the seventh angel sounded: And there were loud voices in heaven, saying, "The kingdoms of this world have become *the kingdoms* of our Lord and of His Christ, and He shall reign forever and ever!"

1 Cor 15:51-52 [51]Behold, I tell you a mystery: We shall not all sleep, but we shall all be changed – [52]in a moment, in the twinkling of an eye, at the last trumpet. For the trumpet will sound, and the dead will be raised incorruptible, and we shall be changed.

The sounding of the seventh angel, or last trumpet, indicates a culmination. *It comprises the conclusion of the Church Age and, at the same time, the initiation of the age of the Feast of Tabernacles.* Remember, the Feast of Tabernacles is the "feast to end all feasts." It constitutes the convocation which foreshadows the Millennium. We will celebrate this Feast through the 1000-year reign of Christ and His Holy Ones, along with mortal humans living during this age.

JACOB'S LADDER IS A PROPHECY FOR THE CHURCH

Let's recall one of the best-known passages from Genesis:

Gen 28:11-15 [11]So he came to a certain place and stayed there all night, because the sun had set. And he took one of the stones of that place and put it at his head, and he lay down in that place to sleep. [12]Then he dreamed, and behold, a ladder *was* set up on the earth, and its top reached to heaven; and there the angels of God were ascending and descending on it. [13]And behold, the LORD stood above it and said: "I *am* the LORD God of Abraham your father and the God of Isaac; the land on which you lie I will give to you and your descendants. [14]Also your descendants shall be as the dust of the earth; you shall spread abroad to the west and the east, to the north and the south; and in you and in your seed all the families of the earth shall be blessed. [15]Behold, I *am* with you and will keep you wherever you go, and will bring you back to this land; for I will not leave you until I have done what I have spoken to you."

John 1:51 And He said to him, "Most assuredly, I say to you, hereafter you shall see heaven open, and the angels of God ascending and descending upon the Son of Man."

In the context of the Genesis passage, it is reasonable to conclude that Jesus' version or interpretation of Jacob's Ladder is found with His statement in John 1:51. The ladder is Jesus: the Greek says "on the Son of Man." The angels of God ascending and descending on Jesus, the Son of man. In Genesis, He is not only the ladder but in verse 13, He stands *at the top of the ladder*. Do you see how this proclamation might also convey what we have just considered? The Body of Christ, like the angels in times past, moves between heaven and earth with their Head, the Lord Jesus. The usual conception of the events after the Rapture, has the Church safeguarded and "stashed away" in heaven, with no interaction with those on the earth. Perhaps we have missed the "types" presented in the Old Testament and its fulfillment in the Church who reigns with Christ:

Eph 1:20-23 [20]Which He worked in Christ when He raised Him from the dead and seated *Him* at His right hand in the heavenly *places,* [21]far above all principality and power and might and dominion, and every name that is named, not only in this age but also in that which is to come. [22]And He put all *things* under His feet, and gave Him *to be* head over all *things* to the church, [23]which is His body, the fullness of Him who fills all in all.

The word "angels" in both "Jacob's Ladder" accounts likely references angels, God's messengers, as in this verse:

> **Mat 22:30** For in the resurrection they neither marry nor are given in marriage, but are like angels of God in heaven.

> **Gen 28:16-19** [16]Then Jacob awoke from his sleep and said, "Surely the LORD is in this place, and I did not know *it.*" [17]And he was afraid and said, "How awesome *is* this place! This *is* none other than the house of God, and this *is* the gate of heaven!" [18]Then Jacob rose early in the morning, and took the stone that he had put at his head, set it up as a pillar, and poured oil on top of it. [19]And he called the name of that place Bethel; but the name of that city had been Luz previously.

Jacob proclaims enthusiastically that the Lord was in this place, God's presence was surely manifested here. Therefore, he calls it the House of God (Bethel) and the Gate of Heaven. Yahweh dwelt there – but now Yahweh through Y'shua dwells in the church, the Body of Christ, the House of God. His presence in the Church will be increasingly manifest as the distress of the last days grows worse (discussed in more detail in the final chapter). The story of Jacob's ladder also conveys a typology of the church – the church is the gateway of Heaven – *it is the portal, or doorway through which the blessings of God will be manifested.* To use the biblical metaphor, *He is building a house with **lively stones*** (that's you and me) in which He dwells:

> **1 Pet 2:5-6** [5]You also, as living stones, are being built up a spiritual house, a holy priesthood, to offer up spiritual sacrifices acceptable to God through Jesus Christ. [6]Therefore it is also contained in the Scripture, *"Behold, I lay in Zion* a chief cornerstone, elect, precious, *and he who believes on Him will by no means be put to shame."*

> **Eph 2:19-22** [19]Now, therefore, you are no longer strangers and foreigners, but fellow citizens with the saints and members of the

household of God, ²⁰having been built on the foundation of the apostles and prophets, Jesus Christ Himself being the chief corner*stone,* ²¹in whom the whole building, being fitted together, grows into a holy temple in the Lord, ²²in whom you also are being built together for a dwelling place of God in the Spirit.

The metaphor of the stone is, if you will, a "mega-metaphor." In Greek, *mega* means giant and *meta* means multi-layered, or "deep." Therefore, "stones" conveys an especially deep truth, steeped in meaning. Jacob took the stone upon which he rested and set it down, anointed it with oil. *This stone is Christ* upon which Jacob rested which also represents the *head of the corner* (I Pet 2:6) in the House of God, the Body of Christ. *Christ*, or Messiah, means *anointed one.* Oil is a symbol of the anointing of the Holy Spirit, so oil was poured on the rock at Bethel – the House of God. Jesus was anointed so that He could pour His Holy Spirit on the disciples and form the church, His Body. The Oil was poured on the Chief Cornerstone, the Rock, at the House of God. The Oil was poured on the Head of the Body so that, if each member of the Body is properly fitted in place, the entire Body will be anointed also:

> **Psa 133:1-2** ¹Behold, how good and how pleasant *it is* for brethren to dwell together in unity! ² *It is* like the precious oil upon the head, running down on the beard, the beard of Aaron, running down on the edge of his garments.

(We will talk more about this notion – the unity of the Body as expressed in Psalm 133 – in an upcoming chapter.)

> **Eph 4:11-13** ¹¹And He Himself gave some *to be* apostles, some prophets, some evangelists, and some pastors and teachers, ¹²for the equipping of the saints for the work of ministry, for the edifying of the body of Christ, ¹³till we all come to the unity of the faith and of the knowledge of the Son of God, to a perfect man, to the measure of the stature of the fullness of Christ.

We know that the Body of Christ is not yet built into a perfect man, so Jacob's Ladder cannot be fulfilled until that occurs. Likewise, God's promise to Abraham in Genesis 13:15 will not be fulfilled until the resurrection – these two are directly connected (see Gen 28:12-14):

> **Gen 13:15** For all the land which you see I give to you and your descendants forever.

The Body of Christ was truly great in the days of the Apostles but we know that the glory of the latter House (God's House) will be greater still. It will outshine the former for *all its lively stones will be glorified:*

> **Hag 2:9** "The glory of this latter temple shall be greater than the former,' says the LORD of hosts. 'And in this place, I will give peace,' says the LORD of hosts."

> **John 14:2-3** [2]In My Father's house are many mansions ["dwelling places", but not conveying separate dwellings. See Strong's G3438, also translated as "make our *abode*" in John 14:23]; if *it were* not *so*, I would have told you. I go to prepare a place for you. [3]And if I go and prepare a place for you, I will come again and receive you to Myself; that where I am, *there* you may be also.

The Parousia can't be fulfilled until the Body is built up in unity. We aren't meant to dwell in an apartment complex, time-share, or condominium; for God didn't intend we be split up and made to dwell in many separate units. Instead, we are to be *one unified house.*

> **Eph 2:20-22** [20]Having been built on the foundation of the apostles and prophets, Jesus Christ Himself being the chief corner*stone,* [21]in whom the whole building, being fitted together, grows into a holy temple in the Lord, [22]in whom you also are being built together *for a dwelling place of God in the Spirit.*

Eph 4:13 [Until] we all come to the unity of the faith and of the knowledge of the Son of God, to a perfect man, to the measure of the stature of the fullness of Christ.

This verse could be seen to challenge the aspect of "imminence" within the Pre-Tribulation Rapture point of view. (The imminence of the Rapture means that the LORD can come for His church at any moment. No sign must necessarily occur before the Rapture.) The maturity of the Church (whether it is or isn't fully mature) will not frustrate the timing of God. And yet, Paul seeks to see the church perfected. To be clear, we do not know how perfected the Church will be at the time it is "snatched up" by the LORD. Nevertheless, we have presented here that when the Church is glorified and joined into one (both the resurrected and the raptured members of the Body of Christ) at the Parousia, it will not be idle. It will continue to serve others who become believers during the Great Tribulation. Because of the hostility of the Antichrist toward Israel, it is only logical that the Body of Christ will minister to Jacob's people.

Rev 22:17 And the Spirit and the bride say, "Come!" And let him who hears say, "Come!" And let him who thirsts come. Whoever desires, let him take the water of life freely.

Psa 20:1-2 May the LORD answer you in the day of trouble; May the name of the God of Jacob defend you; [2]May He send you help from the sanctuary, and strengthen you out of Zion.

The God of Jacob will send help from the sanctuary, or Holy of Holies (where His glory dwells)! There will be help for Jacob in the time of Jacob's Trouble. Members of the Body of Christ, as pictured in Jacob's ladder will be ascending and descending (or from the earthly perspective, "appearing and disappearing") in accordance to what the Head of the Body wills. Thus, it seems probable that this "Parousia" ministry will be primarily focused on Israel (Jacob), but will certainly include others whose hearts are open to receive and drawn by the Spirit. This is from whence the second and complete fulfillment of Isaiah 61:1

191

will come. The Body of Christ, taking commands from our LORD, will demonstrate the love and glory of God to Jews and all others who, because of the pressure of world events, turn to the Savior.

Isa 61:1-3 [1]"The Spirit of the Lord GOD *is* upon Me, Because the LORD has anointed Me to preach good tidings to the poor; He has sent Me to heal the brokenhearted, to proclaim liberty to the captives, and the opening of the prison to *those who are* bound; [2]to proclaim the acceptable year of the LORD, and the day of vengeance of our God; to comfort all who mourn, [3]to console those who mourn in Zion, to give them beauty for ashes, the oil of joy for mourning, the garment of praise for the spirit of heaviness; that they may be called trees of righteousness, the planting of the LORD, that He may be glorified."

The Feast of Tabernacles presages an accompanying *cloud of glory* as the place of refuge from harm in Zion. *God has not forgotten His people, Israel.* While there may be protection in the wilderness, *there will be a cloud and smoke protecting those in Zion.* There will be a place of refuge, a tabernacle of shade, and a shelter from storm and rain.

Isa 4:2-6 [2]In that day the Branch of the LORD shall be beautiful and glorious; and the fruit of the earth *shall be* excellent and appealing, for those of Israel who have escaped. [3]And it shall come to pass that *he who is* left in Zion and remains in Jerusalem will be called holy – everyone who is recorded among the living in Jerusalem. [4]When the Lord has washed away the filth of the daughters of Zion, and purged the blood of Jerusalem from her midst, by the spirit of judgment and by the spirit of burning, [5]*then the LORD will create above every dwelling place of Mount Zion, and above her assemblies,* **a cloud and smoke by day and the shining of a flaming fire by night.** *For over all the glory there will be a covering.* [6]*And there will be a tabernacle for shade in the daytime from the heat, for a place of refuge, and for a shelter from storm and rain.*

7: ALL ISRAEL SHALL BE SAVED

ARE YOU SAVED IF YOU ARE BORN A JEW?

All Israel shall be saved. What does this mean? Will all Jews, both those living and deceased, be saved even if they never believed on Christ? Might it mean that at some future point, all those living Jews will accept Christ as Messiah and trust that salvation is through Him and Him alone? How could that happen? When could it happen? Will the Church, the "people called out for His name," (Acts 15:14) have a part to play in this future "about face"?

The idea that all Israel shall be saved goes against the theology of both the Old and New Testaments. Only those with faith, those who believe, will be saved. Living within a particular nation state, or being of a select race, does not automatically mean salvation is yours, whether you want it or not. The LORD does not force Himself upon anyone that does not want Him. We read Paul's oft-quoted statement. "For therein is the righteousness of God revealed from faith to faith: as it is written, "The just shall live by faith." Paul cites Habakkuk 2:4 in Romans and in Hebrews 10:38 (assuming Paul is its author).

This is the cornerstone of salvation as taught in the Bible. "Abraham believed God and it was counted unto him as righteousness." (Romans

4:3) And yet, Paul's extensive argument advanced in Romans 9 – 11, culminates in several pivotal statements, one of which is this:

> **Rom 11:26-27** And so all Israel will be saved, as it is written: *"The Deliverer will come out of Zion,* And He will turn away ungodliness from Jacob; [27]*For this is My covenant with them, When I take away their sins."*

Notwithstanding, much of the love and commitment Evangelicalism has had toward Israel for the past 150 years (beginning primarily with Darbyism aka Dispensationalism) appears due in part to the prophetic interpretation that one day, Israel shall be saved, and its connection to the second coming of Jesus Christ. Indeed, early Dispensationalists were strong Zionists leading up to the first Zionist Conference at Basel in 1897. However, the belief that Israel will come back to its land goes back further. It was advanced by English Puritans in the seventeenth century.[*] It was known as *Protestant Restorationism*.

> **Zech 12:10** And I will pour upon the house of David, and upon the inhabitants of Jerusalem, the spirit of grace and of supplications: and they shall look upon me whom they have pierced, and they shall mourn for him, as one mourneth for his only son, and shall be in bitterness for him, as one that is in bitterness for his firstborn." (KJV)

To support Israel, to restore it to its land, is to hasten the coming of the Lord. At least so many eschatology students have believed. But is this what is meant by "All Israel shall be saved?"

---

* John Owen, a prominent 17th century English Covenant theologian, for example, wrote: "Moreover, it is granted that there shall be a time and season, during the continuance of the kingdom of the Messiah in this world, wherein the generality of the nation of the Jews, all the world over, shall be called and effectually brought unto the knowledge of the Messiah, our Lord Jesus Christ; with which mercy they shall also receive deliverance from their captivity, restoration unto their own land, with a blessed, flourishing, and happy condition therein." See https://en.wikipedia.org/wiki/Christian_Zionism.

Michael Heiser discusses the rejection of Israel leading to Gentile salvation. One of his essential points is that Israel was God's elect in the Old Testament. When the Scripture spoke of the "elect" it was speaking of Israel corporately.[†] We see this terminology used by the prophet Isaiah:

> **Isa 65:9,22** [9]And I will bring forth a seed out of Jacob, and out of Judah an inheritor of my mountains: and *mine elect* shall inherit it, and my servants shall dwell there... [22]They shall not build, and another inhabit; they shall not plant, and another eat: for as the days of a tree are the days of my people, and *mine elect* shall long enjoy the work of their hands. (KJV)

Most Jews who understand their Bible recognize that they were to be a "light unto the Gentiles." But *unbelief* caused Israel to reject the Messiah during his visitation (Luke 19:44). This led to apostasy. And the elect might commit sin, but they still chose to follow Yahweh. The forsaking of Yahweh, consciously deciding that you no longer wish to call on the name of the Lord, or believe in Him at all, is *the rejection* that leads to condemnation and ceasing to be numbered among the elect. Therefore, rejection resulted in Gentiles coming into the fold of God's elect. So, who is God's elect now? Those who believe in Jesus Christ, in whom there is no distinction between Jew and Gentile:

> **Rom 10:12-13** [12]For there is no distinction between Jew and Greek; for the same Lord is Lord of all, bestowing his riches on all who call on him. [13]For "everyone who calls on the name of the Lord will be saved." (ESV)

---

†There is also reference to the Messiah as the elect, in our view, when Isaiah says, "Behold my servant, whom I uphold; mine elect, in whom my soul delighteth; I have put my spirit upon him: he shall bring forth judgment to the Gentiles." (Isaiah 42:1)

Says Heiser,

> The apostasy of the elect led to many Gentiles being saved and, in fact, replacing those elect Israelites as Yahweh's people, the inheritors of the Abrahamic promises (Galatians 3). The result was one people of God (Jew and Gentile = the "Church"). This meant in turn that the one people of God was therefore ultimately composed of elect and non-elect. Paul, in prelude to his explanation of all this in Romans 9-11, gives us the famous "foreknowing, predestinating, justification, etc." chain of concepts in Romans 8. There's no indication that he was speaking only of Jews there, as what he says in Romans 8 is true of all believers. The wording of Paul is interesting given the position we suggest. He does not use the word "election" in the description. He does not speak of Jew only. He tells us more broadly that God predestined the salvation of ... some ... a remnant ... the composition of which he will explain (*in Romans 9 – 11*) ...[‡]

Rom 11:20-24 [20]They [the elect Israelites who were set aside] were broken off because of their unbelief, but you stand fast through faith. So do not become proud, but fear. [21]For if God did not spare the natural branches, neither will he spare you. [22]Note then the kindness and the severity of God: severity toward those who have fallen, but God's kindness to you, provided you continue in his kindness. Otherwise you too will be cut off. [23]And even they, if they do not continue in their unbelief, will be grafted in, for God has the power to graft them in again. [24]For if you were cut from what is by nature a wild olive tree, and grafted, contrary to nature, into a cultivated olive tree, how much more will these, the natural branches, be grafted back into their own olive tree. (ESV)

[‡] (Retrieved from http://drmsh.com/election-salvation-unbelief-and-eternal-security/ on 01/16/17)

Returning to Heiser's commentary:

(Quoting Heiser) What do we learn here?

1. That the Israelites, who were elect, forfeited salvation because of their unbelief (see Jude 5 here as well). As elect people, if they would have believed, they would have been (spiritually) saved and not condemned as unfaithful.

2. If God was able and willing to set aside these elect who did not believe, He will not spare "you". Who is Paul addressing? Gentiles who were allowed entrance into the people of God through faith. Paul says God expects them to "continue in his kindness" – in my view, this refers to God's offer of salvation to them – the non-elect.

3. Paul also curiously says that if the unbeliever (in context, the failing Jew who was elect) *does not continue in their unbelief* they will be "grafted in, for God has the power to graft them in again."

... I think it noteworthy in light of this that, in the long list of what cannot separate us from God's love, unbelief does not appear. Why? Because that can separate us from God's love – in fact it keeps us from God's love shown to us in Christ. No sins of the flesh can remove us from the family of God. The only thing that keeps us from God's family is unbelief. Salvation is BY grace, THROUGH faith; God's part and our part. Both are essential, but one is primary.[§]

[§] Ibid. Dr. Heiser believes that Israel, about whom Paul speaks, refers to the Israelites that were blended into the Gentile nations after 722 B.C. To make a long story short, Heiser asserts that Israel refers to the mixture of Hebrews from the Northern Kingdom of Israel who were dispersed into "all the nations" (aka the *Diaspora*). Strictly speaking *Jews* refer to the two tribes of the Southern Kingdom: Judah and Ephraim. In Acts 2, we see those who practice Judaism back in Jerusalem for Passover. They are from "every nation." These likely had Israelite ancestors, and were certainly "Jews" in the modern sense of practicing the Jewish religion with a Hebrew heritage. The non-Hebrew world referred to all those with a Hebrew ancestry as Jews during the "Second Temple Period" forward (the second temple was erected in the sixth century B.C. through Zerubbabel and the remnant returning from Babylon). Thus, the phrase "all Israel shall be saved," for Heiser, references *all believers* from

WHAT IS GOD'S PLAN TO BRING ISRAEL TO FAITH?

But we believe that God has a plan to bring many, living in Israel, to faith in Jesus Christ. And he will do this in a spectacular and glorious way!

> **Rom 11:31** Even so these also have now been disobedient, that through the mercy shown you they also may obtain mercy.

"Through the mercy shown you" (to Gentiles to whom Paul speaks) "they" the Jews "may obtain mercy." Could Paul be stating that a day is coming when Gentiles will take the message to the Jews? Then will the hearts of the Jews be opened, scales fall from their eyes, and their ears unstopped regarding Jesus of Nazareth being their Messiah? When might this time be? How might preaching of the gospel by Gentiles become effective? Romans 11:26-27, cited earlier, refers to Isaiah 59:20-21:

> **Isa 59:19-21** [19]So shall they fear the name of the LORD from the west, And His glory from the rising of the sun; When the enemy comes in like a flood, The Spirit of the LORD will lift up a standard against him. [20]"The Redeemer will come to Zion, and to those who turn from transgression in Jacob," Says the LORD. [21]"As for Me," says the LORD, "this *is* My covenant with them: My Spirit who *is* upon you, and My words which I have put in your mouth, shall not depart from your mouth, nor from the mouth of your descendants, nor from the mouth of your descendants' descendants," says the LORD, "from this time and forevermore."

> **Isa 60:1-3** Arise, shine; For your light has come! And the glory of the LORD is risen upon you. [2]For behold, the darkness shall cover the

---

all nations regardless of race. For starters, he cites the fulfillment of Old Testament prophecy in the coming of the Holy Spirit upon those gathered to whom Peter preached, referencing the prophecies of Joel (cited by Peter). For more information, listen to Dr. Heiser's podcast, "What does All Israel shall be saved, mean?" The view advanced in this book does not totally or exclusively align with Dr. Heiser's perspective on this one point. Dr. Heiser colorfully asserts that Pentecost (Acts 2) "kick-started" the Kingdom.

earth, and deep darkness the people; *But the LORD will arise over you, And His glory will be seen upon you.* [3]The Gentiles shall come to your light, and kings to the brightness of your rising.

The visible, manifest glory of God plays a prominent role in the salvation of Israel. Unlike what we have typically been taught, this presence may even appear over Israel in the very last of the last days:

Ezek 38:23 Thus I will magnify Myself and sanctify Myself, and *I will be known in the eyes of many nations.* Then they shall know that I *am* the LORD."'

Ezek 39:7-8 [7]So *I will make My holy name known in the midst of My people Israel,* and I will not *let them* profane My holy name anymore. *Then the nations shall know that I am the LORD, the Holy One in Israel.* [8]Surely it is coming, and it shall be done," says the Lord GOD. "This *is* the day of which I have spoken.

Ezek 39:28-29 [18]Then they shall know that I *am* the LORD their God, who sent them into captivity among the nations, but also brought them back to their land, and left none of them captive any longer. [29]*And I will not hide My face from them anymore*; for I shall have poured out My Spirit on the house of Israel,' says the Lord GOD."

Dan 9:24-27 [24]"Seventy weeks are determined for your people and for your holy city, to finish the transgression, to make an end of sins, to make reconciliation for iniquity, to bring in everlasting righteousness, to seal up vision and prophecy, and to anoint the Most Holy. [25] Know therefore and understand, *that* from the going forth of the command to restore and build Jerusalem until Messiah the Prince, *there shall be seven weeks and sixty-two weeks;* The street shall be built again, and the wall, even in troublesome times. [26]And after the sixty-two weeks Messiah shall be cut off, but not for Himself; and the people of the prince who is to come shall destroy the city and the sanctuary. The end of it *shall be* with a flood, and till the end of the war

199

desolations are determined. *²⁷Then he shall confirm a covenant with many for one week; But in the middle of the week He shall bring an end to sacrifice and offering.* And on the wing of abominations shall be one who makes desolate, even until the consummation, which is determined, is poured out on the desolate."

Ezek 38:3 And say, 'Thus says the Lord GOD: "Behold, I *am* against you, O Gog, the prince of Rosh, Meshech, and Tubal.

The War of Gog and Magog, as it is usually labeled, has long been seen by Jewish scholars as the Messianic war. At its peak, Messiah comes to save Israel from destruction. Most Christian eschatology teachers in the twentieth century supposed that this war occurs at the outset of Daniel's Seventieth Week (quoted above, Daniel 9:24-27) or some time before (see chart following). Israel is saved, but not by Messiah's visible return (which comes later), but by God's invisible work through natural means or as a result of a third-party that intercedes on Israel's behalf. The traditional scenario speculates that Gog would be a distinct leader from the Antichrist, and specifically, would be a Russian leader.

During the past decade, however, the traditional scenario fingering Gog as a Russian leader from the land of Magog, has given way to a different point of view held by many who believe Magog is not Russia but Turkey. Gog is a Turkish "king" attempting to put the Ottoman Empire back together again. We know this outlook as the Islamic Antichrist Theory. Co-author Woodward uses the acronym, IAT, discussing the pros and cons of this perspective in his book, *Mistaken Identity: The Case Against the Islamic Antichrist. (Faith Happens Books, 2016.* The IAT also asserts that Gog and the Antichrist are *one and the same person*, and the War of Gog and Magog is just another name for the last battle, what Christians call, the Battle of Armageddon. Consequently, the IAT considers the last war *a regional war.* Russia and the United States, along with Europe, play no role in an Islamic assault against Israel. The core argument lies in disagreeing with the translation of Rosh as a tribal name, and seeing it merely as a compound adjective, the *"chief* prince." It also views Bible prophecy as "regional" only.

However, these authors believe the traditional scenario remains the preferred interpretation (#4 or #5) A preponderance of eschatology

When Gog and Magog Happens	Noted Eschatology Experts
1. **During or at the End of the Great Tribulation** (Commences the Armageddon Campaign/War and transpires for several months or years)	E.W. Bullinger David Dolan Clarence Larkin Harry Rimmer Robert Van Kampen
2. **At or After the Midpoint** (Upon the revealing of the Antichrist and his claim to divinity and global command – Gog and Magog rebel)	Hal Lindsey Noah Hutchings J. Vernon McGee J. Dwight Pentecost Jack Van Impe David Webber
3. **Just Prior to the Midpoint** (The seven-year covenant of peace breaks down. Gog attacks Israel and is defeated, clearing the way for Antichrist to rule.)	Ed Hindson Mark Hitchcock Salem Kirban Renald Showers John F. Walvoord Warren Wiersbe
4. **At the Beginning of 70th Week** (Gog rebels at the announcement of the seven-year covenant and attacks immediately. His weapons will be burned by Israel for seven years.)	J.R. Church Peter Goodgame Thomas McCall Charles R. Taylor Zola Levitt
5. **Sometime Before the 70th Week** (Israel has been gathered from the nations. Israel seeks protection and covenants with Antichrist. Gog attacks Israel and his defeat is major catastrophe for Islam, clearing the way for the Temple to be rebuilt.)	Arnold Fruchtenbaum Emil Gaverluk John Hagee Grant Jeffrey Tim LaHaye Chuck Missler Randall Price Chuck Smith

Figure 4 - *The Various Views on the Timing of the Gog/Magog War*
© S. Douglas Woodward (Credit also to Douglas Berner)

scholars agree (note the names). We reproduce a chart summarizing the views of *when* the War of Gog and Magog happens relative to other last days' events, on the preceding page. It is from Woodward's book, *The Next Great War in the Middle East* (2016). The analysis of these various views is considered carefully in Woodward's volume.

But to pick up the story once again as foretold by the traditional scenario, once Israel is safe (after God has defeated Gog and his hordes from surrounding nations), the traditional scenario suggests that this uneasy peace will supply a perfect occasion for the Antichrist to step to the foreground and covenant with Israel, promising protection them from further calamity. Some speculate that the covenant will include a provision for Israel to rebuild the Temple. For what seems a necessary pre-condition for the revealing of Antichrist is a rebuilt Jewish Temple. For the Bible seems clear that half-way through this covenant, Antichrist turns against Israel and declares war on Israel and the Jewish people – perhaps globally so. Antichrist enters the rebuilt Temple (or perhaps a partially completed Temple) announcing he is God and must be worshipped (See Daniel 9 and 2 Thessalonians 2). This occurs exactly at the mid-point of the "week." (Daniel 9:27) After 42 months of Great Tribulation (aka *The Time of Jacob's Trouble*), Messiah returns at the Battle of Armageddon, the visible Second Coming of Christ, to save Israel and usher in the Millennial Kingdom.

THE REJECTION OF ISRAEL AND THE RETURN OF THE KING

Jesus spoke of his rejection by Israel, and their acceptance of the false Messiah, the Antichrist. Jesus appears to speak of this Antichrist here:

John 5:43 I have come in My Father's name, and you do not receive Me; *if another comes in his own name, him you will receive.*

Again, after 3½ years, the Antichrist betrays the Jews, blasphemes God with unequaled, unspeakable blasphemies (Daniel 9:27). After this event, many in Israel will conclude that he is the false Messiah while the true Messiah, was indeed Jesus Christ.

Zech12:2-3 [2]"Behold, I will make Jerusalem a cup of drunkenness to all the surrounding peoples, when they lay siege against Judah and Jerusalem. [3]And it shall happen in that day that I will make Jerusalem a very heavy stone for all peoples; all who would heave it away will surely be cut in pieces, though all nations of the earth are gathered against it.

Zech 13:8-9 [8]And it shall come to pass in all the land," Says the LORD, "*That* two-thirds in it shall be cut off *and* die, but *one*-third shall be left in it: [9]I will bring the *one*-third through the fire, Will refine them as silver is refined, And test them as gold is tested. *They will call on My name, And I will answer them. I will say, 'This is My people'; And each one will say, 'The LORD is my God.'*"

Zech12:8-10 *In that day the LORD will defend the inhabitants of Jerusalem;* the one who is feeble among them in that day shall be like David, and *the house of David shall be like God, like the Angel of the LORD before them*. [9]It shall be in that day *that* I will seek to destroy all the nations that come against Jerusalem. [10]"And I will pour on the house of David and on the inhabitants of Jerusalem the Spirit of grace and supplication; *then they will look on Me whom they pierced. Yes, they will mourn for Him as one mourns for his only son, and grieve for Him as one grieves for a firstborn.*

And then, the promise of the Kingdom given to Israel shall finally come to pass. Messiah inaugurates the Davidic Kingdom, and rules Israel and the nations, after Israel is redeemed, Jeremiah, Isaiah, and Hosea prophesy:

Jer 31:31-34 [31]"Behold, the days are coming, says the LORD, when I will make a new covenant with the house of Israel and with the house of Judah – [32]not according to the covenant that I made with their fathers in the day *that* I took them by the hand to lead them out of the land of Egypt, My covenant which they broke, though I was a husband to them, says the LORD. [33]*But this is the covenant that I will make with the house of Israel after those days, says the LORD: I will put My law in their minds, and write it on their hearts; and I will be their God, and they shall be My people.* [34]No more shall every man teach his neighbor, and every man his brother, saying, 'Know the LORD,' for they all shall know Me, from the least of them to the greatest of them, says the LORD. For I will forgive their iniquity, and their sin I will remember no more."

Isa 59:19-20 [19]*So shall they fear The name of the LORD from the west, And His glory from the rising of the sun;* when the enemy comes in like a flood, The Spirit of the LORD will lift up a standard against him. [20]*"The Redeemer will come to Zion, And to those who turn from transgression in Jacob,"* Says the LORD.

Isa 10:20-21 [20]*"The Redeemer will come to Zion, And to those who turn from transgression in Jacob,"* Says the LORD. [21]"As for Me," says the LORD, "this *is* My covenant with them: My Spirit who *is* upon you, and My words which I have put in your mouth, shall not depart from your mouth, nor from the mouth of your descendants, nor from the mouth of your descendants' descendants," says the LORD, "from this time and forevermore."

Hosea 3:4-5 [4]For the children of Israel shall abide many days without king or prince, without sacrifice or sacred pillar, without ephod or teraphim. [5]*Afterward the children of Israel shall return and seek the LORD their God and David their king. They shall fear the LORD and His goodness in the latter days.*

This salvation is often interpreted as the time in which "all Israel shall be saved." In fact, this is the consensus view of most "futurists" (those that believe a significant portion of biblical prophecy is yet to be fulfilled). Consequently, the concept of the salvation of Israel in this context can be, and often is seen as, a "national" as well as individual moment of repentance when belief in the true Messiah of the Jews finally comes to pass.

THE TRIGGER POINT FOR JEWISH REPENTANCE

Remember, the Angel of the Lord was in the pillar of fire by night and cloud by day – the visible glory of God. The glory of Yahweh was evident to Israel as they dedicated the Temple of Solomon. God became an undeniable, visible presence. Therefore, it is our proposal that perhaps as early as the mid-point in Daniel's 70th Week (or not long after the Rapture of the Church), Israel will witness God's glory returned, and that this glory belongs to Yahweh, to His Messiah Jesus (and we contend, His holy ones – the glorified believers translated some time before *the Presence is revealed*). Then many Jews will turn to God, repent, and proclaim that Yahweh and Y'shua are one. Many Jews trust in the LORD and look to Him for salvation.

This occurrence does not necessarily happen separately from the provision the LORD will make for the protection of many believing Jews. Scores will flee to Jordon (ancient Edom), to the region of Mount Seir, to the city we know as Petra, where God has prepared a place for them. The flight to Petra is, in fact, one of the themes often heard from mainstream teachers of eschatology. Of course, the debate continues today regarding whether Christ's instruction to flee Jerusalem (when Jerusalem is surrounded by armies) references solely the Jewish War of 67-70 A.D., or whether it refers to a future "flight" at the beginning of the Great Tribulation. On this matter, we turn to famous Evangelical scholar and teacher Lambert Dolphin for his breakdown of what happens at this point.

DEEP DIVE: THE FLIGHT OF THE REMNANT FROM JERUSALEM AT MID-TRIBULATION

Lambert Dolphin

- ### The Flight of the Remnant

(I) pointed out that Revelation 12 is a symbolic overview of all of Israel's history. In Revelation 12:6 we read, "The woman fled into the desert to a place prepared for her by God, where she might be taken care of for 1,260 days." The woman is symbolic of Israel. 1260 days is exactly three and one half years--the standard lunar (prophetic) years of the Bible, with 360 days each. Later in the same chapter, this event is described this way:

The woman was given the two wings of a great eagle, so that she might fly to the place prepared for her in the desert, where she would be taken care of for a time, times and half a time, out of the serpent's reach. Then from his mouth the serpent spewed water like a river, to overtake the woman and sweep her away with the torrent. But the earth helped the woman by opening its mouth and swallowing the river that the dragon had spewed out of his mouth. (Revelation 12:14-16)

This also corresponds to Jesus' warning in His Olivet Discourse, a sermon by Jesus to his disciples known as the "Olivet Discourse" – so-called because Jesus was seated with his disciples on the Mt. of Olives opposite the Second Temple when he gave this sweeping outline of the future.

So when you see standing in the holy place 'the abomination that causes desolation,' spoken of through the prophet Daniel--let the reader understand--then let those who are in Judea flee to the mountains. Let no one on the roof of his house go down to take anything out of the house. Let no one in the field go back to get his cloak. How dreadful it will be in those days for pregnant women and nursing mothers! Pray that your flight will not take place in winter or on the Sabbath. For then there will be great distress, unequaled from the beginning of the world until now--and never to be equaled again. If those days had not been cut short, no one would survive, but for the sake of the elect those days will be shortened. (Matthew 24:15-22, NIV)

• **Jerusalem Surrounded by Armies**

The parallel passage in Luke 21 adds what Matthew does not tell us, that Jerusalem will be surrounded by hostile armies at the time of the end.

When you see Jerusalem being surrounded by armies, you will know that its desolation is near. Then let those who are in Judea flee to the mountains, let those in the city get out, and let those in the country not enter the city. For this is the time of punishment in fulfillment of all that has been written. How dreadful it will be in those days for pregnant women and nursing mothers! There will be great distress in the land and wrath against this people. They will fall by the sword and will be taken as prisoners to all the nations. Jerusalem will be trampled on by the Gentiles until the times of the Gentiles are fulfilled. (Luke 21:20-24, NIV)

This same scene is depicted by the Old Testament prophet Zechariah:

Behold, a day of the LORD is coming, when the spoil taken from you will be divided in the midst of you. For I will gather all the nations against Jerusalem to battle, and the city shall be taken and the houses plundered and the women ravished; half of the city shall go into exile, but the rest of the people shall not be cut off from the city. Then the LORD will go forth and fight against those nations as when he fights on a day of battle. (Zechariah 14:1-3)

Jerusalem, "trodden down by the Gentiles" again and again since the time of the Babylonian captivity is yet to suffer one last final, terrible invasion by the Gentiles.

• **Flight of Jews from Judea**

The prophet Joel foresaw this calamity.

Blow the trumpet in Zion; sound the alarm on my holy hill. Let all who live in the land tremble, for the day of the LORD is coming. It is close at hand--a day of darkness and gloom, a day of clouds and blackness. Like dawn spreading across the mountains a large and mighty army comes, such as never was of old nor ever will be in ages to come. Before them fire devours, behind them a flame blazes. Before them the land is like the garden of Eden, behind them, a desert waste--nothing escapes them. They have the appearance of horses; they gallop along like cavalry. With a noise like that of chariots they leap over the mountain tops, like a crackling fire consuming stubble, like a mighty army drawn up for battle. At the sight of them, nations are in anguish; every face turns pale. They charge like warriors; they scale walls like soldiers. They all march in line, not swerving from their course. They do not jostle each other; each marches straight ahead. They plunge through defenses without breaking ranks. They rush upon the city; they run along the wall. They climb into the houses; like thieves they enter through the windows. Before them the earth shakes, the sky trembles, the sun and moon are darkened, and the stars no longer shine. (Joel 2:1-10, NIV)

The size of this believing remnant at the mid-tribulation point is open to discussion, but for the sake of argument it would seem to be some thousands or perhaps tens of thousands of believing Jews who are warned to flee from Jerusalem.

The words and teachings of Jesus to His people Israel were not heeded when He was with them during His First Advent. We cannot expect the entire nation to take this warning to leave Jerusalem seriously even though it will no doubt be heralded again by a new generation of prophets in the end time. Those Jews in Israel who have come to know Y'shua personally during the first half of the tribulation *will* be responsive and it is to this believing remnant that Jesus makes His appeal.

Lambert Dolphin, *The Kingdom* (on-line). See http://ldolphin.org/kingdom/ch11.html.

The following passages from Zechariah set forth many events that will happen during the Time of Jacob's Trouble – however, they don't necessarily present a sequence of events in chronological order. This is the nature of Hebrew prophecy. What is important for our study is that these passages lead up to the Presence of God, the Pillar of Cloud and Fire, being revealed to Israel sometime in their day of trouble:

Zech 14:1-9 [1]Behold, the day of the LORD is coming, and your spoil will be divided in your midst. [2]For I will gather all the nations to battle against Jerusalem; The city shall be taken, the houses rifled, And the women ravished. Half of the city shall go into captivity, But the remnant of the people shall not be cut off from the city. [3]Then the LORD will go forth and fight against those nations, as He fights in the day of battle. [4]And in that day His feet will stand on the Mount of Olives, which faces Jerusalem on the east. And the Mount of Olives shall be split in two, from east to west, *making* a very large valley; Half of the mountain shall move toward the north and half of it toward the south. [5]Then you shall flee *through* My mountain valley, for the mountain valley shall reach to Azal. Yes, you shall flee as you fled from the earthquake in the days of Uzziah king of Judah. *Thus, the LORD my God will come, and all the saints with You.* [6]It shall come to pass in that day *that* there will be no light; The lights will diminish. [7]It shall be one day which is known to the LORD – neither day nor night. But at evening time it shall happen t*hat* it will be light. [8]*And in that day it shall be that living waters shall flow from Jerusalem,* Half of them toward the eastern sea and half of them toward the western sea; In both summer and winter it shall occur. [9]*And the LORD shall be King over all the earth. In that day, it shall be – "The LORD is one," And His name one.*

Zech 13:1-2 *"In that day a fountain shall be opened for the house of David and for the inhabitants of Jerusalem, for sin and for uncleanness.* [2]"It shall be in that day," says the LORD of hosts, "that

I will cut off the names of the idols from the land, and they shall no longer be remembered. I will also cause the prophets and the unclean spirit to depart from the land.

- **Living Water will flow out of Jerusalem during the Parousia (through the church, God's pipeline), and after that, through the next 1000 years.**

   Rev 14:1 Then I looked, and behold, a Lamb standing on Mount Zion, and with Him one hundred *and* forty-four thousand, having His Father's name written on their foreheads.

   Isa 30:18-21 [18]Therefore the LORD will wait, that He may be gracious to you; And therefore, He will be exalted, that He may have mercy on you. For the LORD *is* a God of justice; Blessed *are* all those who wait for Him. [19]For the people shall dwell in Zion at Jerusalem; You shall weep no more. He will be very gracious to you at the sound of y our cry; When He hears it, He will answer you. [20]And *though* the Lord gives you The bread of adversity and the water of affliction, Yet your teachers will not be moved into a corner anymore, But your eyes shall see your teachers. [21]*Your ears shall hear a word behind you, saying, "This is the way, walk in it," Whenever you turn to the right hand or whenever you turn to the left.*

- **The church will fulfill this at the Parousia, when it accompanies Israel (like the pillar of cloud and fire) through the tribulation wilderness.**

   Isa 30:26 Moreover the light of the moon will be as the light of the sun, And **the light of the sun will be sevenfold**, As the light of seven days, *In the day that the LORD binds up the bruise of His people, and heals the stroke of their wound.*

Isa 30:30 *The LORD will cause His glorious voice to be heard,* and show the descent of His arm, *With the indignation of His anger; And the flame of a devouring fire,* With scattering, tempest, and hailstones.

The LORD will be there in glory with rivers of Living Water for a thirsty Israel. In this context, we should "reread" what Paul says in the Book of Colossians:

Col 3:4 When Christ *who is* our life appears, **then you also will appear with Him in glory.**

Traditionally, many assume this is Christ's visible second coming, when he appears with the clouds of heaven to judge the enemies of Israel and to destroy the Antichrist. However, consider the possibility that this appearance occurs sometime after the Rapture, but before the coming of Christ to throw Antichrist and the False Prophet into the lake of fire. In other words, we propose that the reappearance of the pillar of fire occurs at some point during the period of Great Tribulation. Therefore, when He appears, we (the Body) will appear with Him (the Head) in glory! Might this not be the fulfillment of prophecy and the typology we have covered throughout our study? In Romans 11, we learned that "all Israel shall be saved" *through our mercy (the Gentiles who have made the Jews jealous)* and that the Deliverer comes from Zion to remove ungodliness from Jacob:

Isa 33:20-22 [20]*Look upon Zion, the city of our appointed feasts;* Your eyes will see Jerusalem, a quiet home, A tabernacle *that* will not be taken down; not one of its stakes will ever be removed, nor will any of its cords be broken. [21]But *there the majestic LORD will be for us, a place of broad rivers and streams,* in which no galley with oars will sail, nor majestic ships pass by [22](For the LORD *is* our Judge, the LORD *is* our Lawgiver, *The LORD is our King; He will save us*);

1 Th 4:15-17 [15]For this we say to you by the word of the Lord, that we who are alive *and* remain until the **coming** of the Lord will by no means precede those who are asleep. [16]For the Lord Himself will descend from heaven with a shout, with the voice of an archangel, and with the trumpet of God. And the dead in Christ will rise first. *[17]Then we who are alive and remain shall be caught up **together with them in the clouds to meet the Lord in the air**. And thus, we shall always be with the Lord.*

We know from the passage in 1 Thessalonians quoted above, that from the *Parousia* forward, we will *ever be with the Lord* (Note: *Parousia* is the word translated "coming" in verse 15). Where He is, so shall we be. If Y'shua (gleaming with God's glory) resides on Mount Zion with 144,000 in Revelation 14, the Church is this 144,000. The number is symbolic and a holy number: *144,000 is a multiple of 144, which is a multiple of 12 x 12 (not one, **but two 12s**). And 12 is the number that often signifies the people of God).*

1 Th 3:13 That He may establish your hearts blameless in holiness before our God and Father at the *coming of our Lord Jesus Christ with all His saints.*

At the end of the seven years there is no question that all will witness the brightness or outshining of His *parousia* (2 Thessalonians 2:8), "And then the lawless one will be revealed, *whom the Lord will consume with the breath of His mouth and destroy with the brightness of His coming."*

It should not be missed that Peter referenced the transfiguration of Jesus in glory on the holy mount as the "parousia" of our Lord Jesus Christ (II Pet 1:16). We recall how in the gospels, Jesus stated that some of those "standing here" will see *the coming of the Kingdom of God.* (Matthew 16:28; Luke 9:27) Peter reinforces the correlation of the coming Kingdom with the "majesty" (glory) in his second epistle:

2 Pet 1:16 For we did not follow cunningly devised fables when we made known to you the power and **coming** of our Lord Jesus Christ, but were eyewitnesses of His majesty.

Meeting the Lord "in the air" seems reasonable that it would be in the first heaven, "in the clouds" (for clouds don't exist in the second heaven). It follows that *His parousia with us in glory* will be at Zion, the holy mount (either the Temple Mount or the higher mount in Jerusalem where current tradition holds it is Mount Zion.** This is also where the armies of the antichrist gather to battle against Israel, their Messiah and His holy ones (glorified believers). While the Battle of Armageddon is thought to transpire in Jezreel, it likely pertains to the area surrounding Jerusalem, the Valley of Jehoshaphat, (aka Kidron Valley and the "Valley of Decision,") running along the east wall of Jerusalem.

> **Rev 16:16** "And they gathered them together to the place called in Hebrew, Armageddon."

> **Rev 19:19** And I saw the beast, the kings of the earth, and their armies, gathered together to make war against Him who sat on the horse and against His army.

The issue is, "What does *Armageddon* actually mean?"

OH WHERE, OH WHERE CAN ARMAGEDDON BE?

Michael Heiser makes a very strong argument that Armageddon is not in the plain of Jezreel, at Mount Megiddo, but at Jerusalem. He begins,

> In fact, *magedon* does indeed point to Jerusalem, in an especially dramatic way. *Har-magedon* is Jerusalem. The key is remembering that the term derives from Hebrew. To those who do not know Hebrew, "Megiddo" seems like an obvious explanation for *magedon* since both words have *m-*

** "Mount Zion is a hill in Jerusalem just outside the walls of the Old City. The term Mount Zion has been used in the Hebrew Bible first for the City of David and later for the Temple Mount, but its meaning has shifted and it is now used as the name of ancient Jerusalem's Western Hill. In a wider sense, the term is also used for the entire Land of Israel." See https://en.wikipedia.org/wiki/Mount_Zion.

g-d. But in Hebrew there are actually two letters that are transliterated with "g" in Greek (and English translations). [††]

Heiser then explains that these two different Hebrew letters (*gimel*) and (*ʿayin*) are both represented by "g" in English (such as "Gomorrah") and *that* is what has created the mystery of the location of Armageddon (we will not go into the details of the Hebrew here).

Dr. Heiser explains that the Hebrew phrase employed by John in the Book of Revelation is in fact a "transliteration of our mystery Hebrew term is actually *h-r-m-ʿ-d*. Since there is a reference to the first portion of this name (h-r) in Hebrew where the word *har* means mountain, it is only logical to connect the dots to see what we see. And discovering the connection is rather startling. In Hebrew, the phrase *har moʿed is found amidst the famous passage concerning Lucifer (aka Satan):*

> **Isa 14:12-15** [12] How you have fallen from heaven, morning star, son of dawn! You are cut down to the ground, conqueror of nations! [13] And you yourself said in your heart, "I will ascend to heaven; I will raise up my throne above the stars of God; and I will sit on the mountain of assembly [*har moʿed*] on the summit of Zaphon; [14] I will ascend to the high places of the clouds, I will make myself like the Most High." [15] But you are brought down to Sheol, to the depths of the pit.

Heiser then decodes this connection:

> (Earlier) we saw that the phrase *har moʿed* was one of the terms used to describe the dwelling place of Yahweh and his divine council – the cosmic mountain. The phrase obviously would have been filled with theological meaning to anyone who knew Hebrew and the Old Testament

---

[††] This passage and other quotations from Dr. Heiser in this section are from *The Unseen Realm*, op. cit., p. 370-373)

well. But why would Yahweh's dwelling place be called "the summit of Zaphon"? Didn't we just learn in the last chapter that was Baal's abode?

Heiser points out that *Yahweh desires Zaphon to be His own*, just as He did with "Mount Bashan" (Mount Hermon, the notorious landing spot for the Watchers and likely location of the Mount of Transfiguration) as declared in Psalm 68:15–16. When Jesus scaled this evil mountain with his disciples, he reclaimed the mountain, and it then became "the holy mountain" as Peter testifies in 2 Peter 1:6. But we can't stop there. Next, Heiser has us make note of the mountain talk from Psalm 48:

> **Psa 48: 1-2** ¹Yahweh is great and very worthy of praise in the city of our God, in his holy mountain. ² Beautiful in elevation, the joy of the whole earth, is *Mount Zion, in the far north* (Lit., "heights of the north"), the city of the great king.

Says Heiser:

> Psalm 48 makes a bold theological statement. It evicts Baal from his dwelling and boots his council off the property. The psalmist has Yahweh ruling the cosmos and the affairs of humanity, not Baal. Psalm 48 is a backhanded smack in the face to Baal. So is Isaiah 14.

Heiser then establishes that these passages are examples of how the biblical writers used the pagan literature of their day to exalt Yahweh and slight the lesser gods of the pagan nations. Associating Armageddon with Jerusalem literally constitutes a confrontation of biblical proportions. Jerusalem is indeed a mountain, a high place of elevation around 2,500 feet above sea level. Jerusalem has been, at least during the history of Israel, Mount Zion. It would not be surprising then that Baal and other gods (think Heiser's teaching on "the Divine Counsel" gone bad) will counterattack Yahweh's claim to Mount Zaphon as Mount Zion, by attempting to capture

Jerusalem. Heiser indicates this is exactly what happens at the fulfillment of Revelation sometime in our future:

> Armageddon is about how the unbelieving nations, empowered by the antichrist, empowered by the prince of darkness – Lord (*ba'al*) of the dead, prince Baal (*zbl ba'al*), Beelzebul – will make one last, desperate effort to defeat Jesus at the place where Yahweh holds council, Mount Zion, *Jerusalem*. Revelation and Zechariah agree.[4] Armageddon is a battle for all the supernatural and earthly marbles at Jerusalem...

While there are many different notions concerning what "All Israel shall be saved" might mean, the salvation of the people of Israel in Jerusalem and those who are "holed up" in Petra, stands undeniably as one aspect of God's salvation. In other words, the salvation Paul discusses may not be the single meaning of his teaching in Romans 11:26 that "all Israel shall be saved." Many sincere prophecy students believe that this "corporate salvation" captures the precise meaning of Romans 11:26.

However, our understanding of "all Israel will be saved" must be broader than this. Nevertheless, for all those who are "futurists" – believing that the prophecies of the Old Testament will be fulfilled in the future, specifically, in space-time – this rescue of the remnant of Israel is fundamental to sound eschatological interpretation in Pre-Millennialism. Yahweh/Y'shua saves those alive in the nation of Israel from total annihilation. Those who have died believing, they shall be resurrected to life and participate in the Kingdom. Israel will indeed be saved, and "nationally" this salvation leads to establishing the promised Messianic Kingdom in which *all* the promises of the prophets for the regathering of the House of Judah and Israel are fulfilled. The Church will somehow be in the middle of this salvation process – for we, the Body, are then fully ONE with the Head, Jesus Christ.

Says DeVern Fromke:

> You will agree, when you survey the whole of Christendom today, that there are very few believers who have light or revelation concerning the Body of Christ or the calling to full-sonship. The adversary has used every blinding, darkening, withholding and divisive effort to keep us from the light of the Church's true nature, calling and destiny. We must see that this is not an optional truth which we may look into if time permits, but it is truth central to the very purpose of realizing a temple for His glory. How many believers have gotten a glimpse of some glory they will receive, but have been blinded to living only unto His glory. Graduation from the school of sonship will be to the throne. It was this which the noble-father had in view as he awaited the "*huiothesia*" of his son. For this was the day when the father began to share his authority and government with his son. For this reason our Father has waited while the Holy Spirit "leads us into all truth." In His school room we pass through spiritual infancy and childhood, where everything is done for us, until we arrive unto a place where God's purpose can be accomplished in and through us. When we graduate from this school it will be together as a class. As one new man we will reach the time of adoption as a corporate Body.[‡]

We will address the oneness of the corporate body in the last chapter.

[‡] Fromke, DeVern F. *The Ultimate Intention* (Kindle Locations 2636-2646). Hauraki Publishing. Kindle Edition.

8: THE WOMAN ISRAEL AND HER MALE CHILD

A GENERATION LOST AND FOUND

There is a mystery hidden in Matthew's genealogy of the lineage of Jesus Christ. Some would suggest that something is missing, or that Matthew wasn't a very good math student. Skeptics would propose that we have stumbled across an error in the text, proving the Bible is not inerrant. The issue: Matthew chronicles 42 generations in the lineage of David, from the great King down to Jesus. Or so he says. But when we analyze it carefully, the tax collector who should have been especially good at accounting (and even better at counting), seems to have come up one short.

Allow us to point out the mystery in Matthew 1:1-17. To discover the enigma of the messiah's generations, Huffman eliminated the verse numbers and then numbered the generations. This allows us to do the sums easily.

Mat 1:1-17 The book of the genealogy of Jesus Christ, the Son of David, the Son of Abraham: [2]Abraham <1> begot Isaac <2>, Isaac begot Jacob <3>, and Jacob begot Judah and his brothers <4>. [3]Judah begot Perez and Zerah by Tamar <5>, Perez begot Hezron <6>, and Hezron begot Ram <7>. [4]Ram begot Amminadab <8>, Amminadab begot Nahshon <9>, and Nahshon begot Salmon <10>. [5]Salmon begot Boaz by Rahab <11>, Boaz begot Obed by Ruth <12>, Obed begot Jesse <13>, ⁶and Jesse begot David the king <14>. David the king begot Solomon by her *who had been the wife* of Uriah <15>. ⁷Solomon begot Rehoboam <16>, Rehoboam begot Abijah <17>, and Abijah begot Asa <18>. ⁸Asa begot Jehoshaphat <19>, Jehoshaphat begot Joram <20>, and Joram begot Uzziah <21>. ⁹Uzziah begot Jotham <22>, Jotham begot Ahaz <23>, and Ahaz begot Hezekiah <24>. ¹⁰Hezekiah begot Manasseh <25>, Manasseh begot Amon <26>, and Amon begot Josiah <27>. ¹¹Josiah begot Jeconiah and his brothers <28> about the time they were carried away to Babylon. ¹²And after they were brought to Babylon, Jeconiah begot Shealtiel <29>, and Shealtiel begot Zerubbabel <30>. ¹³Zerubbabel begot Abiud <31>, Abiud begot Eliakim <32>, and Eliakim begot Azor <33>. ¹⁴Azor begot Zadok <34>, Zadok begot Achim <35>;, and Achim begot Eliud <36>. ¹⁵Eliud begot Eleazar <37>, Eleazar begot Matthan <38>, and Matthan begot Jacob <39>. ¹⁶And Jacob begot Joseph <40> the husband of Mary, of whom was born Jesus <41> who is called Christ. ¹⁷So all the generations from Abraham to David *are* fourteen generations, from David until the captivity in Babylon *are* fourteen generations, and from the captivity in Babylon until the Christ *are* fourteen generations. *

Verse 17 states there are three sets of fourteen generations – 42 in all. But doing the math carefully, we count 41. The third set of 14 is missing a generation (only 13 are listed). Did Matthew make a mistake?

Let's look at Psalms 22 (generally considered an amazing prophecy of the death of the Messiah, Y'shua). We will run across the "lost generation" there. And its identification may astound you.

Psa 22:7-8 All those who see Me ridicule Me; They shoot out the lip, they shake the head, *saying,* ⁸"He trusted in the LORD, let Him rescue Him; Let Him deliver Him, since He delights in Him!"

---

* See Bill Britton, *The 42nd Generation*, Springfield, MO.

220

Psa 22:14-18 I am poured out like water, and all My bones are out of joint; My heart is like wax; It has melted within Me. [15]My strength is dried up like a potsherd, And My tongue clings to My jaws; You have brought Me to the dust of death. [16]For dogs have surrounded Me; the congregation of the wicked has enclosed Me. They pierced My hands and My feet; [17]I can count all My bones. They look *and* stare at Me. [18]They divide My garments among them, and for My clothing they cast lots.

Psa 22:27-31 [27]All the ends of the world shall remember and turn unto the LORD: and all the kindreds of the nations shall worship before thee. [28]For the kingdom is the LORD's: and he is the governor among the nations. [29]All they that be fat upon earth shall eat and worship: all they that go down to the dust shall bow before him: and none can keep alive his own soul. [30]*A **seed** shall serve him; it shall be accounted to the Lord **for a generation**.* [31]They shall come, and shall declare his righteousness unto a people that shall be born, that he hath done this.

Verses 7 and 8 record how those surrounding Christ mocked Him. Verses 14-18 are incredibly specific as they predict that those that kill the Messiah pierce His hands and His feet and He would be extraordinarily thirsty. Those around Him will stare at Him in disdain, while his clothing would be divvied up – except for his robe. And history tells us that these prophecies all came true. Recall that his robe was one piece, seamless. To tear it in two would ruin it completely. So, for this garment the soldiers cast lots. (Note: this fact became the basis of a famous film in the 1950s, *The Robe*, starring Richard Burton, the first film to be released in super wide-screen, aka CinemaScope).

If you should read Psalm 22, adjacent to the account of the crucifixion of Christ from the Gospels, it is hard to believe any objective person could fail to see the remarkable parallels between the person David describes in Psalm 22 and what the Gospels tell us about the death of Christ. David was not a prophet – but this Psalm is one of the most amazing prophecies in the Bible.

SO HOW CAN A SON WITH NO NATURAL CHILDREN – BE AN EVERLASTING FATHER?

But hidden amid these verses is one that stands out and brings us back to the lost generation – verse 30, *"A seed shall serve him; it shall be accounted to the Lord for a generation."* What does this strange statement mean? By looking closely at Isaiah 53, we see two references that talk *of this seed as a generation* or as *descendants*.   These two passages provide astonishing prophecies of the Messiah, and hint at what this strange phrase means:

> **Isa 53:8** He was taken from prison and from judgment, and *who will declare His generation?* For He was cut off from the land of the living; For the transgressions of My people He was stricken.

> **Isa 53:10** Yet it pleased the LORD to bruise Him; He has put *Him* to grief. When You make His soul an offering for sin, *He shall see His* **seed**, He shall prolong *His* days, And the pleasure of the LORD shall prosper in His hand.

"Who shall declare His generation?" or "Who will be His sons, since He died, having none." And yet, *He shall see His seed – Jesus has offspring.*

> **Isa 9:6** For unto us a Child is born, unto us a Son is given; And the government will be upon His shoulder. And His name will be called Wonderful, Counselor, Mighty God, *Everlasting Father,* Prince of Peace.

The prophet Isaiah proclaims that the Son will be called the "Everlasting Father." **Jesus will have children.** His mystical lineage becomes the 42nd generation. *The lost generation is the completed generation of Christ – the Head, Jesus, and His unified body, the Church.* We know that the Church is called the Body of Christ in many passages. (See the "Deep Dive" on The Body of Christ a few pages hence). Of course, Jesus and the Father are one.

Whether plant or animal, we begin with a seed. For plants, this is literally so. For animals, the fertilized egg is where life begins. However, the male contribution to conception is often referred to as *seed*, and descendants are also called *seed*. The word for seed, *zera'*, is used in the KJV 229 times, but translated seed, 221 times. And seed is a masculine noun which ties the word back to the human male.

Some better-known verses from Genesis (which means, *beginnings*) speak of offspring or descendants (all references here are KJV):

Gen 3:15 And I will put enmity between thee and the woman, and between *thy* **seed** and *her* **seed**; it shall bruise thy head, and thou shalt bruise his heel.

Gen 4:25 And Adam knew his wife again; and she bare a son, and called his name Seth: For God, *said she*, hath appointed me another **seed** instead of Abel, whom Cain slew.

Gen 9:9 And I, behold, I establish my covenant with you, and with your **seed** after you [Noah]

Gen 12:7 And the LORD appeared unto Abram, and said, "Unto thy **seed** will I give this land:" and there builded he an altar unto the LORD, who appeared unto him. [Abraham]

Gen 46:6 And they took their cattle, and their goods, which they had gotten in the land of Canaan, and came into Egypt, Jacob, and all his **seed** with him: [Jacob aka Israel]

And the Word tells us that Christ has seed. God is reproduced in us when we are born again – Jesus is reproduced when He is formed in us. *The seed that serves Jesus in the last days will be His children. We are Christ's seed.* And His seed wars against the seed of the Nachash, the "shining one" commonly referred to as serpent (Satan – Genesis 3:15). So, when we speak of seed in the Bible, we are typically dealing with lineage, ancestry, genealogy, or "the family tree." The New Testament picks up this same usage with the following scriptures (all references here are KJV). Note how these New Testament verses refer to those in Genesis:

Jhn 7:42 Hath not the scripture said, That Christ cometh of the *seed* of David, and out of the town of Bethlehem, where David was?

Rom 1:3 Concerning his Son Jesus Christ our Lord, which was made of the *seed* of David according to the flesh;

Gal 3:16 Now to Abraham and his seed were the promises made. He saith not, "And to *seeds*, as of many;" but as of one, "And to thy *seed*, which is Christ."

2 Tim 2:8 Remember that Jesus Christ of the seed of David was raised from the dead according to my gospel:

Rev 12:17 And the dragon was wroth with the woman, and went to make war with the *remnant* of her *seed*, which keep *the command-ments of God,* and have the *testimony of Jesus Christ.*

DEEP DIVE: THE BODY OF CHRIST

There is a wealth of passages that use the metaphor, the Body of Christ. These are descriptive and definitive of the two truths that Christ dwells in each one of us individually; but also *among us* - The Church – *corporately.* "For where two or three are gathered together in my name, there am I in the midst of them." (Matthew 18:20, KJV). It is important, as we will discuss later in more depth, that we emphasize both the inward dwelling within the individual believer of Christ, and the outward dwelling (outward to the individual but within) the Church itself.

First, in reviewing the following verses, we notice that the metaphor of the Body of Christ was the teaching of Paul, hinted at by Jesus, but the theological basis upon which Paul built all his churches. *Christ dwells in you; Christ dwells in the Body. And that Body is one.*

1 Cor 12:13 For by one Spirit are we all baptized into one body, whether we be Jews or Gentiles, whether we be bond or free; and have been all made to drink into one Spirit.

1 Cor 12:27 Now ye are the body of Christ, and members in particular.

I Cor 12:12 For as the body is one, and hath many members, and all the members of that one body, being many, are one body: so also is Christ.

And the Body has Christ as its head, *and it is to be unified.* In Christ, there is no distinction any longer between Jew and Gentile. Indeed, Paul emphasizes how important the metaphor of the Body is, indicating that from a spiritual perspective, we are one. As the Christian folk song says, "We are one in the Spirit, we are one with the Lord. And we pray that our unity will one day be restored."

Col 1:18 And he is the head of the body, the church: who is the beginning, the firstborn from the dead; that in all things he might have the preeminence.

Rom 12:4-5 For as we have many members in one body, and all members have not the same office: So we, being many, are one body in Christ, and every one members one of another.

Eph 1:22 And hath put all things under his feet, and gave him to be the head over all things to the church.

Eph 4:4 There is one body, and one Spirit, even as ye are called in one hope of your calling.

Eph 5:23 For the husband is the head of the wife, even as Christ is the head of the church: and he is the saviour of the body.

Eph 2:19-22 Now therefore ye are no more strangers and foreigners, but fellow citizens with the saints, and of the household of God; And are built upon the foundation of the apostles and prophets, Jesus Christ himself being the chief corner stone; In whom all the building fitly framed together groweth unto an holy temple in the Lord: In whom ye also are builded together for an habitation of God through the Spirit.

Eph 5:29-30 For no man ever yet hated his own flesh; but nourisheth and cherisheth it, even as the Lord the church: For we are members of his body, of his flesh, and of his bones.

Col 2:19 And not holding the Head, from which all the body by joints and bands having nourishment ministered, and knit together, increaseth with the increase of God.

And yet, while there is to be unity, we are not all to do the same things. Within the Church, there is diversity – there are different duties to be performed and personal gifts with which we bless one another:

Rom 12:6-8 Having then gifts differing according to the grace that is given to us, whether prophecy, let us prophesy according to the proportion of faith; Or ministry, let us wait on our ministering: or he that teacheth, on teaching; Or he that exhorteth, on exhortation: he that giveth, let him do it with simplicity; he that ruleth, with diligence; he that sheweth mercy, with cheerfulness.

1 Cor 12:13-21 For by one Spirit are we all baptized into one body, whether we be Jews or Gentiles, whether we be bond or free; and have been all made to drink into one Spirit. For the body is not one member, but many. If the foot shall say, Because I am not the hand, I am not of the body; is it therefore not of the body? And if the ear shall say, Because I am not the eye, I am not of the body; is it therefore not of the body? If the whole body were an eye, where were the hearing? If the whole were hearing, where were the smelling? But now hath God set the members every one of them in the body, as it hath pleased him. And if they were all one member, where were the body? But now are they many members, yet but one body

Eph 4:15-16 But speaking the truth in love, may grow up into him in all things, which is the head, even Christ: From whom the whole body fitly joined together and compacted by that which every joint supplieth, according to the effectual working in the measure of every part, maketh increase of the body unto the edifying of itself in love.

Eph 4:11-13 And he gave some, apostles; and some, prophets; and some, evangelists; and some, pastors and teachers; For the perfecting of the saints, for the work of the ministry, for the edifying of the body of Christ: Till we all come in the unity of the faith, and of the knowledge of the Son of God, unto a perfect man, unto the measure of the stature of the fulness of Christ.

Pastor Tony Evans makes an important observation in this comment:

> Christ's body, the church, is not an organization, but an *organism*. We can create a robot and have organization. The parts connect to each other so that it works. But the problem with the robot is that it has no life. It is organizationally connected, but it's not a living being. A human body, in contrast, has organization that makes it function, but it also is an organism. It's a living, breathing life. *Connection in the body is necessary for function and for life, and it is essential if we are to leave a lasting impact and impression on our society and in our world.*

Retrieved May 21, 2017, http://tonyevans.org/the-body-of-christ/.

THE SEEDS OF TWO BIRTHS

When we are born of the Spirit and born into the family of God – we are His children, and He is our Father. We are brethren with our Lord Jesus Christ (Hebrews 2:11-12).

Rom 8:15-17 [15]For you did not receive the spirit of bondage again to fear, but you received the Spirit of adoption by whom we cry out, "Abba, Father." [16]The Spirit Himself bears witness with our spirit that we are children of God, [17]and if children, then heirs – heirs of God and joint heirs with Christ, if indeed we suffer with *Him*, that we may also be glorified together.

Heb 2:11-12 [11]For both He who sanctifies and those who are being sanctified *are* all of one, for which reason He is not ashamed to call them brethren, [12]saying: *"I will declare Your name to My brethren; In the midst of the assembly I will sing praise to You."*

John 12:24 Most assuredly, I say to you, unless a grain of wheat falls into the ground and dies, it remains alone; but if it dies, it produces much grain.

When Jesus died as the grain of wheat to bring forth fruit, He became the parent of that fruit. In this way, *Jesus is the Everlasting Father*, and we are *His seed*, or *His generation*. We see that to become adopted as sons of God and to be become perfect reproductions of the grain of wheat, we must mature:

1 John 3:1-2 [1]Behold what manner of love the Father has bestowed on us, that we should be called children of God! Therefore the world does not know us, because it did not know Him. [2]Beloved, now we are children of God; and it has not yet been revealed what we shall be, but we know that *when He is revealed, we shall be like Him, for we shall see Him as He is.*

The Father wants this fruit to mature and grow into the likeness of His son:

Eph 1:4-5 [4]Just as He chose us in Him before the foundation of the world, that we should be holy and without blame before Him in love, [5]having predestined us *to adoption as sons* by Jesus Christ to Himself, according to the good pleasure of His will,

Heb 2:13 And again: *"I will put My trust in Him."* And again: *"Here am I and the children whom God has given Me."*

Hebrews 2:13 references Isaiah 8:18:

Isa 8:18 Here am I *and the children whom the LORD has given me! We are for signs and wonders in Israel* from the LORD of hosts, who dwells in Mount Zion.

The writer of Hebrews reveals that Isaiah speaks of Jesus and His children. *We, along with Jesus, are meant for* **signs and wonders** *in Israel, when He dwells in Mount Zion.* Again, this passage causes us to conclude that we will be with Jesus on Mount Zion, manifesting the glory of God to Israel at His Parousia!

Dan 11:32 Those who do wickedly against the covenant he shall corrupt with flattery; but *the people who know their God shall be strong, and carry out great exploits.*

That's us! If we follow on to know the Lord, we will be strong, and do exploits, even during the time of Jacob's Trouble.

CHRIST IN YOU, THE HOPE OF GLORY

In the prior section devoted to Jacob's Ladder, we saw that the Body of Christ would minister God's presence at the place where Jacob rested. Also, we concluded that this "ladder climbing" referred to the Parousia. When I (Huffman) think of the word "Christ," I think of Jesus – but when I think of the word "Messiah," I think of the Anointed One, the Savior of the Jews. Both words mean "Anointed One," but, "Messiah" helps me see it as more than just a name. Many verses take on new significance when I substitute "Messiah" for "Christ." Consider 1 Cor 12:12.

1 Cor 12:12 For as the body is one and has many members, but *all the members of that one body*, being many, *are one body*, so also *is* Christ.

Gal 4:19 My little children, for whom I labor in birth again until *Christ is formed in you.*

Col 1:27 To them God willed to make known what are the riches of the glory of this mystery among the Gentiles: which is *Christ in you, the hope of glory.*

The Messiah in us is – the hope of glory. But let's consider all these "ins and outs."

- We are *in Christ* from the standpoint of salvation: *justification, sanctification, and glorification.*
- Christ is *in us*, through the Spirit who dwells in us. We are His seed.
- And we are *in the Body of Christ*, members of it, such that we are to be a *living organism*, so connected to one another are we to be.

Now, Jesus Christ is the Messiah of Israel, *but we are part of His Body. Consequently, it would be wrong to suppose that we have no relationship toward Israel, nor any role to play in its salvation, its "grafting back in."* And that role is more than just making Jews jealous!

As the Body of the Messiah, we will play an important role in the deliverance of Israel.

THE *CHURCH* WILL RULE WITH A ROD OF IRON?

Now let's jump to the strange dream of Joseph that irritated both of his parents upon his recounting. In this dream, the implications are clear by their reaction: one day, he would obtain a status greater than they. They would bow down to him. He would be a ruler over the Tribe of Israel during an "interim" period while they sojourned in Egypt:

Gen 37:9-10 Then he dreamed still another dream and told it to his brothers, and said, "Look, I have dreamed another dream. And this time, the sun, the moon, and the eleven stars bowed down to me." [10]So he told *it* to his father and his brothers; and his father rebuked him and said to him, "What *is* this dream that you have dreamed? Shall your mother and I and your brothers indeed come to bow down to the earth before you?"

Of course, that is exactly what happened. For the sake of calling out Israel as a nation, separating it from the other nations enslaved by sin and corrupted by the "elohim" (little "g" gods) who ruled them – the 70 corrupted members of the Divine Council – Joseph would be carried away to Egypt as a slave. Later, his family would follow him there to avoid the killing drought in "Canaan Land." And there is no need to recite the details for we remember the rest of the story: slavery for Israel in Egypt, Moses arises as the deliverer, the Exodus of the children of Israel, and Joshua leads Israel in taking the promised land from the giants who resided there. Israel would enjoy glory and then end up in shame. Eventually, virtually all of Israel would be dispersed after it failed to receive its Messiah.

While Israel has been scattered, in our day she has also been regathered, not in belief, but in unbelief. Nevertheless, one day Israel will be saved in such a way that it, along with believers from the Church translated in the Rapture, shall rule the nations with its Messiah.

A favorite among classic dispensational teachers is Arthur Pink (1885 – 1952). Pink provides this excellent summary of the biblical truth that *Israel shall be the "head of the nations" during the Davidic Kingdom*, aka the Messianic King, during the next age, the time we know as The Millennium:

> It is a ground for thanksgiving that during the last three or four generations the people of God have given considerable attention to the prophecies of Scripture which treat of the future of Israel. The old method of "spiritualizing" these predictions, and making them apply to the Church of the present dispensation, has been discarded by the great

231

majority of Pre-Millennarians. With a steadily increasing number of Bible students it is now a settled question that Israel, as a nation, shall be saved (Rom. 11:26), and that the promises of God to the fathers will be literally fulfilled under the Messianic reign of the Lord Jesus (Rom. 9:4). Jerusalem, which for so many centuries has been a by-word in the earth, will then be known as "the city of the great King" (Matt. 5:35). His throne shall be established there, and it shall be the gathering point for all nations (Zech. 8:23; 14:16-21). Then shall the despised descendants of Jacob be "the head" of the nations, and no longer the tail (Deut. 28:13); then shall the people of Jehovah's ancient choice be the center of His earthly government; then shall the Fig Tree, so long barren, "blossom and bud, and fill the face of the world with fruit" (Isa. 27:6).[†]

The promise to be rulers is no small thing. Stunningly, like Joseph, there is a definite sense in which rulership will not just be characteristic of Israel in the Millennium – it being the "head of the nations" – but equally of the Church, the Body of Christ, as well. We read:

> **Rev 2:26-29** [26]And he who overcomes, and keeps My works until the end, *to him I will give power over the nations –* [27]*'He shall rule them with a rod of iron; They shall be dashed to pieces like the potter's vessels'* – as I also have received from My Father; [28]and I will give him the morning star. [29]"He who has an ear, let him hear what the Spirit says to the churches."'

This promise catches us unaware. We think of Jesus ruling the nations with a rod of iron. But the Church? Yes. Revelation states plainly: "To him who overcomes, to that person (and collectively to those doing so as part of the Church), I will give power over the nations." In other words, prophecy links the Head of the Church and the Body of the Church together as rulers

---

[†] Arthur Pink, *The Antichrist*. Retrieved on May 21, 2017, from http://www.bible believers.com /Pink/antichrist19.htm

over the nations. This amounts to yet another astounding promise for those who believe in Jesus Christ, to those who partake of the divine nature, and who dwell with Him for "time and eternity" after the Rapture (or resurrection).

And another witness to the same gracious gift is found when assembling the following three verses (all KJV). They parallel the truth that we will share in Christ's glory, as they convey we are to be seated with Christ on His throne:

Heb 8:1 Now of the things which we have spoken this is the sum: We have such an high priest, **who is set on the right hand of the throne of the Majesty** in the heavens.

Heb 12:2 Looking unto Jesus the author and finisher of our faith; who for the joy that was set before him endured the cross, despising the shame, and **is set down at the right hand of the throne of God**.

Rev 3:21 To him that overcometh *will I grant to sit with me in my throne*, even as I also overcame, and **am set down with my Father in his throne.**

THE SIGN IN THE HEAVENS – COULD THE CHURCH BE THERE?

However, there are other magnificent discoveries hiding in the book of Revelation about which the reader may not be aware.

Rev 12:1-5 ¹Now *a great sign appeared in heaven*: a woman clothed with the sun, with the moon under her feet, and on her head a garland of twelve stars. ²Then being with child, she cried out in labor and in pain to give birth. ³*And another sign appeared in heaven*: behold, a great, fiery red dragon having seven heads and ten horns, and seven diadems on his heads. ⁴His tail drew a third of the stars of heaven and threw them to the earth. And the dragon stood before the woman who was ready to give birth, to devour her Child as soon as it was born. ⁵She bore a male Child who was to rule all nations with a rod of iron. And her Child was caught up to God and His throne.

Almost all scholars would equate the woman with Israel. But who is *the male child*? That question generates controversy among scholars. Is it Jesus? Or is it the Church? It remains an important question to ask.

The frequent view is that the male child is Christ. Certainly, that would seem to be apparent. Jesus was born of Israel and then resurrected and ascended unto the Throne of God. *But might the passage have a double fulfillment?* Dr. Heiser asserts that, from his research, Revelation 12 constitutes an *astral* prophecy (astral in the sense of a *sign in the stars*, being astronomical, but not pertaining to the occult as in astral projection). He believes it foretold the birth and resurrection of Jesus. We would agree that the sign of Revelation 12 was present at the birth of Jesus.[‡] According to Heiser (and Ernest Martin in his book, *The Star of Bethlehem: The Star that Astonished the World*), this sign occurred on September 11, 3 B.C. One commentator summarizes the remarkable information in these words:

> While Dr. Martin's date for the birth of Yeshua (Jesus) agrees exactly with what is in the Bible code, can we infer that the birth of Yeshua took place exactly between 6:15 to 7:49 pm on September 11, 3 BC? I believe that we can accept the time of birth as being 7 pm plus or minus an hour based on the exact sign in the sky.
>
> What about the death of Herod as it relates to all this? After all, many scholars have said that king Herod died in 4 BC or 5 BC? Dr. Ernest L. Martin in his book, laboriously goes through each possibility for the death of king Herod and with a number of other scholars, proves that Herod died a couple of weeks after the total lunar eclipse of January 10, 1 BC. He pinpoints the date of death of Herod to about January 29, 1 BC plus or minus a couple of days[§]

[‡] Heiser, Michael, "September 11: Happy Birthday to Jesus". See http://drmsh.com/september-11-happy-birthday-to-jesus/.

[§] Roy A Reinhold, "Other Scholarship Proving the Exact Date of the Birth of Yeshua." March 28, 2002, Retrieved from http://ad2004.com/prophecytruths /Articles/Yeshua/yeshuabirth5.html.

However, we believe that Revelation 12:1-5, points to a *double fulfillment.* To be more specific, the signs in the heavens can refer to both the birth and resurrection (glorification) of Jesus, the messiah, as the "already,", while the "not yet" is the soon to be accomplished glorification of the Body of Christ. The first fulfillment serves as the typology for the future realization of the second fulfillment. As you will see below, there are many classic commentaries that agree with the idea of a double fulfillment and that the second pertains to the birth of a child that is yet future, i.e., the Church. In this sense, Acts Chapter 2 (the coming of the Holy Spirit) can be viewed as the "conception" and the 2,000 years "in between" as incubation, the final portion of that era as Labor pains (an analogy that even Jesus used), with the birth occurring at the second fulfillment of Revelation 12:1-5.

For those who believe that the Church has a distinctive role, separate and apart from Israel, the male child also comprises the Body of Christ, the Church. In verse 5, the Child is "caught up" to heaven. The word used in Greek for this event is *harpazo,* "snatching up." It is the very same word used in the "rapture verses" of Paul (1 Corinthians 15, 1 Thessalonians 4). Could this image in Revelation 12 also be a reference to the Body of Christ and its rapture? Remember Luke's account of Jesus ascension in Acts 1. Recall that Jesus *wasn't really snatched up.* He ascended as His disciples watched, in a cloud until disappearing out of their sight.

From the *Faith Life Study Bible:* "In Revelation, the number 12 is associated with the 12 tribes of Israel and also the 12 apostles as the Church's foundation (Rev 21:14). Thus, the woman could symbolize the faithful people of God. The Messiah is born from God's people, Israel, and His work continues with God's people, the Church."

Barnes' Notes on the Bible, on Revelation 12:5, voices the same opinion:

And she brought forth a man child - Representing, according to the view above taken, the church in its increase and prosperity - as if a child were born that was to rule over all nations. See the notes on Revelation 12:2. **Who was to rule all nations** - That is, according to this view, the church thus represented was destined to reign in all the earth, or all the earth was to become subject to its laws. Compare the notes on Daniel 7:13-14.[**]

Gill's Exposition of the Entire Bible, regarding Revelation 12:5 agrees. The **male child** is the "mystical Christ", i.e., "his members, who are called by his name." Reading this statement in context:

And she brought forth a man child.... Not Christ, literally and personally considered, or Christ in his human nature, as made of a woman, and born of a virgin, which was a fact that had been years ago; but *Christ mystically, or Christ in his members, who are called by his name, because he is formed in them, and they are the seed of the woman, the church.*[††]

Another source who proposes identifying the male child with the Church is scholar Michael J. Svigel. We include more of his commentary because his is more current. We draw from his paper, *The Apocalypse of John and the Rapture of the Church: A Reevaluation.* In his study, Svigel writes:

Within the smaller unit of chapter 12 itself, the woman and dragon are first introduced and the events of 12:1-6 appear to follow a general chronological order. The war in heaven of 12:7-12 appears to be an expansion of the fate of the dragon upon the catching up of the male child to heaven. Then, 12:3-18 recapitulates the events after the catching up of the male child, filling in details regarding the pursuit of the woman and the preservation initially described in 12:6 (pp. 27-28).

[**] Retrieved from http://biblehub.com/commentaries/revelation/12-5.htm.

[††] Ibid.

Svigel goes on to argue that Rev 12:5 refers the reader to Isaiah 66:7:

> Thus, John's use of "poor grammar" in Revelation 12:5 is intended to point the reader back to the images of Isaiah 66:7, which reads: "Before she travailed, she brought forth; before her pain came, she gave birth to a boy." The next verse demonstrates that the woman and child are not intended to represent individuals, but rather assemblies: "Who has heard such a thing? Who has seen such things? Can a land be born in one day? Can a nation be brought forth all at once? As soon as Zion travailed, she also brought forth her sons." The passage switches from the singular "son" to the plural "sons," and describes the birth of "a land" and "a nation" (p. 29).

On the identity of the Male Child, Svigel says:

> **"The Male Child**. The crux of the argument of this paper lies with the identification of the male child born to the woman, Israel. The following section will examine this identification in greater depth. In preview, it will be argued that the male child born to the woman has, like the dragon, and possibly the woman, a double referent, one an individual, Jesus Christ, the other a corporate body, the Church. Five main arguments for this identification will be given: 1) the consistency in symbolism in Revelation 12; 2) the significance of the allusion to Isaiah 66:7-8; 3) the lexical issues involving the snatching up of the male child; 4) the identification of the male child as the one who will "rule over all the nations with an iron rod;" and 5) the absence of the death and resurrection of the Messiah argues for the identification of the male child with the Church. (p.30)

Svigel's paper continues to expand those five points to insist that the **male child** *is the raptured body of Christ along with its head, Jesus Christ.* The paper is well worth reading, as he goes through the major views of the Rapture and looks at when it may occur in the timeline of Revelation.[‡‡]

[‡‡] Svigel, Michael J., "The Apocalypse of John and the Rapture of the Church: A Reevaluation." *Trinity Journal 22* (2001). 23-74. See https://bible.org/article/apocalypse-john-and-rapture-church-reevaluation.

Thus, we conclude that the man-child the woman (Israel) brings forth is one who overcomes, and who believes (many so believe) – as written to the Seven churches in Revelation, chapters 2 and 3). We know that God the Father, brought forth one Son by Israel (in Mary) but that He must be joined to *many mature sons* to be one Body for the Messiah, Jesus. And when He comes in glory with them, they will rule and reign with Him.

> **Rev 20:4** And I saw thrones, and they sat on them, and judgment was committed to them. Then I saw the souls of those who had been beheaded for their witness to Jesus and for the word of God, who had not worshiped the beast or his image, and had not received *his* mark on their foreheads or on their hands. And they lived and *reigned with Christ for a thousand years*.

To expand further: the "man-child," in the Greek says, "male son," or *vios* (meaning a *mature son*, ready to rule the Father's house).

> **Rev 12:6** Then the woman fled into the wilderness, where she has a place prepared by God, that **they** *should feed her there* one thousand two hundred and sixty days.

"That **they** should feed her there." Could the "they" be members of the Body of Christ? Might they participate in the care of those Jews that flee to the wilderness? Might the "man-child" nourish the woman in the wilderness for 3½ years? We know that this period lasts for a 3½ years. And, likewise, it is agreed that a biblical, prophetic year is 360 days. Therefore, 1260 days = 3½ x 360 days, or 3½ years. There is no question that this period of safekeeping transpires during the same period that the Antichrist seeks to destroy Jews and those who have become believers during the Great Tribulation. But, consider yet one more scripture which seems to reinforce that those who have fled will be comforted by the LORD. Might he minister through His body to those living in Petra, awaiting the return of the Messiah to conquer the Antichrist and bring an end to his rule of terror and the persecution and killing of those who have been martyred for the cause of Christ?

Hosea 2:14 "Therefore, behold, I will allure her, *will bring her into the wilderness, and speak comfort to her.*

We believe that this possibility is worthy of serious consideration. We think it may indeed be a ministry of the already glorified saints. They will care for the mortal Israelis in the wilderness of Edom. The "male child" will manifest His glory to the remnant in Petra; that is, those mature sons of God, the Body of the Messiah. God in His lovingkindness and providence, provides a place for the woman and children to serve her.

THE SIGN OF THE SON OF MAN

Just as the Angel of God (the pre-incarnation second person of the Trinity, The WORD, Jesus Christ) was in the cloud of glory over the tabernacle in the wilderness to lead Israel (Exodus 14:19, Hebrews 1:3), *the Body of the Messiah, the Church, will appear with their Lord in the cloud of glory over mount Zion, leading Israel.* While many propose differing candidates for the Sign of the Son of Man, we put forth the possibility that the sign of *the Glory of Christ and His Body* is the Sign of the Son of Man. It would occur at such time that all may witness the glorious presence of the God of Abraham, Isaac and Jacob. However, we believe the world *will still not repent.* The "earth dwellers" will still deny the truth of God. Many passages speak of God appearing over Zion. If Jesus Christ appears over Zion in glory, *the Body of Christ will be there too.*

Isa 4:1-6 And in that day seven women shall take hold of one man, saying, "We will eat our own food and wear our own apparel; Only let us be called by your name, to take away our reproach." [2]In that *day the Branch of the LORD shall be beautiful and glorious;* And the fruit of the earth *shall be* excellent and appealing For those of Israel

239

who have escaped. ³And it shall come to pass that *he who is* left in Zion and remains in Jerusalem will be called holy – everyone who is recorded among the living in Jerusalem. ⁴When the Lord has washed away the filth of the daughters of Zion, and purged the blood of Jerusalem from her midst, by the spirit of judgment and by the spirit of burning, ⁵*then the LORD will create above every dwelling place of Mount Zion, and above her assemblies,* **a cloud and smoke by day and the shining of a flaming fire by night**. *For over all the glory there will be a covering.* ⁶And there will be a tabernacle for shade in the daytime from the heat, for a place of refuge, and for a shelter from storm and rain.

Mat 24:30 Then the *sign of the Son of Man will appear in heaven,* and then all the tribes of the earth will mourn, and they will see the *Son of Man coming on the clouds of heaven with power and great glory.*

Heb 1:3 Who being t*he brightness of His glory and the express image of His person,* and upholding all things by the word of His power, when He had by Himself purged our sins, sat down at the right hand *of the Majesty on high.*

Exo 14:19 *And the Angel of God, who went before the camp of Israel, moved and went behind them; and the pillar of cloud went from before them and stood behind them.*

Chapter 14 of the book of Revelation testifies of 144,000 that are not defiled, who follow the Lamb wherever He goes. They are redeemed from among men, being firstfruits to God and to the Lamb. They are before the throne of God. They are without fault before God because their sins have been washed away by the blood of the Lamb. Are these the 144,000 "Jewish witnesses?" from Revelation 7:4? *No, this is the Church.* The number should not be taken literally, but metaphorically, being a multiple of 12. There were 12 tribes and there were 12 apostles. 12 x 12 = 144,000. These are hints of the ultimate unity of all the redeemed; that is, the Church and Israel.

Rev 14:1-5 [1]Then I looked, and behold, a Lamb standing on Mount Zion, and with Him one hundred *and* forty-four thousand, having His Father's name written on their foreheads. [2]And I heard a voice from heaven, like the voice of many waters, and like the voice of loud thunder. And I heard the sound of harpists playing their harps. [3]They sang as it were a new song before the throne, before the four living creatures, and the elders; and *no one could learn that song except the hundred and forty-four thousand who were redeemed from the earth.* [4]These are the ones who were not defiled with women, for they are virgins. *These are the ones who follow the Lamb wherever He goes.* These were redeemed from *among* men, *being* firstfruits to God and to the Lamb. [5]And in their mouth was found no deceit, for they are without fault before the throne of God.

Zec 12:8-10 [8]In that day the LORD will defend the inhabitants of Jerusalem; the one who is feeble among them in that day shall be like David, and the house of David *shall be* like God, *like the Angel of the LORD before them.* [9]It shall be in that day *that* I will seek to destroy all the nations that come against Jerusalem. [10]"And I will pour on the house of David and on the inhabitants of Jerusalem the Spirit of grace and supplication; then they will look on Me whom they pierced. Yes, they will mourn for Him as one mourns for *his* only *son,* and grieve for Him as one grieves for a firstborn.

Zec 14:3-5 [3]Then the LORD will go forth and fight against those nations, As He fights in the day of battle.[4] And in that day His feet will stand on the Mount of Olives, which faces Jerusalem on the east. And the Mount of Olives shall be split in two, from east to west, *making* a very large valley; Half of the mountain shall move toward the north and half of it toward the south. [5]Then you shall flee *through* My mountain valley, For the mountain valley shall reach to Azal. Yes, you shall flee as you fled from the earthquake in the days of Uzziah king of Judah. *Thus, the LORD my God will come, and* **all the saints with You**.

Isa 26:15-21 [15]You have increased the nation, O LORD, you have increased the nation; You are glorified; You have expanded all the borders of the land. [16]LORD, in trouble they have visited You, they poured out a prayer *when* Your chastening *was* upon them. [17]*As a woman with child Is in pain and cries out in her pangs, when she draws near the time of her delivery*, so have we been in Your sight, O LORD. [18]We have been with child, we have been in pain; We have, as it were, brought forth wind; We have not accomplished any deliverance in the earth, nor have the inhabitants of the world fallen. [19]Your dead shall live; *Together with* my *dead body they shall arise.* Awake and sing, you who dwell in dust; For your dew *is like* the dew of herbs, And the earth shall cast out the dead. [20]*Come, my people, enter your chambers, and shut your doors behind you; Hide yourself, as it were, for a little moment, until the indignation is past.* [21]For behold, *the LORD comes out of His place to punish the inhabitants of the earth for their iniquity;* The earth will also disclose her blood, and will no more cover her slain.

Here we see the wording of Isaiah referenced in the words of John, written almost 800 years later. Revelation 12:2-4 and 12:7-9 reflect Isaiah 26:15-21. Isaiah 26:19 speaks of the resurrection. But notice verse 20 speaks of the Parousia. It is one of the most notable Old Testament hints of the Rapture for that portion of God's people, the Church – the firstfruits of the resurrection – who enter into *chambers* (in Hebrew, *cheder* pronounced kheh'der), the innermost room such as bedchamber, into which the groom and the bride retire). They remain in their chambers until the *indignation* is past. Recall that the "indignation" comprises another term for *Jacob's Trouble* –3½ year *Great Tribulation*, or *Day of the Lord*. Therefore, John 14:2-3 appears to confirm Isaiah's prophecy. These are the very words of Christ.

John 14:2-3 [2]In My Father's house are many mansions (Greek, *monē*, pronounced monay); if *it were* not *so,* I would have told you. I go to prepare a place for you. [3]And if I go and prepare a place for you, I will come again and receive you to Myself; that where I am, *there* you may be also.

Monē conveys *dwelling places,* or *chambers* – rooms in God's house (we are God's house). When we encountered this word earlier in our study, we emphasized that there shall be unity in the Body of Christ, that we not think in terms of "apartments." The word can mean this, but it would be inconsistent to underscore with a heavy line that these chambers (plural) suggest some differentiation, i.e., perhaps there are differing degrees of glory for each believer. Nonetheless, *not all stars shine with equal brilliance.*

Dan 12:2-3 [2]And many of those who sleep in the dust of the earth shall awake, Some to everlasting life, Some to shame *and* everlasting contempt. [3]Those who are wise shall shine Like the brightness of the firmament, and those who turn many to righteousness Like the stars forever and ever.

1 Cor 15:39-43 [39]All flesh *is* not the same flesh, but *there is* one *kind of* flesh of men, another flesh of animals, another of fish, *and* another of birds. [40]*There are* also celestial bodies and terrestrial bodies; but the glory of the celestial *is* one, and the *glory* of the terrestrial *is* another. [41]*There is one glory of the sun, another glory of the moon, and another glory of the stars;* **for one star differs from another star in glory.** [42]So also *is* the resurrection of the dead. *The body* is sown in corruption, it is raised in incorruption. [43]It is sown in dishonor, *it is raised in glory.* It is sown in weakness, *it is raised in power.*

1 Pet 5:4 And when the Chief Shepherd appears, *you will receive the crown of glory that does not fade away.*

Isa 28:5 In that day *the LORD of hosts will be for a crown of glory* and a diadem of beauty *to the remnant of His people.*

243

While there are many proposals for "the sign of the Son of Man," *we believe that the pillar of cloud by day and the fire by night may be such a sign.*[§§] More simply, it may be the brilliance of glory of Christ and His Body, The Church glorified with Christ Jesus. It may be the sign of the Son of Man, appearing at or after the Parousia, during the final 3½ years. Appearing over Zion, the glory of the LORD shall be as apparent as it was to those who gathered for the dedication of Solomon's Temple. To assert otherwise because this is too strange and unusual to be true – would be unbelief. Regardless of whether this glory of Zion happens in this way, the emphasis remains: The Church "follows the Lamb wherever He goes."

THE DAY OF ATONEMENT

Recalling the Day of Atonement, the second part of the Feast of Tabernacles, we remember that the sins of Israel were taken away or imputed to the scapegoat. As we discussed, this feast has not been fulfilled in the Church. However, just as the other feasts exemplified events fulfilled in the life of Christ and in His Body, this one will be fulfilled too.

The period between the Blowing of Trumpets and the Day of Atonement was 10 days. *Ten is the number of trial or testing in the Bible.* This is symbolic for the testing occurring in the body of Christ during the fulfillment of these feast-days. (1) The ten commandments were the

---

[§§] Friend Scott Clarke has developed wonderful research and brilliant graphics to illustrate his proposal that the sign of Revelation 12 lies in the stars, with a most usual alignment of the constellation Virgo and several of the planets, comprising a "crown" of 12 stars. This alignment occurs on Rosh Hashanah, September 23, 2017. While Scott is careful to not "set a date," he cites many reasons why this event may be the "snatching away" of the Church. We will know soon enough. As this book is published in June 2017, this sign lies only a few months away. Scott corrected us when we wrote this footnote in an early draft. We indicated he saw the September alignment as the sign of the Son of Man. No, not so, said Scott. Yet, it is a significant sign in the stars. But what does it mean? Does it foretell the rapture?

greatest test for man. (2) Daniel said, "Prove thy servants, I beseech thee, ten days" (Daniel 1:12). (3) Jesus promised the church in Smyrna tribulation 10 days (Revelation 2:10). (The Greek word appearing here, translated *tribulation,* is the word *Thlipsis.* It is the same word Jesus used for great *tribulation* in Matthew 24:21 and 24:29). *Thlipsis* in Greek *may be translated as tribulation, affliction, trouble, anguish, or persecution.* Likewise, (4) the disciples tarried for the Holy Spirit ten days – in fasting and prayer – and their faith was tested during that time. In chapter six (p. 183), we discussed link between the Last Trumpet /Seventh Angel to the Day of Atonement. These speak to the same event.

The part the church plays in the restoration of Israel begins at this time, and fulfills the verse in Romans with which we began this chapter:

Rom 11:26-27 [26]And so all Israel will be saved, as it is written: "The Deliverer will come out of Zion, And He will turn away ungodliness from Jacob; [27]For this is My covenant with them, when I take away their sins."

1 John 3:1-9 [1]Behold what manner of love the Father has bestowed on us, that we should be called children of God! Therefore, the world does not know us, because it did not know Him. [2]Beloved, now we are children of God; *and it has not yet been revealed what we shall be, but we know that when He is revealed, we shall be like Him,* for we shall see Him as He is. [3]And everyone who has this hope in Him purifies himself, just as He is pure. [4] Whoever commits sin also commits lawlessness, and sin is lawlessness. [5]And you know that He was manifested to take away our sins, and in Him there is no sin. [6]Whoever abides in Him does not sin. Whoever sins has neither seen Him nor known Him. [7]Little children, let no one deceive you. He who practices righteousness is righteous, just as He is righteous. [8] He who sins is of the devil, for the devil has sinned from the beginning. For this purpose, the

Son of God was manifested, that He might destroy the works of the devil. [9]Whoever has been born of God does not sin, *for His seed remains in him;* and he cannot sin, because he has been born of God.

This passage certainly constitutes a significant statement confirming the witness of these authors. As we stand today, we have parts in our soul that are alive in God and parts that are not. *But in Christ Jesus, we are alive and without sin.* We are commanded to reckon ourselves dead to sin (Romans 6:11). Recall our earlier discussion about *seed.* John tells us that God's seed has been placed within us. *And that seed is Christ.* Apart from Him, we are not sinless. But once we are totally living in the power of the Spirit and Christ dwells in us fully, we should sin no more. *This sanctification leads to glorification.* God works in us, that we may live according to His good pleasure.

Phi 2:12-13 [12]Wherefore, my beloved, as ye have always obeyed, not as in my presence only, but now much more in my absence, work out your own salvation with fear and trembling. [13]For it is God which worketh in you both to will and to do of *his* good pleasure. (KJV)

Gal 5:5 For we through the Spirit eagerly wait *for the hope of righteousness by faith.*

Eph 4:11-16 [11]And He Himself gave some *to be* apostles, some prophets, some evangelists, and some pastors and teachers, [12]for the equipping of the saints for the work of ministry, for the edifying of the body of Christ, [13]*till we all come to the unity of the faith and of the knowledge of the Son of God, to a perfect man, to the measure of the stature of the fullness of Christ;* [14]that we should no longer be children, tossed to and fro and carried about with every wind of doctrine, by the trickery of men, in the cunning craftiness of deceitful plotting, [15]but, speaking the truth in love, *may grow up in all things into Him who is the head – Christ –* [16]from whom the whole body, joined and knit together by what every joint supplies, according to the effective working by which every part does its share, causes growth of the body for the edifying of itself in love.

God will bring His church to perfection, that is a "mature man, unto the measure of the stature of the fullness of Christ". This is corporate maturity – not individual, The Lone Ranger is not a model for perfection. It comes to us in part as we join with the Body of Christ and participate in it.

Rev 12:4-13 [4]His tail drew a third of the stars of heaven and threw them to the earth. And the dragon stood before the woman who was ready to give birth, to devour her Child as soon as it was born. [5]*She bore a male Child who was to rule all nations with a rod of iron. And her Child was caught up to God and His throne.* [6]Then the woman fled into the wilderness, where she has a place prepared by God, that *they* should feed her there one thousand two hundred and sixty days.

This book doesn't seek to pick one perspective on the Rapture amid the Pre-Trib, Pre-Wrath, or Mid-Trib positions. But we do believe in the "catching up," And we aren't oblivious to passages that reinforce our view that the Rapture is a separate event from the visible Second Coming (when Jesus defeats His enemies, the enemies of Israel, and establishes His rule). Because of this, we would point out that we believe the reason that Satan is finally thrown out of heaven (that there is no longer a place for him there), *is because the glorified Body of Christ has been translated and transported to heaven.* It isn't a "space" problem – it is that the convicted is no longer out on bail. There is no place for accusations against God's elect. The revealing of the true Sons of God, shows them spotless and clothed in white. They can be accused no longer. Likewise, the false gods that have led the nations astray for thousands of years are no longer rulers in the heavens, the "powers and principalities," the corrupted Divine Council, are thrown out as well. The Body of Christ begins its rule when Michael and his angels cast Satan out of heaven – forever.

Rev 12:7-13 [7]And war broke out in heaven: Michael and his angels fought with the dragon; and the dragon and his angels fought, [8]but they did not prevail, nor was a place found for them in heaven any longer. [9]So the great dragon was cast out, that serpent of old, called the Devil and Satan, who deceives the whole world; he was cast to the earth, and his angels were cast out with him. [10]Then I heard a loud voice saying in heaven, "Now salvation, and strength, and the kingdom of our God, and the power of His Christ have come, for the accuser of our brethren, who accused them before our God day and night, has been cast down. [11]*And they overcame him by the blood of the Lamb and by the word of their testimony*, and they did not love their lives to the death. [12]*Therefore rejoice, O heavens, and you who dwell in them!* Woe to the inhabitants of the earth and the sea! For the devil has come down to you, having great wrath, because he knows that he has a short time." [13]Now when the dragon saw that he had been cast to the earth, *he persecuted the woman* who gave birth to the male Child.

This powerful passage pictures the Day of Atonement made manifest – *the blood of the Lamb and the Word of their Testimony is the Day of Atonement fulfilled in the church.* Notice the man-child is caught up (*harpazo*) to the throne of God. This is where God dwells – in the Holy of Holies where His presence is manifest (the *kabod*, the shekinah glory of God). *Again, this holiest place could only be entered on the Day of Atonement.* That is why we draw the conclusion that it is here that we see the Day of Atonement fulfilled. Again, when the church is sinless before the throne of God (the man-child, or *vios*), there is no room for the accuser, his henchmen, or his accusations in heaven (for the sins have been covered by the blood of the Lamb). The scape goat will no longer be necessary. There is no reason for him. He is cast out.

Job 1:9-11 [9]Then Satan answered the LORD, and said, Doth Job fear God for nought? [10]Hast not thou made an hedge about him, and about his house, and about all that he hath on every side? thou hast blessed the work of his hands, and his substance is increased in the land. [11] But put forth thine hand now, and touch all that he hath, and he will curse thee to thy face. (KJV)

Until then, Satan continues his favorite pastime: *accusing believers before God.* This is the only legal right God has granted him for which he appears in the Third Heaven.

John 14:30 I will no longer talk much with you, for the ruler of this world is coming, and he *has nothing in Me.*

Jesus was sinless, so Satan had no legal hold or right to Him. Satan could no longer accuse Christ. Jesus gave Himself willingly to die for us. Satan will have nothing in the Church either. The blood of the Lamb has freed us from his accusations. No more dissing from the devil!

Satan has been the Accuser of the Brethren for a very long time. But when the Day of Atonement is fulfilled in the Church, he loses his job! He forfeits all legal rights to accuse or otherwise torment the church. When he loses his standing – *he comes down to earth hopping mad.* For he knows, the epic story of the ages will soon be concluded.

2 Cor 10:4-6 [4]For the weapons of our warfare *are* not carnal but mighty in God for pulling down strongholds, [5]casting down arguments and every high thing that exalts itself against the knowledge of God, bringing every thought into captivity to the obedience of Christ, [6]and being ready to punish all disobedience when your obedience is fulfilled.

9: MANY SONS ARE BROUGHT TO GLORY: THE BOOK OF HEBREWS

JESUS CHRIST BUILDS A NEW HOUSE FOR HIS BRIDE

Among those who study the Bible intensely, the New Testament's Book of Hebrews is often selected as a personal favorite. It's teaching requires a solid appreciation for the Old Testament, and some understanding of classical Greek philosophy.

Indeed, the concepts of the book undoubtedly come forth from a great mind that bridges the ancient Greek and Hebrew worlds. This dual mindset leads many to suppose that the Apostle Paul is its author, as he was trained in both "oriental" and "occidental" thinking. Other than the Book of Romans and the Gospel of John, Hebrews arguably has had more impact than any other book in the New Testament. For our purposes, it comprises an excellent way to summarize the material we've covered in *The Revealing*.

Heb 1:3 Who being the brightness of *His* glory and the express image of His person, and upholding all things by the word of His power, when He had by Himself purged our sins, sat down at the right hand of the Majesty on high,

Heb 2:10 For it was fitting for Him, for whom *are* all things and by whom *are* all things, *in bringing many sons to glory*, to make the captain of their salvation perfect through sufferings.

Heb 2:12-13 [12]Saying: *"I will declare Your name to My brethren; In the midst of the assembly I will sing praise to You."* [13]And again: *"I will put My trust in Him."* And again: **"Here am I and the children whom God has given Me."**

Not only was Jesus the "express image" of Yahweh, who sustains the very creation by His presence throughout it, He himself will bring many sons – brethren – children – to that glory. Jesus (the brightness of God's glory), took the form of flesh and blood to be a faithful high priest to make reconciliation such that He can bring to the Father "the children whom God has given Me."

Heb 3:2-6 [2]Who was faithful to Him who appointed Him, as Moses also *was faithful* in all His house. [3]For this One *has been counted worthy of more glory than Moses,* inasmuch as He who built the house has more honor than the house. [4]For every house is built by someone, but He who built all things *is* God. [5]And Moses indeed *was* faithful in all His house as a servant, for a testimony of those things which would be spoken *afterward,* [6]but Christ as a Son over His own house, *whose house we are* if we hold fast the confidence and the rejoicing of *the hope firm to the end.*

Jesus is the builder of the house. Moses constitutes one part of that house. But the whole house consisting of believers from all time, will one day comprise the eternal Bride of Christ. But in this age, the members assembled to date are the Body of Christ. Israel's redemption and the assembling of all believers into one "bride" awaits the Messianic Kingdom for its fruition.

Heb 3:7-19 [7]Therefore, as the Holy Spirit says: *"Today, if you will hear His voice,* [8]*Do not harden your hearts as in the rebellion,* In the day of trial in the wilderness, [9]*Where your fathers tested Me, tried Me, and saw My works forty years.* [10]*Therefore I was angry with that generation, and said, 'They always go astray in their heart, and they have not known My ways.'* [11]*So I swore in My wrath, 'They shall not enter My rest.'"* [12]Beware, brethren, lest there be in any of you an evil heart of unbelief in departing from the living God; [13]but exhort one another daily, while it is called *"Today,"* lest any of you be hardened through the deceitfulness of sin. *[14]For we have become partakers of Christ if we hold the beginning of our confidence steadfast to the end,* [15]while it is said: *"Today, if you will hear His voice, do not harden your hearts as in the rebellion."* [16]For who, having heard, rebelled? Indeed, *was it* not all who came out of Egypt, *led* by Moses? [17]Now with whom was He angry forty years? *Was it* not with those who sinned, whose corpses fell in the wilderness? [18]And to whom did He swear that they would not enter His rest, but to those who did not obey? [19]So we see that they could not enter in *because of unbelief.*

Hebrews teaches that Israel missed the promised land and with it God's rest because of unbelief. Likewise, by definition, *believers are not believers unless they believe!* Unbelief means we are **not** in the Body of Christ.

Heb 4:1-2 [1]Therefore, since a promise remains of entering His rest, let us fear lest any of you seem to have come short of it. [2]For indeed the gospel was preached to us as well as to them; but the word which they heard *did not profit them, not being mixed* **with faith** *in those who heard it.*

We have a promise from the Father. We may enter into His rest *by faith* (the promised land of *dwelling with Christ* in Heaven upon our death or upon the earth as part of Christ's kingdom). It has a corporate, future fulfillment.

Heb 4:9 There remains therefore a rest for the people of God.

Rest is on the seventh or sabbath. *The Feast of Tabernacles* is the seventh feast, or the **feast of rest**.

Heb 5:6-8 [6]As He also *says* in another *place: "You are a priest forever According to the order of Melchizedek";* [7]who, in the days of His flesh, when He had offered up prayers and supplications, with vehement cries and tears to Him who was able to save Him from death, and was heard because of His godly fear, ⁸though He was a Son, *yet He learned obedience by the things which He suffered.*

EVEN CHRIST HAD TO "LEARN" OBEDIENCE

As priest of the New Covenant, Christ Jesus still had *to learn obedience* during his earthly life through the things that He suffered. Will we learn obedience by any other means? This does not mean that our Savior was predisposed to be disobedient. He did not have a "sin nature." However, he could not avoid His Passion (His suffering) to bring many sons to glory.

Heb 6:12 That you do not become sluggish, but imitate those who *through faith and patience inherit the promises.*

We inherit the promises through faith and patience. See what James says about patience:

James 1:4 But let patience have *its* perfect work, that you may be perfect and complete, lacking nothing.

When we become *perfect* (fulfilling our mission – see the definition below) *through patience* (aka *longsuffering*) – *we inherit the promises.*

Perfect: τελειοσ (Strong's 5046): 1) brought to its end, finished; 2) wanting nothing necessary to completeness; 3) perfect; 4) that which is perfect; 4a) consummate human integrity and virtue; 4b) of men, 4b1) full grown, adult, of full age, mature.

"Mature and complete" Those who are suffering should have joy (James 1:2) because trials serve as a path to Christian maturity. Complete and mature individuals show integrity and single-minded devotion to God; godliness characterizes them. (*Logos Faithlife Study Bible, James 1:4*)

Heb 6:17 Thus God, determining to show more abundantly to the *heirs of promise* the immutability of His counsel, confirmed *it* by an oath.

We are the heirs of the promise. God's oath confirms we will receive it.

Heb 6:18-20 [18]That by two immutable things, in which it *is* impossible for God to lie, we might have strong consolation, who have fled for refuge to lay hold of the hope set before *us*. [19]*This hope we have as an anchor of the soul, both sure and steadfast, and which enters the Presence behind the veil*, [20]where the forerunner has entered for us, *even* Jesus, having become High Priest forever according to the order of Melchizedek.

Our hope (of receiving the promise) is an anchor for our soul. It lies within the veil in the Holy of Holies. I (Huffman) picture this anchor (our hope), set down solidly in the Holy of Holies, "hooked" to the heavenly Ark of the Covenant itself (of which the earthy Ark was but a replica). *God's shekinah presence dwells there.* What must we do to share in it? *Hang on tight. And soon, we will lay hold (secure or obtain) this hope.* Once more, this comprises nothing less than God's presence – His manifested glory – which Jesus has entered into and received:

Heb 12:2 Looking unto Jesus, *the author and finisher of our faith, who for the joy that was set before Him endured the cross, despising the shame,* and has sat down at the right hand of the throne of God.

Jesus, who gives us this hope (the anchor that is), stands there, if you will, pulling on the rope. We are at the other end, holding on tight and looking to Him for empowerment. This is only our analogy. But it illustrates this truth.

A SUPERIOR PREISTHOOD – THE ORDER OF MELCHIZEDEK

Heb 7:14 For it *is* evident that our Lord arose *from Judah*, of which tribe *Moses spoke nothing concerning priesthood.*

Jesus is a high priest of a new order of priesthood. It is known as *the Order of Melchizedek*, the King of Salem (Jeru-*salem*), and of the tribe of *Judah, not Levi*, from which the Levitical priesthood originates. It should be remembered that Judah also means *peace*. (While not in the scope of our study to identify this "combo" King and Priest, it is fundamental to know that Jesus uniquely comprises both a King and Priest). The model for government in ancient Israel was to keep these offices separate. But in Christ, we see the two offices combined.

Heb 7:21 For they have become priests without an oath, but He with an oath by Him who said to Him: "The Lord has sworn And will not relent, 'You are a priest forever According to the order of Melchizedek'").

Heb 7:25 Therefore, He is also able to save to the uttermost those who come to God through Him, since He always lives to make intercession for them.

He was made high priest by an oath of God. He ever lives to make intercession for us to save or deliver us forever and to the uttermost- completely, perfectly, totally – that we might receive the promises.

Heb 8:4-6 [4]For if He were on earth, He would not be a priest, since there are priests who offer the gifts according to the law; [5]who serve the copy and shadow of the heavenly things, as Moses was divinely instructed when he was about to make the tabernacle. For He said, *"See that you make all things according to the pattern shown you on the mountain."* [6]But now He has obtained a more excellent ministry, inasmuch as He is also Mediator of a better covenant, which was established on better promises.

The new covenant is better than the old covenant. The Old Covenant, with its tabernacle and sacrifices, were but a shadow and pattern of heavenly things – the things that we have received in part now but will receive in full. Moses was instructed to pay attention to detail, so that we would have the correct Pattern to observe.

> **Heb 8:10-11** [8] "For this is the covenant that I will make with the house of Israel after those days, says the Lord: *I will put My laws in their mind and write them on their hearts; and I will be their God, and they shall be My people.* [11]None of them shall teach his neighbor, and none his brother, saying, 'Know the Lord,' for all shall know Me, from the least of them to the greatest of them."

A NEW TABERNACLE, A PERFECT WAY INTO THE HOLIEST PLACE

The New Covenant will entirely fulfill the promises...or should I say has fulfilled"? Once more, we encounter a truth that is an *"already, but not yet" aspect of New Covenant promises.* Now, recall the old tabernacle of Moses:

> **Heb 9:2-4** [2]For a tabernacle was prepared: the first *part,* in which *was* the lampstand, the table, and the showbread, which is called the sanctuary; [3]and behind the second veil, the part of the tabernacle which is called *the Holiest of All,* [4]*which had the golden censer and the ark of the covenant overlaid on all sides with gold,* in which *were* the golden pot that had the manna, Aaron's rod that budded, and the tablets of the covenant...

Notice in this description, *the altar of incense is missing in the Holy Place but appears in the Holy of Holies.* The altar of incense was taken into the Holy of Holies once a year – on the Day of Atonement. *This implies that the promises about which the writer speaks relate to this special day.* Recalling that the minutest detail the Holy Spirit intentionally inspires in the biblical writers, this "missing element" has significance which amounts to this: *we must offer the sacrifice of praise and worship.* Reflect once more on the tribe of Judah as we enter the Holiest place. Our entry connects us with the transcendent *heavenly Day of Atonement.* Its meaning? Praise and worship are essential to *enter into the promise – the glory of God, which comprises our inheritance:*

Heb 9:6-15 [6]Now when these things had been thus prepared, the priests always went into the first part of the tabernacle, performing *the services.* [7]But into the second part the high priest *went* alone once a year, not without blood, which he offered for himself and *for* the people's sins *committed* in ignorance; [8]the Holy Spirit indicating this, that *the way into the Holiest of All was not yet made manifest while the first tabernacle was still standing.* [9]It *was* symbolic for the present time in which both gifts and sacrifices are offered which cannot make him who performed the service perfect in regard to the conscience – [10]*concerned* only with foods and drinks, various washings, and fleshly ordinances imposed until the time of reformation. [11]But Christ came *as* High Priest of the good things to come, with *the greater and more perfect tabernacle* not made with hands, that is, *not of this creation.* [12]Not with the blood of goats and calves, but with His own blood He entered the Most Holy Place once for all, having obtained eternal redemption. [13]For if the blood of bulls and goats and the ashes of a heifer, sprinkling the unclean, sanctifies for the purifying of the flesh, [14]how much more shall the blood of Christ, who through the eternal Spirit offered Himself without spot to God, cleanse your conscience from dead works to serve the living God? [15]And for this reason *He is the Mediator of the new covenant*, by means of death, for the redemption of the transgressions under the first covenant, *that those* **who are called may receive the promise of the eternal inheritance.**

The priests entered into the Holy Place (the first, earthly tabernacle). But only once a year did the high priest go into the Holy of Holies (aka the *Most Holy Place*). The continual method of accessing the Most Holy Place (Jesus being that perfect method, of which the author of Hebrews writes) *had not yet been revealed.* We are told in verse 9 that, (paraphrasing) the prior "old covenant" holy method for approaching God's presence and glory" was *symbolic* only (it was not "the real thing" – it was earthly not heavenly – and thus it was inferior). Christ, however, was a high priest of good things to come. *He entered the holiest place to fulfill the Day of Atonement, to secure our atonement, and to guarantee our inheritance. He preceded us, clearing the way for the body of Christ "to enter in."*

We must be crystal clear about what all this means. There are Greek, high-minded philosophical conceptions behind the writer's argument. These are based on Plato's concept of "heavenly ideas" (i.e., our earthly concepts of transitory "things" depend upon their heavenly counterparts, perfected ideas for earthly concepts or things to have meaning). We mustn't let that confuse us, since it is hard for us to understand. While the writer talks of the "heavenly way" to stress the New Covenant's superiority to the "earthly way" of the Old Covenant; he is not inferring that "entering in" can only happen for believers in a future state, in heaven, or in the Millennium. *No, the access to God has been granted to us right now!* For we are sinless in God's eyes. *And if we are learning obedience through our work in progress we call sanctification, then access to God's glorious presence has been forever established.* The work is finished. It is done.

Heb 9:23-28 [23]Therefore *it was* necessary that the copies of the things in the heavens should be purified with these, but the heavenly things themselves with better sacrifices than these. [24]*For Christ has not entered the holy places made with hands, which are copies of the true, but into heaven itself, now to appear in the presence of God for us;* [25]not that He should offer Himself often, as the high priest enters the Most Holy Place every year with blood of another – [26]He then would have had to suffer often since the foundation of the world; but now, *once at the end of the ages,* He has appeared to put away sin by the sacrifice of Himself. [27]And as it is appointed for men to die once, but after this the judgment,

[28]so Christ was offered once to bear the sins of many. *To those who eagerly wait for Him He will appear a second time, apart from sin, for salvation.*

Allow us to highlight verses 23 and 28 from *The Amplified Bible:*

Heb 9:23, 28 [23]By such means therefore it was necessary for the [earthly] copies of the heavenly things to be purified, but the actual heavenly things themselves [required far] better and nobler sacrifices than these. [28] Even so it is that Christ having been offered to take upon Himself and bear as a burden the sins of many once and once for all, will appear a second time, not carrying any burden of sin nor to deal with sin, but to bring to full salvation those who are (eagerly, constantly and patiently) waiting for and expecting Him.

This means Christ appeared in the heavenly Holy of Holies to present a better sacrifice to the Father – His own blood. Christ will appear a second time bringing full, complete salvation and deliverance to us who wait for Him. *This is the fulfillment of the Day of Atonement and the Feast of Tabernacles.*

Heb 10:19 Therefore, brethren, *having boldness to enter the Holiest by the blood of Jesus,*

We have liberty (boldness) and freedom, to enter the Holy of Holies by Jesus' blood.

Heb 10:22-25 [2]Let us draw near with a true heart in full assurance of faith, having our hearts sprinkled from an evil conscience and our bodies washed with pure water. [23]Let us hold fast the confession of *our* hope without wavering, for He who promised *is* faithful. [24]And let us consider one another in order to stir up love and good works, [25]not forsaking the assembling of ourselves together, as *is* the manner of some, but exhorting *one another,* and so much the more as you see the Day approaching.

HOLD THE ROPE – DON'T GIVE UP HOPE – THE KING IS COMING

Then, the writer returns from his "heavenly excursion" to everyday reality. He instructs his readers that part of the process of gaining access and preparing ourselves for the day when Christ returns, requires we participate in the local assembly of believers. Moreover, he insists the unity of the local assembly remains essential. Of what day is he speaking? The Day of the Lord, the day when salvation is perfected, when it truly is "mission accomplished":

Heb 9:28 So Christ was offered once to bear the sins of many. To *those who eagerly wait for Him He will appear a second time,* apart from sin, *for salvation.*

Heb 10:32-34 [32]But recall the former days in which, after you were illuminated, you endured a great struggle with sufferings: [33]partly while you were made a spectacle both by reproaches and tribulations, and partly while you became companions of those who were so treated; [34]for you had compassion on me in my chains, and joyfully accepted the plundering of your goods, *knowing that you have a better and an enduring possession for yourselves in heaven.*

Don't go back. You have something much better waiting for you. *Our inheritance (the glory of God) give us access to heaven (the Sky) even before our bodies are transformed into a body like His (Philippians 3:21).*

Heb 10:35-37 [35]Therefore do not cast away your confidence, which has great reward. [36]For you have need of endurance, so that after you have done the will of God, you may receive the promise: [37]*"For yet a little while, and He who is coming will come and will not tarry.*

We have a great reward. By doing the will of God, with patience, we receive the promise (in part) now. He will come with His reward for us, the promise, the inheritance (Hebrews 9:15, referenced above) and then the promise will be made perfect.

Heb 10:39 But we are not of those who draw back to perdition, but of those who believe to the saving of the soul.

We must "keep on believing" to the experiential deliverance of our soul. We make this distinction because our soul is "legally" delivered – from God's perspective. This fact has been fully established. In other words, the result is binding on all parties as if it were a consummated contract because in the law of God, it is. It constitutes what we mentioned earlier – the "already, but not yet." Peter adds his testimony to this truth:

1 Pet 1:9 Receiving the end [culmination] of your faith – the salvation of *your* souls.

1 Pet 1:22 Since you have purified your souls in obeying the truth through the Spirit in sincere love of the brethren, love one another fervently with a pure heart.

OBTAINING THE PROMISE, IN PART, *NOW* THROUGH FAITH

And then the writer of Hebrews expounds on faith – *"believing unto receiving" our inheritance.* As we shall see, *it is through faith that we receive the promise.*

Heb 11:1-4 ¹Now faith is the substance of things hoped for, the evidence of things not seen. ²For by it the elders obtained a *good* testimony. ³By faith we understand that the worlds were framed by the word of God, so that the things which are seen were not made of things which are visible. ⁴By faith Abel offered to God a more excellent sacrifice than Cain, through which he obtained witness that he was righteous, God testifying of his gifts; and through it he, being dead, still speaks.

Heb 11:8-10 [8]By faith Abraham obeyed when he was called to go out to the place which he would receive as an inheritance. And he went out, not knowing where he was going. [9]By faith he dwelt in the land of promise as *in* a foreign country, dwelling in tents with Isaac and Jacob, the heirs with him of the same promise; [10]for he waited for the city which has foundations, whose builder and maker *is* God.

Heb 11:12-13 [12]Therefore from one man, and him as good as dead, were born *as many* as the stars of the sky in multitude – innumerable as the sand which is by the seashore. [13]These all died in faith, not having received the promises, but having seen them afar off were assured of them, embraced *them* and confessed that they were strangers and pilgrims on the earth.

Abraham's seed (Israel) died – not receiving the promises.

Heb 11:14-16 [14]For those who say such things declare plainly that they seek a homeland. [15]And truly if they had called to mind that *country* from which they had come out, they would have had opportunity to return. [16]But now they desire a better, that is, a heavenly *country*. Therefore, God is not ashamed to be called their God, for He has prepared a city for them.

They also look for a heavenly city *(even those already in heaven!)* So heaven really can't be the final reward. Heaven constitutes a "rest" (an other-worldly rest stop, if you will, to catch our breath). Rather it is the glorified body of believers, the full assembly of all saints (old and new covenant believers) comprising the New Jerusalem, constitutes the reward for which we wait.

Rev 21:9-11 [9]Then one of the seven angels who had the seven bowls, filled with the seven last plagues, came to me and talked with me, saying, "Come, I will show you the bride, the Lamb's wife." [10]And he carried me away in the Spirit to a great and high mountain, and showed me the great city, the holy Jerusalem, descending out of heaven from God, [11]having the glory of God. Her light *was* like a most precious stone, like a jasper stone, clear as crystal.

Even Abraham, Isaac and Jacob are waiting for this heavenly city to be completely formed in and through Christ and His body.

Heb 11:19 Concluding that God *was* able to raise *him* up, even from the dead, from which he also received him in a figurative sense.

Abraham received Isaac from the dead – an illustration that fore-shadowed prophetically – *Jesus receiving His many sons in the resurrection.*

Heb 11:24-27 [24]By faith Moses, when he became of age, refused to be called the son of Pharaoh's daughter, [25]choosing rather to suffer affliction with the people of God than to enjoy the passing pleasures of sin, [26]esteeming the reproach of Christ greater riches than the treasures in Egypt; *for he looked to the reward.* [27]By faith he forsook Egypt, not fearing the wrath of the king; for he endured as seeing Him (through the eyes of faith) who is invisible.

Likewise, knowledge of the reward kept Moses motivated.

Heb 11:35 Women received their dead raised to life again. Others were tortured, not accepting deliverance, that they might obtain a better resurrection.

Heb 11:39-40 [39]And all these, having obtained a good testimony through faith, did not receive the promise, [40]God having provided some-thing better for us, *that they should not be made perfect apart from us.*

They received not the promise. They were not made perfect without us. *They must wait until the end of the age, when God's entire House assembles together.* As stated at the outset, heaven isn't the promise. Neither the Old Testament saints nor the New Testament saints have received the promise by being "in heaven." They still await it – the glorification of our bodies.

RESISTING SIN, RUNNING THE RACE, & "KEEPING OUR FEET"

Heb 12:1-5 [1]Therefore we also, since we are surrounded by so great a cloud of witnesses, let us lay aside every weight, and the sin which so easily ensnares *us,* and let us run with endurance the race that is set before us, [2]looking unto Jesus, the author and finisher of *our* faith, who for the joy that was set before Him endured the cross, despising the shame, and has sat down at the right hand of the throne of God. [3]For consider Him who endured such hostility from sinners against Himself, lest you become weary and discouraged in your souls. [4]You have not yet resisted to bloodshed, striving against sin. [5]And you have forgotten the exhortation which speaks to you as to sons: "My son, do not despise the chastening of the Lord, nor be discouraged when you are rebuked by Him."

We must look away from ourselves and look to Jesus. We are to let the chastening of the Lord work holiness and righteousness. Why?

Heb 12:10-11 [10]For they indeed for a few days chastened *us* as seemed *best* to them, *but He for our profit, that **we may be partakers of His holiness**.* [11]Now no chastening seems to be joyful for the present, but painful; nevertheless, afterward it yields the peaceable fruit of righteousness to those who have been trained by it.

265

Heb 12:14-15 [14]Pursue peace with all *people,* and **holiness, without which no one will see the Lord:** [15]looking carefully lest anyone fall short of the grace of God; lest any root of bitterness springing up cause trouble, and by this many become defiled.

We must not allow sin to rob us of the inheritance. If sin dominates us, we cannot experience holiness. Without holiness that comes through allowing the life of Christ to live through us, we will not be glorified. Allowing the Holy Spirit to work God's holiness into us, *permits the Day of Atonement to be fulfilled for those in the Body of Christ.*

God's voice shook the world when Moses delivered the law of God on Pentecost, beginning the dispensation of Law. His voice sounded so loud and long it frightened the people and made Moses tremble. (Exodus 20:18) But the shaking, which will occur again when God's voice shakes both heaven and earth, will not knock down those who have obtained holiness, to those whom the completed work of the atonement applies. *They cannot be shaken such that they fall to the ground, and break in pieces.* This shaking may anticipate the great earthquake at the Sixth Seal, which may be the same great earthquake prophesied in Ezekiel 38:19 and Revelation 16:18. However, symbolically the people of God will withstand the judgments of God that fall upon those around them.

Heb 12:26-29 [26]Whose voice then shook the earth; but now He has promised, saying, *"Yet once more I shake not only the earth, but also heaven."* [27] Now this, *"Yet once more,"* indicates the removal of those things that are being shaken, as of things that are made, that the things which cannot be shaken may remain. [28]Therefore, since we are receiving a kingdom which cannot be shaken, let us have grace, by which we may serve God acceptably with reverence and godly fear. [29]For our God *is* a consuming fire.

The kingdom of God cannot be moved. It will withstand the "second shaking". Abide there and you will withstand the fearsome voice of God.

Heb 12:22-23 [22]But you have come to Mount Zion and to the city of the living God, the heavenly Jerusalem, to an innumerable company of angels, [23]to the general assembly and church of the firstborn *who are* registered in heaven, to God the Judge of all, to the spirits of just men made perfect.

In Hebrews 13, we find practical steps to deliverance (salvation) and ultimately the promised inheritance. We see three specific instructions in Hebrews, chapter 13, to realize salvation and commence receiving the inheritance (holiness) now. We (1) must offer praise and thanksgiving, (2) do good and share, and (3) submit to our leaders in the Body of Christ.

Heb 13:15-17 [15]Therefore by Him let us continually *offer the sacrifice of praise to God,* that is, the fruit of *our* lips, giving thanks to His name. [16]But do not forget *to do good and to share,* for with such sacrifices God is well pleased. [17]*Obey those who rule over you, and be submissive,* for they watch out for your souls, as those who must give account. Let them do so with joy and not with grief, for that would be unprofitable for you.

Sacrifices from the altar of incense will arise and one day come into the Holiest Place. *This transpires on the Day of Atonement!* Remember this is the second stage of the Feast of Tabernacles. It takes place before the Feast concludes. The prophecy in *Revelation 12 conveys that the Body of Christ enters into the Holy of Holies on the Day of Atonement!*

Recall also that Zechariah prophesied in God's new kingdom on the earth, all the nations of the earth will go up to Jerusalem to keep the Feast of Tabernacles (Zechariah 14:1, 4-5, 9, 16-21). *Thus, we see why the Feast of Tabernacles is the one feast that is kept after the Kingdom is set up on the earth.* The earthly fulfillment of that feast brings the promised inheritance to believers as well as the Kingdom of God upon the earth – the glorified Body of believers will administer the Kingdom under the kingship of the Head, the King, Jesus Christ.

Mat 6:10 Your kingdom come. Your will be done – on earth as *it is* in heaven.

Jesus' prayer will be fulfilled when the Feast of Tabernacles is fulfilled!

THE HEAVENLY TABERNACLE

Now we will jump back to earlier passages in Hebrews to draw out the meaning of the "heavenly tabernacle." The passages are eloquent with deep import to believers.

Heb 8:1-6 [1]Now *this is* the main point of the things we are saying: *We have such a High Priest, who is seated at the right hand of the throne of the Majesty in the heavens,* [2]*a Minister of the sanctuary and of the true tabernacle which the Lord erected, and not man.* [3]For every high priest is appointed to offer both gifts and sacrifices. Therefore, *it is* necessary that this One also have something to offer. [4]For if He were on earth, He would not be a priest, since there are priests who offer the gifts according to the law; [5]*who serve the copy and shadow of the heavenly things,* as Moses was divinely instructed when he was about to make the tabernacle. For He said, *"See that you make all things according to the pattern shown you on the mountain."* [6]But now He has obtained a more excellent ministry, inasmuch as He is also Mediator of a better covenant, which was established on better promises.

The writer asserts that we have a *better* High Priest, Jesus, who serves (continually) in the sanctuary of the True (better) Tabernacle in heaven, the *earthly tabernacle being a mere copy of the heavenly.*

Heb 9:11-12 [11]But Christ came *as* High Priest of the good things to come, with the greater and more perfect tabernacle not made with hands, that is, not of this creation. [12]Not with the blood of goats and calves, but *with His own blood He entered the Most Holy Place once for all,* having obtained eternal redemption.

Heb 9:23-28 [23]Therefore *it was* necessary that the *copies of the things in the heavens should be purified with these, but the heavenly things themselves with better sacrifices than these.* [24]For Christ has not entered the holy places made with hands, *which are copies of the true, but into heaven itself, now to appear in the presence of God for us;* [25]not that He should offer Himself often, as the high priest enters the Most Holy Place every year with blood of another – [26]He then would have had to suffer often since the foundation of the world; but now, once at the end of the ages, He has appeared to put away sin by the sacrifice of Himself. [27]And as it is appointed for men to die once, but after this the judgment, [28]so Christ was offered once to bear the sins of many. *To those who eagerly wait for Him* **He will appear a second time**, apart from sin, for **salvation**.

Christ entered the Holy of Holies in Heaven and presented His blood once and for all. Our salvation is to be made complete (it will be fully perfected) at His second coming. This coming is not about sin, *but glorification for believers and judgment to those who reject Him*. However, we are to reckon that this salvation belongs to us, legally, already. To "reckon" is to calculate and be satisfied that we have indeed arrived at the correct total. Our salvation "adds up" perfectly. We must reckon (count) ourselves dead to sin and alive to Christ. (Romans 6:11)

Heb 10:19-22 [19]Therefore, brethren, *having boldness to enter the Holiest by the blood of Jesus,* [20]by *a new and living way* which He consecrated for us, through **the veil, that is, His flesh,** [21]and *having* a High Priest over the house of God, [22]let us draw near with a true heart in full assurance of faith, having our hearts sprinkled from an evil conscience and our bodies washed with pure water.

Jesus opened the way for us to enter the heavenly Most Holy Place, and draw near to God. Jesus' blood was spilled on the earth, making earth the outer court with its altar of sacrifice (the cross). He took His blood into heaven to offer it before the Father in the heavenly Holy of Holies, just as the High Priest did on earth on the Day of Atonement. We are not amiss to point out an interesting correlation here: *the skin of Jesus* and *the veil of the Temple*. Both cloak the Glory of God residing within the Holiest Place. Additionally, we can acquire a glimpse of cosmology from Hebrews' teaching. We learn the Holy Place seems within earth's reaches, not distant at all. Heaven, like the Lord God, is not "far from us." This notion reminds us of Paul's lecture to the Athenians, in which he quotes the Greek poet Epimenides, "In Him, we live and move and have our being." (Acts 17:28)

Therefore, although we don't wish to delineate the precise nature of where one heaven ends and the next one begins, we can safely assert that the Bible assumes there are "three heavens" just as there are three sections of the heavenly tabernacle: (1) the earth and its surrounding atmosphere; (2) the realm outside the earth inhabited by the "heavenly bodies" (e.g., sun, moon, and stars); and (3) the "third heaven" which is ultra-dimensional. Modern conceptions do not think of Heaven existing at the edge of the galaxy or beyond all matter and energy occupying the universe. It is "right next to us." In some sense, this "other-worldly dimension" resides adjacent to the world we see. This heaven has "immediacy" – it exists all around us, immediately present if we had but eyes to see it or a means to access it. There are many examples of this in the Scripture where the servant of God can see "into" the other dimensions, but those around cannot. We may rightly cite the baptism of Jesus and the conversion of Paul on the road to Damascus. John saw the heavens open and the Spirit descending as a dove. (Mark 1:10) Paul heard Christ and was blinded by His glory, while others were struck down but did not hear the words of Christ, but thought it had only thundered (Acts 9:6-9).

How exciting to see that this heavenly tabernacle fits right into the rest of God's Pattern. Not only does it correspond to the pattern of the earthly tabernacle, but we can discern its spiritual significance too.

Simply put, the born-again experience, symbolized by the Outer Court of the tabernacle, gives the believer access to God's blessing now, even though the body has not yet been transformed. The believer's conscience is cleansed, his spirit reborn, and his mind renewed. It supplies relationships with other believers and a message to non-believers. True, the blessing remains a spiritual experience. However, the principal part of God's blessing remains at the believer's level as he or she exists today. We could say it comprises "ground level." Consequently, earth is the *Outer Court* of the Heavenly Tabernacle. But other levels await the believer.

SPIRITUAL WARFARE IN THE COSMOS

While the concept of the baptism of the Holy Spirit is controversial, it need not be. We all agree the Spirit of Christ gives the believer access to tools that discern and destroy the works of darkness. These tools include the gifts of discernment of spirits, healing, miracles, wisdom, knowledge, faith, prophecy, speaking in tongues and interpretation of tongues. These are listed in 1 Corinthians 12:4-11 and are "distributed to each one individually as He wills" in the assembly of believers.

For those who have experienced "speaking in tongues", they know firsthand that intercessory prayer through tongues is a powerful weapon against the enemy. The other gifts are also powerful "charismata" (instances of *charisma*, derived from the Greek, χάρισμα) primarily used to discern, heal, and build up where the enemy has been tearing down. The opposition that the enemy stirs up against this expression of the fullness of Christ's Spirit which indwells us – the "baptism" (immersion) of the Spirit and His gifts which may flood our Spirit and flow outward – gives us a clue about how powerfully they can be wielded against him. The devil is called the "prince of the power of the air" – he rules the evil spirits of the *aether* (in the Greek), this envelope that surrounds the earth. It should not be surprising that in some exorcisms, the victim coughs until the evil spirit is thrust out, as if it dwelled in the air inside the lungs.

> **Eph 2:2** In which you once walked according to the course of this world, according to the prince of the power of the air, the spirit who now works in the sons of disobedience,

We could say our adversary rules the "evil in the air," since the word "spirit" comes from the Greek word "pneuma," or air. Thus, these power tools of the Holy Spirit, or "air tools," give the believer access to "principalities and powers in the air" to do them damage. (Perhaps we could say that the gifts of the Spirit can literally knock the air out of these evil spirits!) Sometimes the word, "air," is used as the earth's atmosphere, and other times for the upper air, or heaven. Also, we see scholars use the word *heaven* both ways. We know that the Lord confined the devil primarily to earth and its surrounding atmosphere. While not in the scope of this study, aether can refer to what some scientists call "plasma" – the "ether" that resides discretely throughout the universe (i.e., space is not empty).

> **Eph 3:10** To the intent that now the manifold wisdom of God might be made known by the church to the principalities and powers in the <u>heavenly</u> *places,*

> **Eph 6:12** For we do not wrestle against flesh and blood, but against principalities, against powers, against the rulers of the darkness of this age, against spiritual *hosts* of wickedness in the heavenly *places.*

The Holy Spirit also leads the body of Christ in praise and worship in the true Holy Place (*spoken and sung into the air – which also counts as spiritual warfare*), so that we may bring the altar of incense into the true Holy of Holies and experience God's manifest presence. Our praise penetrates the air and takes us into the presence of God. Thus, the Holy Place of the heavenly tabernacle lies beyond the realm where Satan has been confined, but we should not imagine it is distant, or for our praise to reach into the third heaven, that it must climb through the first.

THE PICTURE OF THE COSMOS THE TABERNACLE SUPPLIES

Jesus, our High Priest, serves in the sanctuary of the true heavenly tabernacle. He entered the Holy of Holies in Heaven and presented His blood to the Father on our behalf. Jesus opened the way into the True Holy of Holies, so that we may draw near to God and be sanctified by His holiness and glory. As the Church increasingly fulfills this aspect of God's Pattern, believers access the Holy Place "in the third heaven."

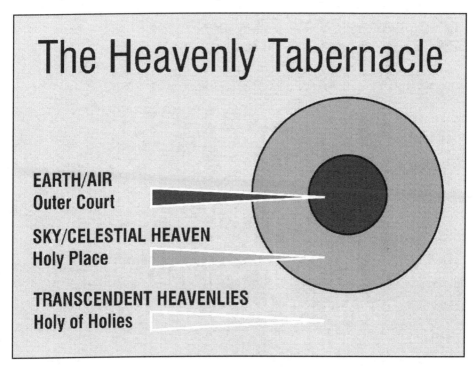

Figure 5 - The Three Heavens Mirrored in the Tabernacle
© Gary L. Huffman, 2017

273

After the rapture of the Body, (which we believe happens at some point before or during the final seven years culminating in Christ's visible return), our bodies will be changed and glorified. We will possess a body identical to Jesus' body after His resurrection.

Phi 3:21 Who will transform our lowly body to be like his glorious body, by the power that enables him even to subject all things to himself. (ESV)

I Cor 15:50-53 [50]Now, this I say, brethren, that flesh and blood cannot inherit the kingdom of God; neither doth corruption inherit incorruption. [51]Behold, I shew you a mystery; we shall not all sleep, but we shall all be changed, [52]In moment, in the twinkling of an eye, at the last trump: for the trumpet shall sound, and the dead shall be raised incorruptible, and we shall be changed. For this corruptible must put on incorruption, and this mortal must put on immortality. (KJV)

1 John 3:2 Beloved, now are we the sons of God, and it doth not yet appear what we shall be: but we know that, when he shall appear, we shall be like him; we shall see him as he is. (KJV)

However, our somewhat unique view we propose is this: we will minister God's glorious healing, grace, and in some cases protective presence anywhere on Earth during this time, as the LORD wills – in the terrestrial "air" or in the celestial "sky" (the first and second heaven). Unlike the traditional view, we assert we will not be resting on our laurels,[*] without vocation, dwelling only in our mansion in the sky. Instead, we will be put to work in the service of the King even as we await His fiery return. Even if you do not quite agree with this model, however, you should still find Figure 5 (previous

---

[*] To be satisfied with one's past success and to consider further effort unnecessary. [A symbol of victory and success in ancient times.] Referenced on May 26, 2017 at http://www.phrases.org.uk/meanings/rest-on-his-laurels.html.

page) instructive regarding how the design of the creation portrays the truth conveyed in the structure of the Heavenly Tabernacle. To spell this out, we draw upon the work of professor of Old Testament at Wheaton College, John H. Walton. His compelling work, *The Lost World of Genesis One*, makes a persuasive argument for the "cosmic temple" in the creation story.

DEEP DIVE: GENESIS 1 AS TEMPLE TEXT IN THE CONTEXT OF ANCIENT COSMOLOGY

Dr. John H. Walton

If we are to reach an understanding of an ancient text such as Genesis 1, we must be able to think about the issues the way they would have. A foundational issue is the way people think about existence. In the ancient world, they believed that something existed when it had a role and a function in an ordered system. This is in stark contrast to our way of thinking, that something exists when it has material properties. In our world, to cause something to exist (i.e., to create), involves giving something material properties. *In the ancient world, to cause something to exist involves giving it a function and a role.* In Hebrew, the word translated "create" *(bara')* expresses this very idea. So, "In the beginning period (the Hebrew expresses a period, not a point, referring to the seven-day period), God created (gave functions to) the cosmos. Thus, in Gen(esis) 1:2 the narrative starts with no functions (not with no matter), and assigns functions by separating and naming.

On day 1, verses 4 and 5 make it clear that a *period* of light is being separated from a *period* of darkness and each period is being named. Thus, on day 1 God created not light, but a period of light, i.e., the basis for time. On day two God sets up the basis for weather, and on day 3, the basis for growing food. After the major functions of human existence are established, he assigns functionaries to their various spheres. All of the functions are relative to human existence and they are declared good as they are put in place to function on behalf of humans.

The cosmos is portrayed in the ancient world and in the Bible as a temple, and temples are designed to be micro-models of the cosmos. Temples are built in the ancient world for the gods to rest in, which does not refer to relaxing, but to enjoying and maintaining security and order.

With the mention of God's rest on day seven, we can see that Genesis 1 is also thinking about the cosmos as a temple. God is creating his dwelling place, putting people into it as his images (representatives), and taking up his place at the helm to maintain the order he has established.

In the ancient world *temple dedications were often seven days in duration.* During those seven days, the functions of the temple would be proclaimed, the furniture and functionaries installed, the priests would take up their role and at the end, the deity would enter and take up his rest. If *the cosmos is being viewed as a temple, Genesis 1 can be understood as presenting creation of the cosmos in terms of a temple dedication.* There is no reason to think of the seven days as anything but normal days. Since the text is not discussing the material creation of the cosmos, the days of Genesis 1 offer no information about the age of the material cosmos. Genesis 1 is about the work God did (a *bara'* work), not about the things God made.

The theology of the text presents God as the one who is the founder and CEO of the cosmos. He has brought order, established functions, and maintains the cosmos moment by moment. The insistence on his purposes and his engagement are the polar opposite of a naturalistic view of creation, which has no room for purpose or divine engagement. The theology also speaks to the real issue of creation: who is in charge. [Emphasis added]

http://www.blackhawkchurch.org/archive/sermon_resources/walton.pdf

Related material from Walton's book, *The Lost World of Genesis One*:

In the biblical text the descriptions of the tabernacle and temple contain many transparent connections to the cosmos. *This connection was explicitly recognized as early as the second century A.D. in the writings of the Jewish* historian Josephus, who says of the tabernacle: "every one of these objects is intended to recall and represent the universe."

...Scholars have also recognized that the temple and tabernacle contain a lot of imagery from the Garden of Eden. They note that gardens commonly adjoined sacred space in the ancient world. Furthermore, the imagery of fertile waters flowing from the presence of the deity to bring abundance to the earth is a well-known image.

The garden of Eden is not viewed by the author of Genesis simply as a piece of Mesopotamian farmland, *but as an archetypal sanctuary*; that is, a place where God dwells and where man should worship him. Many of the features of the garden may also be found in later *sanctuaries particularly the tabernacle of Jerusalem temple.* These parallels suggest that *the garden itself is understood as a sort of sanctuary.*

So, the waters flowing through the garden in Genesis 2 are paralleled by the waters flowing from the temple in Ezekiel 47:1-12 (cf. Ps 46:4; Zech 14:8; Rev 22:1-2). This is one of the most common images in the iconography of the ancient world. Consequently, we may conclude that the Garden of Eden was sacred space and temple/tabernacle contained imagery of the garden and the cosmos. All the ideas are interlinked. The temple is a microcosm, and Eden is represented in the antechamber that serves as sacred space adjoining the Presence of God as an archetypal sanctuary...

1. In the Bible and in the ancient Near East the temple is viewed as a microcosm.

2. The temple is designed with the imagery of the cosmos.

3. The temple is related to the functions of the cosmos.

4. The creation of the temple is parallel to the creation of the cosmos.

5. In the Bible, the cosmos can be viewed as a temple.

... Genesis 1 can now be seen as a creation account focusing *on the cosmos as a temple.* It is describing *the creation of the cosmic temple with all of its functions and with God dwelling in its midst.* This is what makes day seven so significant, because without God taking up his dwelling in its midst, the (cosmic) temple does not exist. The most central truth to the creation account is that this world is a place for God's presence. Though all of the functions are anthropocentric, meeting the needs of humanity, the cosmic temple is theocentric, *with God's presence serving as the defining element of existence.* This represents a change that has taken place over nonfunctional cosmos; God was involved but had not yet taken up his residence. The establishment of the functional cosmic temple is effectuated by God taking up his residence on day seven. This gives us a before/after view of God's role. [Emphasis added][†]

Michael Heiser also shows the relationship of the pattern of the Tabernacle and the Garden of Eden. He says the tent (Hebrew: *mishkan* – "dwelling") was where Yahweh caused His presence to dwell, and corresponded to the cosmic conception of the Garden of Eden, where heaven and earth would meet.

> There are many subtle connections between Eden and the tabernacle, some of them discernible only in the Hebrew text. For our purposes, several of the more obvious are worth noting. To begin, the description of the tabernacle as a tent dwelling is significant. Elsewhere in the biblical world, deities and their councils were considered to live in tents – atop their cosmic mountains and in their lush gardens. The tent of the god or gods was, as with mountains or lush gardens, the place where heaven and earth intersected and where divine decrees were issued. This was a common cultural idea, perhaps akin to how many people think of church – church is a place you'd expect to meet God, or where God can be found.[‡]

Heiser reminds us that Moses was told that the pattern shown to him on the holy mountain must be followed for the construction of the tabernacle and its gear (Exodus 25:9, 40; 26:30). This implies (strongly we

---

[†] John H. Walton, *The Lost World of Genesis One*, pp. 80-83. Downers Grove, InterVarsity Press, 2009.

[‡] Heiser, op. cit., pp. 173-175.

might add), that the earthly tabernacle was *a copy of the one existing in heaven*. Continuing with Heiser's thoughts:

> The heavenly tent prototype was the heavens themselves, as Isaiah 40:22 tells us ("It is he who sits above the circle of the earth, and its inhabitants are like grasshoppers; who stretches out the heavens like a curtain, and spreads them like a tent to dwell in" [ESV]). This kind of language is also why the earth is referred to as God's footstool (Isaiah 66:1). Yahweh sits above the circle of the earth, in his heavenly tent, on his throne above the waters which are above "the firmament," and rests his feet on the earth, which is his footstool (Job 9:8; Psa 104:2). As Eden was the place where humanity experienced the presence of God, *so too was the tabernacle*. This was particularly true for the priests, but God's presence occasionally met Israel's leaders outside the holy of holies (Leviticus 9:23; Numbers 12:5–19;20:6; Deuteronomy 31:15), the most obvious instance *being the glory cloud* (Exodus 40:34–35).[§] [Emphasis added}

Heiser says the menorah ("lampstand") in the tabernacle is analogous to the Edenic tree of life, and therefore it takes little imagination to notice it possesses the appearance of a tree (Exodus 25:31–36). It also corresponded to the Garden because it was set right outside the holy of holies.

The cherubim inside the holy of holies are also a clear connection to Eden. The Edenic cherubim stood guard at the dwelling place of God in Eden. Their position atop the lid to the ark of the covenant is not coincidental. The innermost sanctum of the tabernacle was the place from which God would govern Israel. The cherubim form a throne for the invisible Yahweh. Later, when the tent of the most holy place was moved into the temple, two giant cherubim were installed within for Yahweh's throne, making the ark his footstool.[**]

[§] Ibid.

[**] Ibid.

However, Austin-Sparks brings us back to consider the broader, deeper, dispensational framework of "the heavenlies." We find his statement adds much to the discussion of what it means for us to *dwell in the heavenlies with Christ,* both now (positionally) and in ages to come.

> Then, because Christ risen and exalted is "seated at God's right hand," He is in that position representatively and inclusively of the Church. The Church, therefore, is "seated together with Him in the heavenlies"; that is, in the present and ultimate good of His sovereignty. Further, the blessings of believers are now, not as under the old economy, temporal, material, sentient, but "spiritual." "The riches of His grace"; "the riches of His inheritance"; "the riches of His glory"; "the unsearchable riches of Christ," etc.—these are all phrases in "Ephesians." These blessings are for a Church and its members who have—through union with Christ in His death and resurrection—been spiritually delivered and emancipated from "this present evil world" as the sphere of their natural life, ambition and resource, and whose hearts are "set on things above" (Col. 3:1–3). If you have really come into the good of such "riches," then you have proportionately come into the heavenlies. While we are right in mentally conceiving of "the heavenlies" as being a realm, we must not confine the idea to geography. Like "the Kingdom of Heaven," it is a sphere or realm in which spiritual factors, principles or laws and conditions obtain and take pre-eminence. [††]

Supplemented with the wisdom of Walton and Heiser, we feel safe in concluding The Tabernacle portrays the creation of God and His presence throughout the universe. While often deeply contemplative, the writer to the Hebrews provides a biblical confirmation of this beautiful truth. God created the earth (first heaven) and sky (the celestial, second heaven) to reflect the heavenly temple where he dwells (in the third heaven). In the words of

---

[††] Austin-Sparks, T. op. cit., Kindle Locations 628-638.

Austin-Sparks, we see the profound impact that being with Christ in the heavenlies, even now, has upon our ability to take the fight to the enemy.

However, the "heavenlies" and the "third heaven" and the truer, better "tabernacle in heaven," isn't what is paramount for the believer. Remember the earth is where Yahweh earnestly seeks to dwell with a glorified humanity serving Him in a loving relationship, bringing back order and beauty to His world, uncorrupted with the sin of powers and principalities, installing a society of loving restraint on the mortal men and women alive during the Millennium, restoring all of nature to the Garden of Eden, while simultaneously instituting a new administration in the heavenlies. The King is coming "with many sons (and daughters) brought to Glory." And His reign will be wonderful, beyond our imaginings. It begins on earth – but it appears destined for the stars "in the ages to come."

Ezekiel 48:35

"And the name of the city (Jerusalem) from that time on will be:

THE LORD IS THERE."

DEEP DIVE: THE NEW JERUSALEM

(Selections from the Paper, "The New Jerusalem" by Dr. Randall Price)

Dr. Randall Price is one of the top evangelical and dispensational scholars today. He has written many books, both popular and academic. He is an expert on the Temple, Israel's history, and biblical studies among many things. He has also gone on some extravagant "hikes" like going to Mount Ararat searching for Noah's Ark.

His short paper on the New Jerusalem is packed full of information, providing a comprehensive yet comprehendible analysis of its attributes. We will recap some of his insights and scholarship.

Dr. Price begins with this introductory statement:

The New Jerusalem is described in Scripture as "the Jerusalem above" (Galatians 4:26), "the city of the living God, the heavenly Jerusalem," (Hebrews 12:22) and "the holy city" that "comes down out of heaven from God" (Revelation 21:2, 10). In the Old Testament, it is seen as primarily as the abode of God whereas in the New Testament it is also the heavenly home of the saints. The sacred structures within the heavenly city contributed the heavenly design for the earthly Tabernacle and Temple, and in its future descended form as the "Tabernacle of God among men" (Revelation 21:3) it will constitute a celestial Temple that is both physical (Revelation 21:12-21) and spiritual (Revelation 21:22) ...

The New Testament carries forward the Old Testament understanding of the New Jerusalem as the destination for the godly. "By faith Abraham ... was looking for the city which has foundations, whose architect and builder is God" (Hebrews 11:10). The Scripture appears to convey that this "better city" was pre-existent to the creation of the earthly Jerusalem. It was understood to be the residence of the righteous, where they would dwell with the LORD God.

The New Testament asserts, as does the old, that Jerusalem's earthly sanctuaries were designed by God Himself and supplied to Moses. They were shown to Moses on the mount of God and became the divine pattern. The design included their dimensions (Revelation 21:12-21) and the furniture of the structures also. (Revelation 11:19; cf. 4:5; 5:8; 6:9; 8:3; 9:13; 14:18; 15:5-8; 16:7) ... Dr. Price clarifies this:

Stephen's speech in the Book of Acts alludes to Exodus 25:8-9, 40 when it declares: "He who spoke to Moses directed him to make it [the Tabernacle] according to the pattern (Greek *tupon*) which he had seen" (Acts 7:44). The author of Hebrews in comparing the earthly and heavenly sanctuaries likewise refers to "the copies (Greek *hupodeigmata*) of the things in the heavens" (Hebrews 9:23). In these same contexts, it is declared that "the Most High does not dwell in [houses] made by human hands" (Acts 7:48), but in "the greater and more perfect Tabernacle, not made with hands ... not of this creation" (Hebrews 9:11).

Price notes that both Paul in chapter 4 of Galatians and the author of the book of Hebrews speaks of the "Jerusalem above". The more excellent city stands in contrast to Mount Sinai, a place of "law" while the New Jerusalem if a place of grace. Hebrews 12:22-24a expresses who are residents of this city: "But you have come to Mount Zion and to the city of the living God, the heavenly Jerusalem, and to myriads of angels, to the general assembly of the first-born who are enrolled in heaven, and to God, the judge of all, and to the spirits of righteous men made perfect, and to Jesus, the mediator of a new covenant ... (Hebrews 12:22-24a). Price explains that the "registry" includes the Judge (God the Father), the Mediator (God the Son), angels, Old Testament believers, and New Testament saints as well. This list is in keeping with the destiny identified in the Old Testament. Price lists Job 19:25-27; 2 Kings 2:11; Psalm 11:7; 73:24.

Price notes the vital metaphor of the "bride and groom." In Revelation 21:9, the wife of the Lamb is the New Jerusalem (recall earlier that we pointed out the New Jerusalem is both a place and its people). And the bride has been made ready for the groom (Revelation 21:2). Price affirms that this refers to the "many mansions" Jesus promises His disciples in John 14:2 and those who believe in Him as a result of the preaching of His disciples. The reader may recall the Jewish custom of the groom preparing a place, building a home if you will, for the bride (frequently at/in his father's house) to dwell with him. When the bridegroom returned for his bride, this would commence the wedding feast, with the bridge adorned and prepared to consummate the union. (Jesus parable regarding "the wise and foolish virgins" is based upon this custom.)

The New Jerusalem comprises the focal point for the union of Y'shua and His Body, for which the tabernacle and the Temple served as "shadows" of what is to come. It is the ultimate "meeting place." Price explains:

> The New Jerusalem is therefore called "the Tabernacle (Greek skene for Hebrew *mishkan*, "dwelling") of God" since in it God will forever "dwell" among His people (Revelation 21:3; 22:3-4), and a "temple" comprised of "the Lord God, the Almighty and the Lamb" (Revelation 21:22).

The New Jerusalem is structured as a "cube" of massive proportions. "The predicate adjective 'foursquare' (Greek *tetragonos*), describing the dimensions of the city, is from 'four' (Greek tetra) and 'corner' (Greek *gonos*)... This design of connecting planes of equal size forming a cube has long been recognized as the unique cubical shape of the Holy of Holies in the Temple in which the Presence of God dwelt in the midst of Israel." (Ref: 1 Kings 6:20; 8:10-13; 2 Chronicles 3:8; 5:14-6:2).

Importantly, as we have indicated earlier in several places of our study, the New Jerusalem will be a unified residence for both the Church and for the saints of Israel. We see this as the gates are 12 in number and named for each of the 12 tribes, while the foundation stones – also 12 in number – are named after the Apostles of Jesus Christ (although the names are not identified). Price states, "Even though these are all Jewish, they still represent the dispensations of Israel and the Church (as in Hebrews 12:23)..." And another interesting point he makes, "Part of (Jesus') preparation may be His entrance into the heavenly Holy of Holies as a High Priest in order to qualify us as pure priests to serve the holy God." (Hebrews 9:11-14; Revelation 22:3b).

Randall Price, selections from his paper, "The New Jerusalem." Retrieved on June 4, 2017, from http://www.worldofthebible.com/Bible%20Studies/The%20New%20Jerusalem.pdf.

10: CONCLUSION – FINISHING STRONG WITH THE BODY OF CHRIST

"God's vision is not centered so much on the individual, as on the Church; nor are His mighty works done through the single member, but through the Body."* - DeVern Fromke, *The Ultimate Intention*

n pressing on toward our conclusion, it's time to stress the importance of realizing the fullness of God's glory, *through participation in the Body*. Oneness with Christ is also oneness with all members of His Church.

John 17:1-3 Jesus spoke these words, lifted up His eyes to heaven, and said: "Father, the hour has come. Glorify Your Son, that Your Son also may glorify You, ²as You have given Him authority over all flesh, that He should give eternal life to as many as You have given Him. ³And this is eternal life, that they may know You, the only true God, and Jesus Christ whom You have sent.

John 17:11 Now I am no longer in the world, but these are in the world, and I come to You. Holy Father, keep through Your name those whom You have given Me, *that they may be one as We are.*

John 17:20-23 "I do not pray for these alone, but also for those who will believe in Me through their word; ²¹that they all may be one, as You, Father, *are* in Me, and I in You; that they also may be one in

---

Us, that the world may believe that You sent Me. [22]And the glory which You gave Me I have given them, that they may be one just as We are one: [23]I in them, and You in Me; that they may be made perfect in one, and that the world may know that You have sent Me, and have loved them as You have loved Me.

OUR UNITY – A TESTIMONY TO THE TRUTH OF THE GOSPEL

Jesus prayed for unity of all believers down to our present day (as many as God has given Him). "That the world may know" – on this earth, not in the sweet bye-and-bye (perhaps not in heaven, after the rapture, for example). *Has God answered His son's prayer? Is He going to?*

1 Cor 1:10-13 Now I plead with you, brethren, by the name of our Lord Jesus Christ, that you all speak the same thing, and *that* there be no divisions among you, but *that* you be perfectly joined together in the same mind and in the same judgment. [11]For it has been declared to me concerning you, my brethren, by those of Chloe's *household,* that there are contentions among you. [12]Now I say this, that each of you says, "I am of Paul," or "I am of Apollos," or "I am of Cephas," or "I am of Christ." [13]Is Christ divided? Was Paul crucified for you? Or were you baptized in the name of Paul?

"That there be no divisions among you..." Webster's says denomin-ationalism is sectarianism (a dissenting or schismatic religious body). *Schism: division, separation, discord, disharmony – a picture of today's church.* We do not see much harmony among the denominations of our time. *This is not the work of the Spirit of God.*

T. Austin-Sparks writes eloquently about Paul's specific instructions to his churches, to expect opposition that originates from the evil one:

We must remember that when Paul wrote this Letter [Ephesians] and sent it to the churches in localities, he was very well aware of the trends, or even the actual movements toward "departure" and breakdown in the churches. He had foretold it as to Ephesus when he left the elders of that church near the ship on his way to Jerusalem: "I know that after my departing grievous wolves shall enter in among you... and from among your own selves shall men arise... to draw away... after them" (Acts 20:29,30). That was incipient division. But here from his prison in Rome he will write, "all that are in Asia turned away from me." Two Letters will soon be written to Timothy (who was probably in Ephesus) which will deal with the beginnings of the change from primal Christianity to all that it has become now. They were intended to warn against the ecclesiasticism, clericalism, ritualism, sacramentalism, etc., which have invaded the Church and changed its primitive character. No, Paul's head was not in the clouds and his feet off the earth when he deliberately wrote this Letter as to what the Church is. No doubt his reference to the spiritual warfare was because he knew so well that the battle was on in particular relationship with this very matter, showing of how great a consequence it is to the Satanic forces. It is impressive how any stand for a true expression of the Body of Christ. It is fraught with more conflict than anything else.[†]

Nevertheless, Paul teaches that we should set high, even heavenly standards, because the Church remains an indispensable element to bring us into the fullness of Christ, to bring order and impact. And these standards can only be fulfilled by the Spirit working in us, through us, and with us:

> **1 Cor 12:12-14** For as the body is one and has many members, but all the members of that one body, being many, are one body, so also *is* Christ. [13]For by one Spirit we were all baptized into one body – whether Jews or Greeks, whether slaves or free – and have all been

---

[†] Austin-Sparks, T.; Austin-Sparks, Theodore. The Stewardship of the Mystery - Volume 2 (Kindle Locations 727-728). Austin-Sparks.Net. Kindle Edition.

made to drink into one Spirit. [14]For in fact the body is not one member but many.

1 Cor 12:19-21 And if they *were* all one member, where *would* the body *be?* [20]But now indeed *there are* many members, yet one body. [21]And the eye cannot say to the hand, "I have no need of you"; nor again the head to the feet, "I have no need of you."

1 Cor 12:24-27 [24]But our presentable *parts* have no need. But God composed the body, having given greater honor to that *part* which lacks it, [25]that there should be no schism in the body, but *that* the members should have the same care for one another. [26]And if one member suffers, all the members suffer with *it;* or if one member is honored, all the members rejoice with *it.* [27]Now you are the body of Christ, and members individually.

These verses speak of the loving care that each member is to show the others, because *we are all members of the same body.*

1 Cor 1:2 To the church of God which is at Corinth, to those who are sanctified in Christ Jesus, called *to be* saints, with all who in every place call on the name of Jesus Christ our Lord, both theirs and ours:

2 Thes 1:1 Paul, Silvanus, and Timothy, To the church of the Thessalonians in God our Father and the Lord Jesus Christ:

ONE church in each city – the church at Rome, Corinth, Thessalonica, etc. ONE universal church made up of *all believers worldwide.*

Mat 6:33 But seek first the kingdom of God and His righteousness, and all these things shall be added to you.

In the kingdom of God – God is King. *All subjects are to be in submission to One King in order that unity blossoms among all the subjects.*

AS THE DEW FROM HEAVEN – THE REFRESHING OF THE SPIRIT

Ps 133:1-3 [1]Behold, how good and how pleasant *it is* for brethren to dwell together in unity! [2]*It is* like the precious oil upon the head, running down on the beard, the beard of Aaron, Running down on the edge of his garments. [3]*It is* like the dew of Hermon, descending upon the mountains of Zion; for there the LORD commanded the blessing – life forevermore.

In Psalm 133, we encounter references to the mysterious Mount Herman. But what is the "dew of Hermon"? *NetBible Notes* explains:

> The hills of Zion are those surrounding Zion (see Ps 87:1; 125:2). The psalmist does not intend to suggest that the dew from Mt. Hermon in the distant north actually flows down upon Zion. His point is that the same kind of heavy dew that replenishes Hermon may also be seen on Zion's hills. See A. Cohen, Psalms (SoBB), 439. "Dew" here symbolizes divine blessing, as the next line suggests. (*NetBible Notes*)

Why is Hermon referenced here in relation to Zion? From previous commentary, we know that the LORD will reside on all the "mountains from the north" where the false gods dwell. Hermon is but one. So perhaps there is a reference here to the descent of the watchers upon Mount Hermon as told in the Book of Enoch. Or, perhaps it is a reference to Christ ascending the mount with His disciples to reclaim the territory, then descending the mountain to bring blessings. We know that after the transcendent experience the gospels tell us Jesus was confronted by the failure of his other disciples (who had not gone up the mountain) to cast out a demon. The account in Mark is especially detailed and colorful. (See Mark 9:14-29). This juxtaposition suggests that the "conquering" of the evil near Hermon and

Caesarea (regarded as the "gate of hell"), served notice that the "evil moun-tain" had become "the holy mountain." Christ would teach His disciples how to rid the people of all kinds of evil and evil spirits. It would be the blessing, the dew that comes upon Hermon (leading to snow and frost at its high altitudes); therefore, perhaps the reference only regards the pure white ice as a symbol of cleansing and purity. Recall, the Jews saw water as a blessing.

But the solution to the question of what is the meaning of "Aaron and the oil running down his beard," in this context, much simpler. It symbolizes the Spirit of God and 'the anointing' of Aaron by that Spirit. In this Psalm, Aaron represents the anointing of God's Spirit in the Body.

PRESSURE, PAIN, PERSECUTION: THE APPOINTED PATH TO PARTAKING OF THE DIVINE NATURE

But make no mistake. There will be bumpy roads ahead. God will allow this pressure (fire) to refine and unify His people. [See the simple visual aid for the rationale of tribulation and persecution on the Body of Christ at the end of this chapter. It's simple, but it's meant to cement the point firmly in the reader's memory. Challenges await – but they are necessary to bring the Body of Christ into oneness.] Here, we do well to cite Austin-Sparks once more, where he explains the necessity of tribulations if the Body is to achieve the fullness of the measure of Christ:

In the New Testament, the Church universal and the churches local came out of real travail. The travail, agony, and pain of Christ gave birth to the Church at Pentecost. Those who were its nucleus were baptized into His passion. They suffered the breaking of their souls when Jesus died. Hence their ecstatic joy when He rose again. John 16:21,22 was literally fulfilled in their case. That needs no enlarging upon. But what of the churches? Can we put our finger upon a New Testament church which was not born out of and into suffering? Immediately such a church was in view the battle for its very life, its very existence, began. Stonings, imprisonments, lashes, chasings, intrigues, slanders, persecutions of every kind lay at the emergence of every such potential representation of Christ corporately. Someone had to pay a price and the churches were the price of blood and tears. When power is lost, perhaps through neglect, foolishness, strife, division, formalism, or the loss of the sense of the value of the truth, or for any other reason, the only way of recovery will be that of a fresh baptism into sorrow, remorse, tears and travail. This is surely the right interpretation of the Second Letter to the Corinthians after the First. This also surely is the key to the situation in most of the churches in Revelation two and three. It is definitely implied in the case of Laodicea.[‡]

Acts 14:22 Strengthening the souls of the disciples, exhorting *them* to continue in the faith, and *saying, "We must through many tribulations enter the kingdom of God."*

Heb 12:26-27 [26]Whose voice then shook the earth; but now He has promised, saying, *"Yet once more I shake not only the earth, but also heaven."* [27]Now this, *"Yet once more,"* indicates the removal of those things that are being shaken, as of things that are made, *that the things which cannot be shaken may remain.*

And yet the Church has not been abandoned. It possesses powerful capabilities (gifts) to deal with the tribulation, distress, and persecution.

Eph 4:11-16 [11]*And He Himself gave some to be **apostles,** some **prophets,** some **evangelists,** and some **pastors** and **teachers,** [12]for the equipping of the saints for the work of ministry, for the edifying of the body of Christ, [13]till **we all come to the unity of the faith** and of the knowledge of the Son of God, **to a perfect man, to the measure of the stature of the fullness of Christ;** [14]that we should no longer be children, tossed to and fro and carried about with every wind of doctrine, by the trickery of men, in the cunning craftiness of deceitful*

[‡] Sparks, op. cit., (Kindle Locations 777-787).

plotting, ^{15}but, *speaking the truth in love, may grow up in all things into Him who is the head – Christ – ^{16}from whom the whole body, joined and knit together by what every joint supplies, according to the effective working by which every part does its share, causes growth of the body for the edifying of itself in love.*

The five ministries given by Jesus to the church (apostles, prophets, evangelist, pastors, and teachers) must be dedicated and incorporated into the Church that they may accomplish their work. Their mission, rightly enacted, brings unity and maturity to the church, and keeps the church safe amidst the deception of the last days. But, let us realize it is ultimately the love of God which brings maturity to the church; in other words, *the love of God matures the church!* This is the perfection about which the apostle Paul speaks. God's love will bring unity in the Body. *And unity in the Body better prepares each of us to receive the fullness of God's glory:*

Eph 3:17-19 ^{17}That Christ may dwell in your hearts through faith; that you, **being rooted and grounded in love**, ^{18}may be able to comprehend with all the saints what *is* the width and length and depth and height – ^{19}*to know the love of Christ which passes knowledge; that* **you may be filled with all the fullness of God.**

1 John 4:8-17 ^{8}He who does not love does not know God, for God is love. ^{9}In this the love of God was manifested toward us, that God has sent His only begotten Son into the world, *that we might live through Him.* ^{10}In this is love, not that we loved God, but that He loved us and sent His Son *to be* the propitiation for our sins. ^{11}**Beloved, if God so loved us, we also ought to love one anothe**r. ^{12}No one has seen God at any time. *If we love one another, God abides in us, and His love has been perfected in us.* ^{13}By this we know that we abide in Him, and He in us, because He has given us of His Spirit. ^{14}And we have seen and testify that the Father has sent the Son *as* Savior of the world. ^{15}Whoever confesses that Jesus is the Son of God, God abides in him, and he in God. ^{16}And we have known and believed the love that God has for us.

God is love, and he who abides in love abides in God, and God in him. *¹⁷Love has been perfected among us in this: that we may have boldness in the day of judgment; because as He is, so are we in this world.*

This perfect love is an "already, but not yet" perfection. It causes us to be as He is in this world. That is, we should be loving as He is loving. And like Jesus, we should be bold in the face of the Adversary: "If Christ be for us, who can be against us?" (Romans 8:31) We have been "knighted" by the King. Yet, we must muster as a Body and fight side by side, imbued with Christ's power. "I can do all things through Christ who strengthens me." (Philippians 4:13) *We have been given all authority on heaven and in earth.* (Matthew 28:18). We are not alone. Christ is with us always. (Matthew 28:20)

Likewise, we should think of this exceedingly great power also as an "already, but not yet" state for us. We progress toward it. We realize it fully at the Parousia. Says Austin-Sparks, "But, let there be a movement in the direction of a real corporate expression of a Holy Spirit constituted testimony to Christ corporate, then the battle is on and nothing will be untried to break that up, discredit it, or in some way nullify that testimony."[§]

Psa 102:13-16 ¹³Thou shalt arise, [and] have mercy upon Zion: for the time to favour her, yea, the set time, is come. ¹⁴ For thy servants take pleasure in her stones, and favour the dust thereof. ¹⁵ So the heathen shall fear the name of the LORD, and all the kings of the earth thy glory. *¹⁶When the LORD shall build up Zion, **he shall appear in his glory**. (KJV)*

Jesus will build up Zion (the church), stone upon stone, each in its proper place, and then He will appear in His glory! We need to make this spiritual truth real in our daily experience. i.e., live in love and unity with all

---

[§] Austin-Sparks, T.; op. cit., Volume 2 (Kindle Locations 731-733).

brothers and sisters, regardless of doctrinal differences (Note how we said: brothers and sisters – not cult-members, not denomination members).

We must practice *forgiveness, love, patience, forbearance with one another* ("the four *bearings* that the church runs on" – to reference a saying of Bob Mumford, from times gone by). *These are crucial principles leading to the church's complete maturity. This maturity means perfection of the Body.*

But we must obtain some additional context to this crucial truth. Let's step back and do a "deep dive" into the "reason why" the Body of Christ," how it must be understood, and why it must come together to enable us to receive the fullness of God. The following in depth teaching is from DeVern Fromke, ministering for 70 years in our land. He passed away recently in 2016. He was 93. His book, *The Ultimate Intention*, offers tremendous insight into why God created the universe, brought humanity to life, redeemed us after we sinned, and commissioned us to rule with Christ in the ages to come, *all before the foundations of the world.* He mirrors in many ways the views of Austin-Sparks. You see, the Church wasn't invented after humanity sinned. It was God's plan from before the Creation. It was in *the mind of God.* It was in *the heart of God.* The Triune God had predestined this – *whether or not humanity sinned* – to execute this plan, to create the Body for Christ. Fromke's commentary reflects (and adds much to) our prior study of the Book of Hebrews. Indeed, we have already drawn several quotations, including the epigraph at the beginning of this chapter from, *The Ultimate Intention*.

DEEP DIVE: THE CORPORATE GLORIFICATION OF THE BODY OF CHRIST

DeVern F. Fromke

HOW THRILLING IT IS to live in the larger viewpoint and have the Father explain what He is accomplishing now in this present age.

In His plan of sanctification, we see how He deliberately follows a pattern. Just as the husbandman plants one seed that he might have a harvest of much fruit after its kind, so the eternal Father plants His precious Son that He might in due time *bring many sons to glory*. How often we have become so fascinated with the growth of the grain that we have overlooked the Husbandman and His intention in... THE PLANTING AND THE HARVEST

A wonderful, though seldom detected, theme runs through the book of Hebrews. Briefly, it is the story of two bodies the Father has designed for His Son. As a Husbandman, the Father planted His only begotten Son and waits for the growth and harvest *of His many regenerated sons who will one day come to glory*. God has spoken His full and all-inclusive message by His unique Son, and He will continue to speak throughout the whole universe in ages to come by His coming corporate sons in union with His unique Son.

A summary of this theme is seen as follows: His unique Son [chapter/ verse references from the **Book of Hebrews**]:

- "God hast... spoken... in His Son" (literally, 'sonwise,' 1: 2).
- "Thou art My Son..." (1: 5).
- "But of the Son He saith..." (1: 8).
- "Christ as Son over His (God's) house..." (3: 6). His many sons—
- "... bringing many sons unto glory" (2: 10).
- "My son, regard not lightly... the chastening..." (12: 5).
- "... every son whom He receiveth..." (12: 6).
- "God dealeth with you as with sons..." (12: 7).
- "Ye are come to the church (assembly) of the First-born who are registered [as citizens] in heaven" (12: 23, Amp.)."

Moreover, herein are two bodies: "(When) He (Christ) entered into the world, He said... you have made ready a body for Me [to offer]" (Heb. 10:5, Amp.).

This natural individual body which He received was offered (planted) in death. But there is another Body of which Paul speaks in Colossians 1: 18— the many-membered corporate Body, the Church. God's Word speaks much of the first body which the Lord Jesus sacrificed on the Cross, that we might experience a personal setting apart unto God (Hebrews 10: 10). But here we have only the foothills of truth. The summit of truth reaches far up into a corporate experience of which we only have glimpses at present.

"Till we all come... unto a perfect man," Paul wrote, "unto the measure of the stature of the fulness of Christ" (Eph. 4: 13). *Not unto many perfect men, but one perfect man— all of us together, Head and Body— a perfect man.* "For as the body is one, and hath many members and all the members of that one body, being many, are one body: so also is Christ" (1 Cor. 12: 12). Norman Grubb notes that it does not say, "so also is the body of Christ," but "so also is Christ." Can we conceive of this? *We are led to a final unification with Christ which is beyond our present understanding.* When the Father fulfills the mystery of His will, He will gather together "in one all things in Christ, both which are in heaven and which are on earth" (Eph. 1: 10).

We have barest glimpses of future glories. Perhaps some of these truths were contained in the "unspeakable words" which Paul heard, but was not permitted to utter. Even though there is much we have not been told, the truths revealed take us from *the marvelous truth of "Christ in us" individually to the even more wonderful revelation of **"us in Christ" collectively.*** Who can measure the implications of this? However, we are not left in the dark concerning one fact: God's vision is not centered so much on the individual, as on the Church; nor are His mighty works done through the single member, but through the Body.

Why then, we may ask, do we spend so much time searching into our individual relationship of Him? Why did Jesus and those who followed Him show utmost concern for individuals? Because as was said of Soren Kierkegaard: "When he spoke to the individual, calling him to seek purity of heart and integrity of will, he was doing the thing he believed best calculated to fit men to act as a responsible community. If he spoke more of the individual than of the community, it was because the first thing necessary was to restore the true individuality without which true community is not possible. Individuality, not individualism, was his primary aim." Through inner integration— *that holiness which is wholeness—* we are liberated from self-centeredness in order that the Head of the Body can share with us His body-consciousness. Here we must observe real caution. It is possible to talk the language of external unity while building on foundations of sand. *The truth of the Vine-branch relationship must be an individual experience before the believer can participate in the wider corporate implications.*

It seems in the present hour that men are victims of two extremes. One group emphasizes bringing individuals to Christ. The tremendous emphasis placed by the New Testament writers on the relationship of the individual to Christ justifies us in doing the same. *But we must not stop there. We must move on to see individual integration into the Body.* Others become overanxious to explore the ways to external unity without first being concerned with the spiritual condition of individuals thus united. This is the other extreme. *God's intention is clear: When people are living in union with Christ, they are also in living union with one another.* [

Fromke, DeVern F. *The Ultimate Intention* (Kindle Locations 2353-2406). Hauraki Publishing. Kindle Edition.

THE FAMILY AND THE CHURCH

The family is the basic unit of the church. A church within the church, if you will. To live in union with Christ, we must live in union with one another. The Church is not the only, but it is one of the "winepresses" that readies us for becoming partakers of the divine nature. The word translated *partaker* is a related word to the fellowship in the Church, which is a more familiar word from the Greek, *koinonia,* the spirit inspired fellowship of the brethren. *How interesting that "partaking of the divine nature" is likened to fellowship. Partaking* is the translation of the word koy-no-nos'; (Strong's G2839) meaning "a sharer, i.e. associate: companion, fellowship, partaker, partner." Peter is telling us that partaking of the divine nature is collaborating, partnering, or participating in it. *This strongly suggests a corporate arrangement.* Receiving the fullness of Christ – His glory – isn't a solitary endeavor. It transcends "Christ in us." It means we are "in it (the Body) together." The whole family (Church) participates in completing the fullness of Christ.

Psa 68:6 God sets the solitary in families; He brings out those who are bound into prosperity; But the rebellious dwell in a dry *land.*

Singles are not left out. If church families aren't working right – the Body of Christ NEVER WILL. *Each family must seek to be in loving order and unity before the Body of Christ can be.* However, if you are in a highly dysfunctional family, the Body of Christ should offset these difficulties. God is aware of your stewardship in pursuit of "the Mystery."

Mal 4:5-6 Behold, I will send you Elijah the prophet Before the coming of the great and dreadful day of the LORD. [6]And he will turn the hearts of the fathers to the children, And the hearts of the children to their fathers, Lest I come and strike the earth with a curse."

Note: God is so serious about getting families together He sends prophetic ministries to reconcile families and restore love and fellowship.

1 Tim 3:1-5 This *is* a faithful saying: If a man desires the position of a bishop, he desires a good work. [2]A bishop then must be blameless, the husband of one wife, temperate, sober-minded, of good behavior, hospitable, able to teach; [3]not given to wine, not violent, not greedy for money, but gentle, not quarrelsome, not covetous; [4]one who rules his own house well, having *his* children in submission with all reverence [5]*(for if a man does not know how to rule his own house, how will he take care of the church of God?)*

Michael Heiser weighs in on the future role of the family of God. He asserts that because the corporate body of believers, the Church, inherited the Abrahamic promises (Gal 3:26-29), these believers are the "true Israel" of the New Testament. He says that part of our inheritance is the rulership of the nations at the end of days (Rev 3:21), and that we will displace the corrupt divine sons of God who rule the nations, and are under God's judgment (Psa 82). He notes that it is an "already, but not yet" matter of fact; that is, Yahweh's *new council* on earth.

This structuring helps us make sense of something else Paul said. The rulership of the nations was a higher-ranking task than being a messenger (the meaning of the word *angel*). The destiny of believers who will share Jesus' throne and the rule of nations is the backdrop for Paul's statement that Christians should stop letting the world's courts resolve their disputes. In 1 Corinthians 6:3 he protests: "Do you not know that we will judge angels?" When we are made divine (glorified) on the new earth, *we will outrank angels.* Believers are God's once and future family, once and future council, once and future rulers with Jesus over all the nations. *Israel's release propels this theology.***

He also demonstrates that there is other language in the Bible that communicates the idea of the divine-human family council of Yahweh. The "morning stars" in Job 38:7, Abraham's offspring (Genesis 15:5, 22:17), and the "stars of God" in Isaiah 14:13, are dramatic examples. The sons of Jacob (Israel) in Joseph's dream (Gen 37:9) are stars. Heiser stresses that this simile is not an accident. Heiser notes that *star language* often speaks of divinity, glorification, and existence that surpasses nature. His examples include Revelation 1:20; 22:16; cf. 2:28; Daniel 12:2-3 (the righteous will "shine like the brightness of the sky above ... like the stars, forever and ever"). The star language of Genesis 15 absolutely has an eschatological connotation, he explains, confirming that "Abraham's seed" (Galatians 3:26–29) – Yahweh's children, will eventually reverse the disinheritance of the nations that occurred at the Tower of Babel incident.

2 Th 2:13-17 But we are bound to give thanks to God always for you, brethren beloved by the Lord, because God from the beginning chose you for salvation through sanctification by the Spirit and belief

---

** Heiser, *op. cit.,* (pp. 158-160)

The Body of Christ divided today —
Even the face and message of the body are off...

Pressure from Tribulation
and Persecution help bring unity

Figure 6 – Tribulation and persecution brings unity to the Body.

in the truth, [14]to which He called you by our gospel, *for the obtaining of the glory of our Lord Jesus Christ.* [15]Therefore, brethren, stand fast and hold the traditions which you were taught, whether by word or our epistle. [16]Now may our Lord Jesus Christ Himself, and our God and Father, who has loved us and given *us* everlasting consolation and good hope by grace, [17]comfort your hearts and establish you in every good word and work.

Phil 3:8-11 *⁸Yet indeed I also count all things loss for the excellence of the knowledge of Christ Jesus my Lord*, for whom I have suffered the loss of all things, and count them as rubbish, that I may gain Christ ⁹and be found in Him, not having my own righteousness, which *is* from the law, but that which *is* through faith in Christ, the righteousness which is from God by faith; ¹⁰that I may know Him and the power of His resurrection, and the fellowship of His sufferings, being conformed to His death, ¹¹if, by any means, I may attain to the resurrection from the dead.

APPREHENDING THE HEAVENLY LIFE IN CHRIST

Paul emphasizes that faith in Christ's work on the cross achieves a righteous standing before God. This testifies to righteousness which comes through *having faith in that work*. But we mustn't stop there. We must press forward, to apprehend (catch, capture, arrest) the prize of the upward call. And we in the Body must be of the same mind, having the same goal, setting aside worldly desires and priorities. Paul continues:

Phil 3:12-19 ¹²Not that I have already attained, or am already perfected; but I press on, that I may lay hold of [apprehend] that for which Christ Jesus has also laid hold of [apprehended] me. ¹³Brethren, *I do not count myself to have apprehended*; but one thing *I do*, forgetting those things which are behind and reaching forward to those things which are ahead, ¹⁴*I press toward the goal for the prize of the upward call of God in Christ Jesus.* ¹⁵Therefore let us, as many as are mature, have this mind; and if in anything you think otherwise, God will reveal even this to you. ¹⁶Nevertheless, to *the degree* that we have already attained, *let us walk by the same rule* [keep doing the good things for that have worked for you so far], let us be of the same mind. ¹⁷Brethren, join in following my example, and note those who so walk, as you have us for a pattern. ¹⁸For many walk, of whom I have told you often, and now tell you even weeping, *that they are* the enemies of the cross of Christ: ¹⁹whose end *is* destruction, whose god *is their* belly, and *whose* glory *is* in their shame – *who set their mind on earthly things.*

Then why should we reset our priorities? What is our motivation?

Phil 3:20-21 [20]For our citizenship is in heaven, from which we also eagerly wait for the Savior, the Lord Jesus Christ, [21]*who will transform our lowly body that it may be conformed to His glorious body*, according to the working by which He is able even to subdue all things to Himself.

DEEP DIVE: THE NEW CLOTHING FOR WHICH WE PERSEVERE

G.H. Pember

The sin was irrevocably committed: The Tempter had triumphed. But what of the affirmation, "Your eyes shall be opened, and ye shall be as God, knowing good and evil"? Alas! it had indeed proved true; but in a fashion widely differing from Eve's expectation. For in the impetuosity of her pride she had not tarried to reflect that the knowledge of God must needs be fraught with destructive peril to those who have neither the wisdom nor the power of God. Her eyes and those of her husband were indeed opened; but only to see themselves, to behold their own sad condition of nakedness and shame. For now, they became suddenly conscious of the vileness of that flesh which had been the medium of their transgression; they were bewildered with the painful sense of a fall from the eminence on which God had placed them, of their resemblance to the brutes around them, nay, even of their unfitness to be seen.

And these feelings seem to have been intensified in no small degree by an instant *and visible change in their outward appearance*. For while they remained in obedience, the spirit which God had breathed into them retained its full power and vigor. Its pervading influence defended their whole being from the inroads of corruption and death; while at the same time its brightness, shining through the covering of flesh, shed a lustrous halo around them; so that the grosser element of their bodies was concealed within a veil of radiant glory. (Compare the description of God in Psalm 104: 2; – "Who coverest Thyself with light as with a garment.") And thus, as the rulers of creation, they were strikingly distinguished from all the creatures which were placed under them.

But their sin was only made possible by a league of soul and body which destroyed the balance of their being. The overborne spirit was reduced to the condition of a powerless and almost silent prisoner; and, consequently, its light faded and disappeared. Its influence was gone: it could no longer either preserve their bodies from decay, or clothe them in its glory as with a garment. The threat of God was an accomplished fact; the reign of death had commenced.

Nor is it difficult to prove that *the recovery of a visible glory will be the instant result of the restoration of spirit soul and body to perfect order and harmony, the sign of our manifestation as sons of God.* But it will then shine with far more intense brilliancy than it did in Adam: for, as we have before seen, the body of unfallen man was not a spiritual body. The spirit did indeed exercise a mighty and vigorous influence, but the soul was the ruling power, even as it continues to be: for the first man became a living soul. (1 Cor 15:45) But when the resurrection, or the change consequent upon our Lord's return, takes place, our bodies will become spiritual: (1 Cor 15:44) the God-consciousness will be supreme in us, holding both soul and body in absolute control, and shedding forth the full power of its glory without let or hindrance.

Hence in speaking of that time Daniel says – "And they that be wise shall shine as the brightness of the firmament; and they that turn many to righteousness as the stars for ever and ever. (Dan 12:3) So, too, the Lord Himself declares – "Then shall the righteous shine forth as the sun in the kingdom of their Father." (Matt 13:43)

And yet again; both John and Paul tell us that, when we are summoned into the presence of the Lord Jesus, *we shall be like Him, that He will change the body of our humiliation into the likeness of the body of His glory.* (1 John 3:2; Phil 3:221) Nor are we left in ignorance as regards the nature of the body of His glory; for upon the mount of transfiguration He permitted the chosen three to behold the Son of Man as He will appear when He comes in His kingdom. Then His Spirit, ever restrained and hidden during His earthly sojourn, was suddenly freed, and in an instant His whole person was beaming with splendor; so that His face did shine as the sun, and His raiment was white as the light. (Matt 17:2)

G. H. Pember, M.A., *Earth's Earliest Ages, A Study of Vital Questions*, (pp. 140-141) Hachette UK: Hodder & Stoughton, 1876

Perhaps, you may still ask us to begin to sum up what this book has been about and answer the question, "What was the point in searching out this amazing topic, the glory of God?" It comes down to this specific thing: *we must never forget nor lose sight of the goal we've established.* We believe that this goal stood as the most prominent incentive for the early Christians when the road got rough, or worse, when crucified martyrs began to line its edge. *We believe this was, at that time, and remains – the supreme motivation.*

The apostles were all Jews. They knew the significance of God's glory. They communicated it to the Gentiles as they were inspired by the Spirit. We see it witnessed in virtually all the epistles of the New Testament, but especially in Ephesians and in the book of Colossians. The epistle to Colossae begins with an amazing summation of this Glory, and the reconciliation of humanity to God through the blood of the cross, that we may finally participate in the Body of Christ, and share in this Glory... provided *we continue in the faith – that we persevere – that we overcome.*

Col 1:18-23 [18]And He is the head of the body, the church, who is the beginning, the firstborn from the dead, that in all things He may have the preeminence. [19]For it pleased *the Father that in Him all the fullness should dwell,* [20]and by Him to reconcile all things to Himself, by Him, whether things on earth or things in heaven, having made peace through the blood of His cross. [21]And you, who once were alienated and enemies in your mind by wicked works, yet now He has reconciled [22]in the body of His flesh through death, to present you holy, and blameless, and above reproach in His sight – [23]*if indeed you* *continue in the faith,* grounded and steadfast, and are not moved away from the hope of the gospel which you heard, which was preached to every creature under heaven, of which I, Paul, became a minister.

Throughout, we have learned that Paul suffers for the "mystery which has *been hidden from ages and from generations,* but has been revealed to His saints." (Colossians 1:26) But just to be precise, allow us to say it this way: Moses didn't know of the Mystery when he wrote the Pentateuch. David didn't know of the Mystery as he was composing Psalms. The prophets of God didn't learn of this Mystery when the Spirit fell upon them. It was the Mystery – entirely hidden - until God directly revealed it to Paul. Therefore, please understand: Colossians 1:26 is one of the most strategic and remarkable versions in the New Testament, indeed the entire Bible, for it discloses the "ultimate intention" of God – the reason why the Church was created, justified, sanctified (ongoing), and eagerly awaits the day when it will be glorified and all creation released from the curse. To recite this crucial passage one more time, in context:

> **Col 1:24-28** [24]I now rejoice in my sufferings for you, and fill up in my flesh what is lacking in the afflictions of Christ, for the sake of His body, which is the church, [25]of which I became a minister according to the stewardship from God which was given to me for you, to fulfill the word of God, [26]*the mystery which has been hidden from ages and from generations, but now has been revealed to His saints.* [27]To them God willed to make known what are the riches of the glory *of this mystery among the Gentiles: which is Christ in you, the hope of glory.* [28]Him we preach, warning every man and teaching every man in all wisdom, that we may *present every man perfect in Christ Jesus.*

The mystery is this: "Christ in you, the hope of glory. The "mystery" was not an invention of Paul, a product of his creative genius, a personal gospel concocted for his glory. We know that the other apostles upheld it too. They preached it. They agreed that Paul's words were Scripture (2 Peter 3:16). Indeed, *the Mystery was the Gospel*. As a result, the Church spread everywhere, across the entire Gentile world. Says Austin-Sparks:

> That there was a difference and peculiar importance in Paul's ministry has a number of strong evidences and attestations. He knew it himself and often referred to it, both as to its substance and the way in which he received it. This is expressed in such words as these: "the stewardship (R.V. margin) of that grace of God which was given me to you-ward"; "how that by revelation was made known unto me the mystery... whereby... ye can perceive my understanding in the mystery of Christ"; "Unto me... was this grace given... to make all men see (bring to light—R.V. margin) what is the stewardship of the mystery" (Eph. 3:2–4, 8, 9). While Paul does not say that he alone had the "mystery" made known to him, he does claim that, as a stewardship, a ministry, it was revealed to him in a distinctly personal and direct-from-heaven manner. He claimed that he was divinely apprehended for this particular ministry.[††]

Peter expresses the glory that awaits Christians, using the metaphor "the crown of glory:"

> **1 Pet 5:4** And when the Chief Shepherd appears, *you will receive the crown of glory* that does not fade away.

This crown is literal, but also figurative. The crown symbolizes the full glory of Christ – **the revealing** of each son or daughter of God, shining for all to see, the gift of Christ that He eagerly has shared with us. This glory shone on the face of Moses, reflecting God's glory after their meeting. But unlike Moses, the glory that the Church and its members shall receive, will not fade away. No, absolutely not! The manifest presence of God – His glory - will dwell with us and abide upon us all – we will all *share*, that is, *partake* of this glory for eternity!

[††] Austin-Sparks, T. op. cit., Kindle Locations 230-239.

Recall the meaning of manifest – αποκαλυπσισ (ap-ok-al'-oop-sis): 1) laying bear, making naked; 2) disclosing truth, instruction... 2a) concerning things before unknown; 2b) used of events by which things or states or persons hitherto withdrawn from view, are made visible to all; 3) *manifestation, an appearance, or* **the revealing.**

1 Tim 6:12-16 [12]Fight the good fight of faith, *lay hold* on eternal life, to which you were also called and have confessed the good confession in the presence of many witnesses. [13]I urge you in the sight of God who gives life to all things, and *before* Christ Jesus who witnessed the good confession before Pontius Pilate, [14]that you keep *this* commandment without spot, blameless until our *Lord Jesus Christ's appearing,* [15]which He will manifest in His own time, *He who is* the blessed and only Potentate, the King of kings and Lord of lords, [16]*who alone has immortality, dwelling in unapproachable light, whom no man has seen or can see,* to whom *be* honor and everlasting power. Amen.

Understanding the reward that God has in store for us inspires in us with a greater incentive to "fight the good fight of our faith." *Anticipating the inheritance is the to repeat ourselves, the ultimate spiritual motivation, that we may surely follow Jesus to the end.*

So, we beseech you to find your place in the body. Work patiently toward unity for which Jesus prayed. Receive the five-fold ministries of the Spirit for our leaders. In so doing, along with all other believers, *receive the promise of the inheritance – the glory of God.*

THE CALLING IS UNIMAGINABLE AND WEIGHTY

Dr. Heiser reminds us our future existence is incredible:

How do you describe the indescribable? Paul grasped the problem clearly. I still like the King James Version of his sentiments for their rhythmic, almost lyrical quality: "Eye hath not seen, nor ear heard, neither have entered into the heart of man, the things which God hath prepared for them that love him" (1 Corinthians 2:9).

Heiser identifies several passages which refer to what our resurrection life might be like:

> Daniel 12:2–3 ties resurrection life to the heavens (and stars) without speculating on the nature of resurrection existence: "And many from those sleeping in the dusty ground will awake, some to everlasting life and some to disgrace and everlasting contempt. But the ones having insight will shine like the brightness of the expanse, and the ones providing justice for the many will be like the stars forever and ever."
>
> The New Testament contains similar thinking. (We read in) Matthew 13:43, "Then the righteous will shine like the sun in the kingdom of their Father." The point of the celestial analogy: a believer's body will be like that of Jesus, since Jesus' appearance at the transfiguration is described in similar terms: "His face shone like the sun, and his clothing became bright as the light" (Matt 17:2). *Second Temple Jewish sources describe the same idea with respect to the resurrected righteous.*
>
> In our more modern language, we might say that the body Christ had after the resurrection was his earthly body, healed and transformed into a material form unbound by the limitations of human terrestrial existence. It was a "glorious body" (Phil 3:21), both of earth and not of earth. This resurrection transformation is the final, unimaginably literal expression of being conformed to the image of Christ (2 Cor 3:18). [Emphasis added] [‡‡]

Eph 4:11-13 And He Himself gave some *to be* apostles, some prophets, some evangelists, and some pastors and teachers, [12]for the equipping of the saints for the work of ministry, for the edifying of the body of Christ, [13]till we all come to *the unity of the faith and of the*

[‡‡] Heiser, op. cit., (excerpts, pp. 376-379)

knowledge of the Son of God, to a perfect man, to the measure of the stature of the fullness of Christ;

1 John 3:2-3 Beloved, now we are children of God; and it has not yet been revealed what we shall be, but we *know that when He is revealed, we shall be like Him,* for we shall see Him as He is. [3] And everyone who has this hope in Him purifies himself, just as He is pure.

Perhaps the most vivid picture of the gift of the glory of God to the church is that of the honeymoon. The new husband and wife have kept themselves pure and are eagerly anticipating the ecstasy of their sexual union. Just so, the Bride of Christ is betrothed but not married. The best is yet to come! At the marriage of the Lamb and His Bride, the glory of God will be much more fulfilling and blissful than any physical experience on earth! Also, just as the sexual union is a celebration of the covenant of marriage, the glory of God in the church is a celebration of the fulfilled New Covenant. The symbolism that God has built into the sexual experience – corresponding to that of the highest all-consuming spiritual experience – is one major reason that Satan attempts to twist and pervert this gift of God.

DEEP DIVE: THE WEIGHT OF GLORY

For which cause we faint not; but though our outward man perish, yet the inward man is renewed day by day. For our light affliction, which is but for a moment, worketh for us a far more exceeding and eternal **weight** *of glory; While we look not at the things which are seen, but at the things which are not seen: for the things which are seen are temporal; but the things which are not seen are eternal.* (2 Corinthians 4:16-18)

Through this passage, we stumble across a lesser known quality of what *glory* entails. Paul calls it "the *weight* of glory." What does he mean by this?

The word translated 'weight' in the Greek is *baros* (*bah-ross*) occurring six times in the New Testament. It is translated five times as 'burden' and only once as 'weight.' (See Matthew 20:12, Acts 15:28 for examples). The notion constitutes *assigning 'great weight' to an expert's remarks.* To be more specific, it comprises *authority*; yet possessing authority *combined with responsibility*.

In another passage but within the same letter, Paul indicates how many of his opponents complained about his personal style. They criticized him as a weakling when face-to-face, but stern when admonishing others at a dis-tance (through his letters). 2 Corinthians 10:10 says, "... *his letters are* **weighty** *and powerful" (here Paul mimics his opponents).* The word employed in this verse is *barys*, an adjective form of *baros*. As an adjective, *barys* conveys not just sternness or severity *but strength and power*. His enemies were saying, "Oh, so you are a tough guy when you write, but when you are here in person you are not so big and tough after all, are you?"

If we have 'weight,' however, we are not so easily intimidated. Our strength and 'presence' convey 'weight.' In a manner of speaking, it smacks of bragga-docio: "Do not mess with me! You are tugging on superman's cape!"

C.S. Lewis once wrote a book (something he was often inclined to do!) entitled, *The Weight of Glory*. While he never actually refers to the text of 2 Corinthians in the book, this Pauline text remained his touch-stone.

Christopher W. Mitchell says this, regarding what C.S. Lewis meant by "the weight of glory:" "Lewis longed above all else for the unseen things of which this life offers only shadows, for that weight of glory which the Lord Christ won for the human race. And knowing the extraordinary nature of every human person, Lewis longed for and labored for their glory as well."[§§]

Lewis was an evangelist. He was not always eager and enthusiastic to play that part. But he believed in the eternal value of the 'soul' which, on behalf of

---

[§§] "Bearing the Weight of Glory: The Cost of C.S. Lewis's Witness," Christopher W. Mitchell.

God, he sought. Goodness knows Lewis could look upon many he who attempted to convert, surmising that in their present state, they had no 'weight' at all. But the eyes of faith saw something very different. Lewis could see the potential in all humans in the same way Christ sees them. Wright quotes Lewis from his book, *The Four Loves,*

"But heaven forbid we should work in the spirit of prigs and Stoics," Lewis declared, writing of the ultimate purpose of love in his book *The Four Loves.* "While we hack and prune we know very well that what we are hacking and pruning is big with a splendor and vitality which our rational will could never of itself have supplied. To liberate that splendor, to let it become fully what it is trying to be, to have tall trees instead of scrubby tangles, and sweet apples instead of crabs, is part of our purpose." In his fiction, theology, apologetics and correspondence, Lewis can be seen hacking and pruning with the hope that his efforts might be used to produce "everlasting splendours."[***]

Lewis understood very well what Christ won for us at Calvary was much more than forgiveness of sins—it was an amazing future life *consisting of glory with 'great weight.'* In other words, with the glory of God becoming part of our eternal natures, we will cease being 'light weights.' Our lives will carry a presence felt by other entities we will encounter in the Kingdom to come (be they mortal humans, angelic beings, or God Himself—to His praise and glory).

Perhaps we cannot fathom what 'weight' our lives will convey then.

We know we *are to rule with Christ* in the Kingdom that comes (*"and they lived and reigned with Christ a thousand years"*—Revelation 20:4). We are also informed specifically we will judge angels! (No doubt, to their chagrin since their *might* exceeds ours now—see 1 Corinthians 6:3.) We know after we are glorified, we are called "the Mighty Ones" ... We can surmise the "clouds of heaven" that accompany Christ are made white clouds not just because we are wearing white robes and command white horses. Somehow, our glory will shine forth too as we ride with Him. Our glory—God's ultimate

---

[***] Ibid.

gift through Jesus Christ via His death for us—will also contribute to *the brightness of the shining clouds* encompassing the heavens as the battle of Armageddon is joined.

No wonder the multitude that surrounds the throne in Revelation 4:10, casts their crowns before Jesus Christ. The Saints reflect who truly deserves 'their' crown. *The glory which they possess was won by Jesus Christ,* by His suffering on the cross. Indeed, for all but a few, our sufferings are meager compared to what He suffered on our behalf. And yet, He eagerly wants us (recalling the analogy from earlier in the epistle) to exchange our dilapidated 'house' for the *eternal house of glory* He has prepared for us.

S. Douglas Woodward, *Blood Moon: Biblical Signs of the Coming Apocalypse,* (2014), Oklahoma City: Faith Happens Books, pp. 280-283.

Remember that God created us to live from the beginning in His presence (glory), but we chose (in Adam) to live the lower life of the earth (feed our flesh instead of our spirit), and fell short of the glory of God. The glory of God is the spiritual provision for every need that we have – body, soul, and spirit, for it is the full manifestation of God's presence. God's glory satisfies every need spiritually and in our soul, plus being our clothing (2 Cor 4:17,18; 5:1-4), food, and transportation (think translation in the spirit – e.g., Enoch, Elijah, and Philip). The glorification of the believer does not detract from the Lord Jesus, because He is the one who made it possible for us to receive God's glory, *for He is the Brightness of God's glory (Heb 1:3).* Jesus desires to share His inheritance with us. From the cloud of glory, God says, "this is my beloved Son: HEAR HIM" (Luke 9:35). God wants to give His love in a very real and practical way to those who will open to Him in the last days. *His manifest presence through the body of Christ will minister life to those who are willing to identify with Him even if it means physical death.* This is the "meat in due season" that Jesus spoke about:

Mat 24:42-51 [42]"Watch therefore, for you do not know what hour your Lord is coming. [43] "But know this, that if the master of the house had known what hour the thief would come, he would have watched and not allowed his house to be broken into. [44] "Therefore you also be ready, for the Son of Man is coming at an hour you do not expect. [45] "Who then is a faithful and wise servant, whom his master made ruler over his household, to give them food in due season? [46] "Blessed [is] that servant whom his master, when he comes, will find so doing. [47] "Assuredly, I say to you that he will make him ruler over all his goods. [48] "But if that evil servant says in his heart, 'My master is delaying his coming,' [49] "and begins to beat [his] fellow servants, and to eat and drink with the drunkards, [50] "the master of that servant will come on a day when he is not looking for [him] and at an hour that he is not aware of, [51] "and will cut him in two and appoint [him] his portion with the hypocrites. There shall be weeping and gnashing of teeth.

Psa 24:1-10 [1]*A Psalm of David.* The earth [is] the LORD's, and all its fullness, the world and those who dwell therein. [2] For He has founded it upon the seas, and established it upon the waters. [3] Who may ascend into the hill of the LORD? Or *who may stand in His holy place?* [4] He who has clean hands and a pure heart, who has not lifted up his soul to an idol, nor sworn deceitfully. [5] He shall receive blessing from the LORD, And righteousness from the God of his salvation. [6] This [is] Jacob, the generation of those who seek Him, who seek Your face. Selah [7] *Lift up your heads, O you gates! And be lifted up, you everlasting doors! And* **the King of glory** *shall come in.* [8] *Who [is]* **this King of glory**? *The LORD strong and mighty, The LORD mighty in battle.* [9] Lift up your heads, O you gates! Lift up, you everlasting doors! *And the King of glory shall come in.* [10] *Who is this King of glory? The LORD of hosts,* **He [is] the King of glory.** Selah (Amplified Bible) The next time you hear Handel's Messiah, the chorus that quotes these words will have much more meaning, and dare we say, weight, than ever before.

WITH CLEAN HANDS AND PURE HEARTS, LET US BE THE GENERATION THAT SEEKS HIM. LET US LIFT UP THE GATES OF OUR HEARTS AND LET THE KING OF GLORY COME INTO HIS TEMPLE! SELAH.

FOR FURTHER READING

(Books recommended or referenced in *The Revealing*)

Antichrist Before the Day of the Lord, Alan Kurschner

Blood Moon, S. Douglas Woodward

Earth's Earliest Ages, G. H. Pember

Evidence for the Rapture, Michael J. Svigel

First Fruits and Harvest: A Study in Resurrection and Rapture, G. H. Lang

Five Views on Sanctification by Melvin E. Dieter, Anthony A. Hoekema, Stanley M. Horton, J. Robertson McQuilkin, and John F. Walvoord

Harpazo: The Intra-Seal Rapture of the Church, James Jacob Prasch

Reversing Hermon, Michael S. Heiser

The Antichrist, Arthur Pink

The Kingdom, Lambert Dolphin

The Lost World of Genesis One, John H. Walton

The Sign, Robert Van Kampen

The Star of Bethlehem: The Star that Astonished the World, Ernest Martin

The Stewardship of the Mystery, Volume 2, T. Austin-Sparks,

The Ultimate Intention, DeVern F. Fromke

The Unseen Realm, Michael S. Heiser

What on Earth's Going to Happen? Ray C. Stedman

ABOUT THE AUTHORS

Gary L. Huffman grew up on a farm at Highwood, Montana – 40 miles east of Great Falls. The little Methodist church he attended with his family was greatly

influenced by the Charismatic Movement, and so was he. As a teenager, he was lured into the New Age movement... he blames it on the Beatles! He tried the meditation thing plus yoga as well as other New Age practices. To make a long story short, God delivered him out of all of that and he has been serving the Lord ever since.

As a member of the Christian folk/rock group in Seattle called the New Men, he first heard a teaching on the Feast of Tabernacles that started him on the journey of this book. He has taught this in various forms to small groups in his church. He and his wife, Paula, have 7 children, 10 grandchildren, and 1 great grandchild! They live in Great Falls where he works on Malmstrom Air Force Base as a graphic and web designer. Gary likes to paint and still plays the guitar, harmonica and sings "Dylan" style.

S. Douglas Woodward, Th.M. grew up in Oklahoma City, where he now lives once again, after working in Boston for 6 years and Seattle for 21. Doug's experience

lies primarily in business where he has been an executive for Oracle, Microsoft, and a partner at Ernst & Young. He also founded his own company, Smart Starters, which he ran for 10 years, before becoming an Adjunct Professor at the University of Oklahoma, Price School of Business, where he teaches entrepreneurship.

Over the past seven years, Doug has written 15 books, counting this one, on the topics of America's spiritual history, eschatology, and geopolitics. He loves movies, research, and writing and attempts to stay culturally alert. He appears frequently on radio and television programs and speaks at conferences on topics about which he writes. Doug has 2 married children, 2 grandchildren, and a wonderful wife, Donna, with whom he will celebrate 42 years of marriage this summer.

Made in the USA
Columbia, SC
18 August 2017